D1590103

FROM THE ASHES

FROM THE ASHES

THE STORY OF THE HINCKLEY FIRE OF 1894

GRACE STAGEBERG SWENSON

THE CROIXSIDE PRESS / STILLWATER, MINNESOTA

ACKNOWLEDGMENTS

My sincere thanks to the following: Cecile Maser, Curator of the Hinckley Fire Museum, Lee Guptill and Robert Nelson of Hinckley for giving advice and encouragement and sharing their local expertise; to Dick Von Rueden for photographic work; to other Hinckley citizens for interviews granted; to the library and newspaper staff of the Minnesota Historical Society and the staff of the Archives and Manuscripts Division for research aid; to Earl Kuehnast, Rodney Sando and Joe Gummerson for interviews and information, and to the University of Minnesota Forestry Library for reference aid and long-term loans of resource materials.

Dedication

TO

the memory of

MARY ANDERSON KOFOED

of Hinckley

survivor of the fire

who died November 10, 1977

at the age of

101

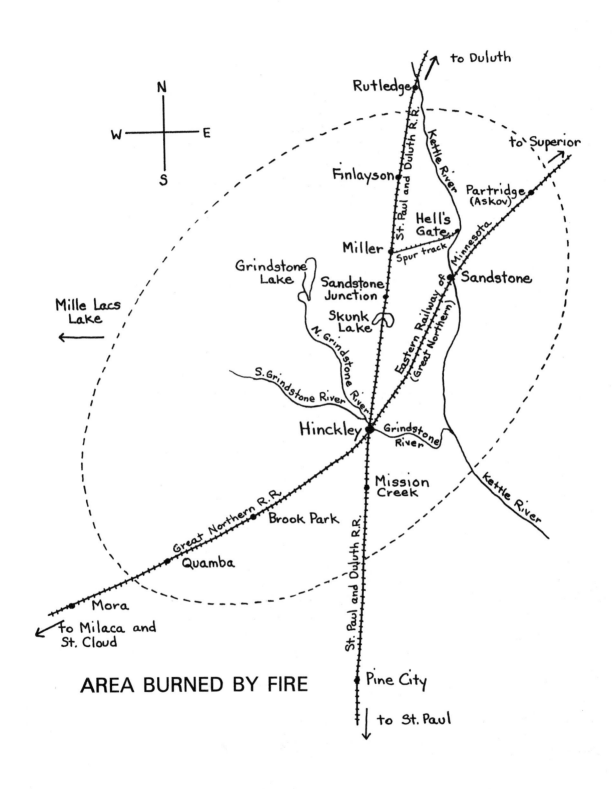

N
W   E
S

to Duluth

Rutledge

to Superior

Finlayson

Kettle River

Partridge
(Askov)

St. Paul and Duluth R.R.

Hell's
Gate

Miller

Spur track

Minnesota

Grindstone
Lake

Sandstone
Junction

Sandstone

Eastern Railway of
(Great Northern)

Skunk
Lake

Mille Lacs
Lake

N. Grindstone River

S. Grindstone River

Hinckley

Grindstone
River

Grindstone River

Mission
Creek

Kettle River

Great Northern R.R.

Brook Park

Quamba

St. Paul and Duluth R.R.

Mora

To Milaca and
St. Cloud

Pine City

to St. Paul

AREA BURNED BY FIRE

Author's Note

From the Ashes is the story of *The Great Hinckley Fire* and a story of people — people who suffered and endured a great disaster. For those who lived through the fire, September 1, 1894, was a date that divided the time line of their lives into two parts — the period *before* and the period *after* the fire.

Since most of the town records were burned in the communities, there remain limited numbers of official local documents, maps and reports from the period prior to the fire. Consequently, information for this chronicle had to come from the few publications on the subject, newspaper accounts, recollections of survivors and their descendants, railroad records and government files.

Among the publications specifically on the subject, most give only a partial and uneven record of the fire. All of the books are out-of-print, except one. The most useful source of information was the book *Memorials of the Minnesota Forest Fires* by the Rev. William Wilkinson, Rector of St. Andrew's Episcopal Church in Minneapolis. Just after the fire Wilkinson took an active part in rescue and burial work in the area and was appointed relief agent at Brook Park. His book, published in 1895, includes accounts of the communities burned and first-hand reports from people who experienced the fire. But his is not a complete story, and some information is contradicted by newspaper reports of the day. Anton Anderson and Clara McDermott in *The Hinckley Fire,* published in 1954, contribute other recollections of survivors, but portions of this book are taken almost verbatim from Wilkinson. The books by Brown, Holbrook and Akermark are helpful in corroborating information found elsewhere, but are sometimes in disagreement with each other and with Wilkinson.

Neither could newspaper reports of the day be relied upon to be the final authority. They were at times exaggerated, contradictory and sensationalized by eager reporters. Initial accounts were often emotional and overstated, only to be refuted by later reports. Misspelled names crept in as messages were telegraphed across the country. Vague terms such as "fires were raging" left much to the imagination, and time was often reckoned imprecisely as "early" or "late" in the day.

Interviews with survivors and their descendants were helpful, but memories can become hazy and oft-told stories take on a legendary quality which can skirt the truth.

This book, then, is a composite gleaned from many sources. Where reports disagreed, I have inferred what is and what is not the truth of *The Great Hinckley Fire* and the people who suffered through it.

G. S. S.

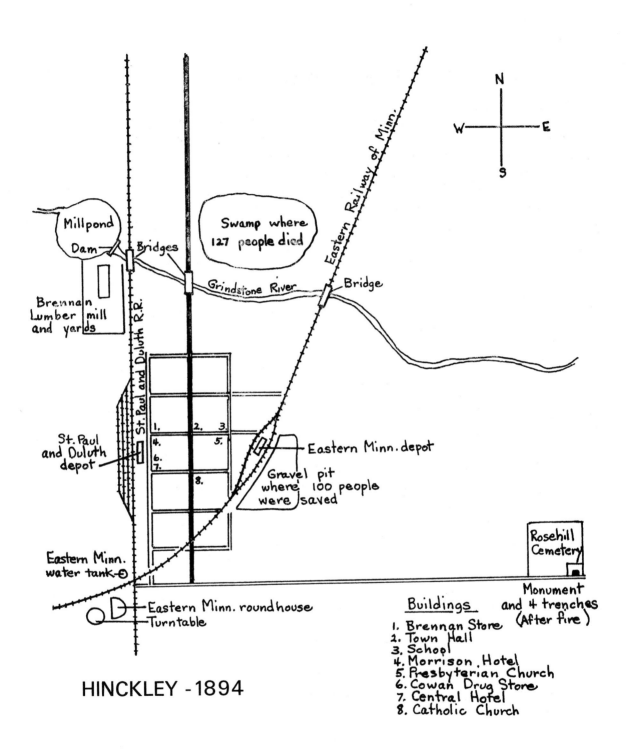

Millpond

Dam

Bridges

Swamp where
127 people died

Eastern Railway of Minn.

Grindstone River

Bridge

Brennan
Lumber mill
and yards

St. Paul and Duluth R.R.

1.   2.   3.

4.   5.

6.
7.

8.

Eastern Minn. depot

Gravel pit
where 100 people
were saved

St. Paul
and Duluth
depot

Eastern Minn.
water tank

Rosehill
Cemetery

Eastern Minn. roundhouse
Turntable

Monument
and 4 trenches
(After fire)

Buildings
1. Brennan Store
2. Town Hall
3. School
4. Morrison Hotel
5. Presbyterian Church
6. Cowan Drug Store
7. Central Hotel
8. Catholic Church

HINCKLEY - 1894

N
W   E
S

Table of Contents

FROM THE ASHES

Hinckley

Hinckley was born in the forests,
    Died in the forests,
And reborn in the ashes
By the spirit of the pioneers.
             Hinckley Fire Museum

CHAPTER **1**

The Times - 1894

I N THE ROSEHILL cemetery one mile east of the village of Hinckley, Minnesota, a slender shaft of gray granite stands a solitary watch over four grass-covered trenches where unidentified fire victims of the Hinckley Fire of 1894 lie buried. The monument, dedicated on September 1, 1900, memorializes the 418 people who lost their lives in the area, 248 from the town of Hinckley. It grimly reminds the few remaining survivors of that day which remains etched indelibly upon their memories. Succeeding generations have paused at the base of the monument, read the inscriptions and paid silent tribute to the indomitable spirit of their forebears.

Although the fire burned several communities and spread over parts of five counties in east central Minnesota, it became known historically as the *Hinckley Fire* since that village sustained the greatest loss in lives and property. At the same time fires burned numerous settlements and acres of forest lands in northern Wisconsin and upper Michigan, but these were not connected to the same fire system and were overshadowed by the disaster at Hinckley.

During the summer of 1894 the Mississippi and Missouri River valleys had experienced extremely hot and dry weather. In the forested regions of northern Minnesota, Wisconsin and Michigan, fires had flared intermittently all summer, leaving small lumbering communities in a state of constant terror. The skies over the Great Lakes had been hazy with smoke, at times creating hazardous shipping conditions on Lakes Superior, Michigan and Huron.

On Saturday, September 1, the fire struck. Two smoldering fire systems converged into one roaring conflagration that devastated in minutes the small lumber town of Hinckley and surrounding settlements. In addition to the 418 reported deaths in the area there were untold numbers of persons

THE TIMES - 1894

3

Hinckley before the fire.

who were never heard from again. In Pine County the fire burned approximately 480 square miles and took swathes into neighboring counties of Aitkin, Carlton, Kanabec and Mille Lacs. Large tracts of virgin white pine were destroyed, and losses were grossly underestimated at $25 million.[1] Casualties and destruction from fires in Wisconsin and Michigan were never determined. The day after the fire all of New England experienced a "dark day" with blackened skies obscuring the sun.

Accounts of the fire were telegraphed immediately across the country and abroad, and newspaper reporters arrived in the burned area from all quarters. On Sunday, September 2, *The New York Times* reported on its front page: "TWO MINNESOTA TOWNS UTTERLY DESTROYED BY FIRE." The Sunday editions of the St. Paul, Minneapolis and Duluth papers spread the shocking news in bold headlines: "INFERNO IN FORESTS" and "HINCKLEY IS IN ASHES." On September 4 *The London Times* told of the "GREAT FOREST FIRES IN AMERICA." Five days after the fire Nellie Bly, the globe-circling journalist from the *New York World,* walked over the ruins of the burned villages and telegraphed a 5,000 word report to her editor. The entire country united in extending sympathy, money and supplies to the destitute fire victims.

At the time of the fire Hinckley was primarily a lumber and railroad town conveniently located in west central Pine County half-way between St. Paul and Duluth. The Grindstone River flowed from west to east on the north edge of the village, joining the Kettle River a few miles to the east. Ten freight and passenger trains ran daily on the two railroads which intersected at the south end of town. They connected Hinckley to Duluth, Superior (Wisconsin), St. Cloud, Minneapolis and St. Paul and made the town a trade and shipping center.

Eastern Hotel at Hinckley
before the fire.

The United States Census of 1890 gave the official population of Hinckley township, including the village, as 912 and Hinckley village as 618. At the time of the fire unofficial reports from citizens and newspapers suggested the town's population was anywhere from 1,000 to 1,700, figures that fluctuated with seasonal work in lumber camps and sawmills.

In 1894 Hinckley was a colorful blend of two ways of life. To the transient mill hands and lumberjacks it was a high-spirited frontier town which provided employment, five or six saloons, five hotels, several boarding establishments and a pleasure house just off the city limits. But to most of the permanent residents Hinckley seemed the ideal place to put down roots and raise a family. All the elements necessary for the good life were there for the enterprising, industrious homesteader.

Spiritual life was nurtured by churches of three denominations, Presbyterian, Roman Catholic and Swedish Lutheran. Children were given a thorough education by a faculty of four teachers and a principal in the new brick schoolhouse built in 1893. Medical care was provided by three doctors —Dr. D. W. Cowan, Dr. E. L. Stephan and Dr. Inez Legg, a woman who also managed a small hospital. The weekly newspaper, *The Hinckley Enterprise,* printed items of big and little significance about the town and surrounding settlements and ran eloquent land promotions and attractive advertisements. Editor Angus Hay was an articulate sounding board for local and national viewpoints.

THE TIMES · 1894

Cigar store at Hinckley
before fire.

Hinckley School, built in 1893.

FROM THE ASHES

6

Dr. D. W. Cowan, Dr. E. L. Stephan,
Editor Angus Hay, and Father E. J. Lawler of Hinckley
Catholic Church at Hinckley before fire

The citizens of Hinckley enjoyed most of the necessities of life. About 250 family dwellings lined the dirt streets. Each of the two railroads had a depot, an express office, a roundhouse and a coal yard. Residents could patronize several general stores and groceries, a bank, two freight companies, a flour and grain dealer, a bakery, an ice cream and candy shop, a meat market, a drug store, a cigar factory, a blacksmith shop, millinery and dressmaking shops, a boot and shoe store, a jewelry shop and a furniture store. There was a town hall, a post office and a volunteer fire department with flashy new uniforms and a modern steam fire engine.

For social activities one could attend the Odd Fellows Lodge, a Literary and Musical Club or Hanson's Opera House which featured traveling shows and weekly dances. The Scandinavian Mission Society supported their good works by festivals and ice cream socials, and a secretive women's "gymnastic society" met behind closed doors away from the prying eyes of inquisitive males. Square dancing to fiddles, accordions or mouth organs was popular at home parties, and the slightly wicked game of "post office" proved an exciting pastime to some. There were baseball games sometimes scheduled at the same hour as Sunday church services, and the sermons of the preachers could scarcely be heard over the cheers of the fans.

THE TIMES - 1894

*Catholic Church
at Hinckley before fire*

Many householders owned a cow or two, maybe a horse, a pig and a few chickens. Some raised potatoes, rutabagas and other vegetables in small garden plots. Deer, partridge and rabbits provided an abundant meat supply and wild raspberries and cranberries were available in season. But to make a living by farming was almost impossible because the land had to be cleared of trees, brush, stumps and rocks. Yet, in an essay contest a Hinckley student in the Senior department wrote glowingly, "Here in Pine County, we have but to tickle the soil with a plough-share and it laughs with a harvest,"[2] and the Hinckley Commerical Union, an organization of business men, boldly advertised on the front page of *The Enterprise:*

Hinckley is surrounded by the most fertile soil that the SUN in its travels shines upon. Natural meadows, filled with red top and blue grass, line its roads. Springs and running waters [at] every farmer's door. No place in the STATE offers a better field for honest endeavor or a RICHER reward to the thrifty farmer. . . .Surrounded with all that nature can bestow, it needs but the strong arm of successful industry to make our Farms Blossom Like Gardens — AND — Our Grain Grow Golden in the Sun![3]

But Hinckley owed its existence not to agriculture but to its strategic location in the center of the white pine timber region. In 1894 the Brennan Lumber Company, the major employer in Hinckley, hired from 300 to 400 workers. Mill hands turned out approximately 200,000 feet of lumber daily in ten-hour shifts. Common laborers earned around $1.00 a day, skilled laborers about $4.00 a day. The mills were fed by logs floated down the north and south branches of the Grindstone to the company millpond. At the time of the fire the Brennan yard was stocked with 28 million feet of lumber awaiting shipment and another 8 million feet of logs ready for the saw. In the Brennan complex there was a sawmill, a planing mill, a lumber yard and a stable of 90 horses all guarded by the "best fire protection available." On July 25, 1894, *The Enterprise* wrote that the Brennan Company had the "most thorough system of waterworks in their plant that can be found. Water mains and hydrants, with hose constantly attached, are placed in all parts of the yards. Under ordinary circumstances it would be impossible for fire to gain any control or headway anywhere in the yards. . . . The fire king would most surely meet defeat from the Brennan Lumber Company."[4]

Yet despite these precautions the fire burned the entire Brennan operation to the ground in minutes, the loss being estimated at around $500,000, half of which was covered by insurance.[5] Several smaller lumber mills in the area suffered the same fate.

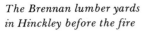

*The Brennan lumber yards
in Hinckley before the fire*

The Brennan mill in Hinckley
before the fire

At the time of the fire, logging camps in the woods were just beginning to gear up for the coming winter season with partial crews at work. When fire burned the forests around them, some lumberjacks and settlers were trapped with no means of escape. The mysterious Tom Corbett perished in such a way. Unidentified charred bodies were found throughout the woods for weeks and months after the fire and many were not included in the official count of deaths. One body was found and identified one mile west of Hinckley four years later. The people and the land paid a tragic toll that fateful afternoon.

By 1894 railroads had given Hinckley local status as a trade center and the "Hub of Pine County." Two lines intersected the town and competed for business. The St. Paul and Duluth Company (later to become the Northern Pacific) carried the major bulk of freight and provided first-rate passenger service between the Twin Cities and Duluth. An especially fast and popular daily passenger train, the Limited, made the run between St. Paul and Duluth in five hours. Hinckley was its mid-point station.

The other railroad, a branch of the Great Northern Company, was the Eastern Railway of Minnesota, which officially extended for seventy miles from Hinckley to Superior, Wisconsin. Although the Eastern operated with its own passenger and freight crews and maintained its own lines, it was entirely under Great Northern control. The Eastern contracted with the parent company to use the tracks from Hinckley to the Twin Cities. James J. Hill, president of the expanding Great Northern system, had appointed his son-in-law, Samuel Hill, to the presidency of the Eastern Minnesota in 1894. Samuel Hill, a promising Minneapolis attorney and no relation of the railroad magnate, had married J. J. Hill's eldest child, Mary Frances, or Mamie as she was called, in 1888. And, as was J. J. Hill's custom, family members were assigned to smaller railroads for training.[6] Earlier he had given his son-in-law the presidency of the Montana Central and later added duties as president of the Eastern. But James J. Hill kept tight control over all branch railroads, and the Eastern was no exception. Just after the fire he accompanied his son-in-law on inspection tours of the burned areas and kept close watch on the repairs of the burned line, especially the rebuilding of the high Kettle River bridge at Sandstone.

In May of 1894 local railroad strikes similar to those in Chicago had occurred on both lines as railroad employees walked off their jobs after drastic cuts in wages. Engineer William Best of the Eastern Railway had been criticized for deserting his train and exposing his passengers to danger.[7] Engineer James Root of the St. Paul and Duluth road had been "arrested and fined on account of some trouble in stopping the 'Limited' at Pine City"[8] presumably during the strike. But three months after the settlement of the strike, these two railroad men, and many others, played leading roles during the fire and earned hero status throughout the state and nation.

In March, 1894, the village of Hinckley had held a spirited election in which Lee Webster, a furniture dealer, had won the mayor's seat by a few votes over the popular Dr. Cowan, who had the endorsement of *The Enterprise*. As the summer progressed, one of the chief concerns of the village council was the local fire situation and the adequacy of the fire fighting equipment. On July 25 when the fire department was called to the south end of town to put out a fire which threatened dwellings, three lengths of hose had burst from the pressure. But the hose had been repaired, and the Waterous steam fire engine stood in the station ready for action.

THE TIMES · 1894

11

PINE COUNTY

Pine County, appropriately named for the extensive pineries of white and red pine that once covered the region, lies in the upper St. Croix Valley on the eastern edge of central Minnesota. Across the St. Croix River to the east is Burnett County, Wisconsin. The 1890 census indicated that 4,052 people resided in the county, 1,830 of foreign birth. Pine City is the county seat.

In 1837 when the United States government made a treaty with the Indians securing the territory north of the Mississippi and west of the St. Croix, splendid white pine, the most highly-prized pine to be found, interspersed with several varieties of hardwoods, grew abundantly. Of the 906,366 acres of land in Pine County, about 665,000 was at one time forest land. Magnificent trees stood well over one-hundred feet tall with diameters from three to five feet. The supply of pine was thought to be limitless and inexhaustible.

The government opened up the land, giving loggers and timbermen stumpage rights, a practice which later proved to be a calamitous procedure. Lumbermen moved in quickly from Maine, Michigan, Wisconsin and Canada and leased or purchased huge timber tracts. Oftentimes trees were cut illegally from adjoining lands on which loggers had no claim. Logging operations were set up, mills built on rivers and the lumber business was on its way to becoming Minnesota's leading industry. In 1895, its peak year, the St. Croix Valley produced 373 million feet of lumber.[9] But as the virgin pine was stripped away, a ravaged land remained with stumps, slashings and brush which supported only a second-rate growth of jack pine. Not only was the valuable timber supply exhausted, but tinder-dry refuse remained as ready fuel for sparks to ignite into full-blown fires. Loggers were not required to replant trees or clear away the brush and debris. The few voices raised in protest were unheeded until the dramatic events of September 1, 1894.

The numerous lumber camps sprinkled through the forests of Pine County attracted a robust species of men. In the 1890's the large majority of lumberjacks were Scandinavians, along with lesser numbers of Germans, Irish, Finns and other nationalities. Many of the men were transients who worked in the lumber camps in the winter and moved on to the Dakota fields in the summer. Others were local settlers who earned extra money by winter logging.

Big load of logs

Logs were hauled over the frozen ground to the rivers and streams to await the spring thaw and the river drive. Occasionally contests developed between the loggers to see which camp could haul the largest load of logs over iced logging roads. Oxen often replaced horses. In 1892 a crew from the Rutledge Lumber Company working north of Hinckley gained national distinction by loading 56 logs scaled at 37,120 feet on one sled drawn by four horses. The load measured 18½ feet in length, 26 feet in height and 20½ feet in width and was larger than the Michigan load displayed at the Chicago Exposition in 1893.[10]

The life of the lumberjack was rigorous, with long hours, crude living conditions, strict camp rules and lonely isolation during winter months. He had a few compensations. One of them was food — it was always ample and usually good. If it wasn't, the cook was fired. There developed a camaraderie with the other men that bolstered the spirit. And the men welcomed the visits of the "sky pilot," a preacher from Duluth who made the rounds of the camps. He led the men in singing lumberjack songs, then hymns, followed by a bit of prudent advice. After leaving a sack full of magazines, he departed for the next camp.

THE TIMES - 1894

13

Lumberjacks generally were paid from $25.00 to $30.00 a month with room and board, while a teamster could earn up to $65.00 a month plus another $35.00 for his team. River drivers, who had the most hazardous job of all, earned approximately $50.00 a month.[11] Since the lumberjack had no place to spend money all winter, he usually had quite a sum on deposit at the end of the season. In the spring when logging stopped, most of the single men headed for the large cities and spent the winter's earnings in a few nights of riotous pleasure.

Lumbermen were highly regarded since it was thought they rendered a valuable service to the development of the area. They provided the wood products that were in great demand by a growing population and cleared the land of the trees that stood in the way of the settlers. Very few individuals were concerned about the depletion of a precious resource. And as fast as the trees were moved out, the people moved in. More than 500 farms were sold in Pine County in four months of early 1894. According to the census, population in Pine County increased dramatically in the twenty years from 1880 to 1900. In 1880 it stood at 1,365, in 1890 it had grown to 4,052, and by 1900 it had reached 11,546.

The Hinckley Fire hastened the premature demise of the lumber industry in Pine County. The people who resettled the blackened land began the transition to an agricultural community. In the first issue of *The Hinckley Enterprise* published after the fire, the editor stated: "The fire on September 1 did in 15 minutes what it would have taken the husbandman 15 years to accomplish. All nature is with us; it seemingly knew our needs, and came to clear the land."[12]

THE STATE OF MINNESOTA

In 1894 Minnesota had been a state for thirty-six years, having been admitted in 1858 as the thirty-second state in the Union. The state flag, designed by Mrs. Edward H. Center of Minneapolis, was adopted by the legislature one year before the fire. Minnesota boasted a population of 1,400,000 and property evaluated at $600 million.[13]

The 1892 election had put Norwegian-born Knute Nelson, Republican, into office as the twelfth governor of the state. He had won decisively over Democrat Daniel Lawler and the enigmatic Ignatius Donnelly of the Populist Party. In the following election in 1894 Nelson won an overwhelming victory for his second term over George Becker, Democrat, and Sidney Owen, Populist candidate. Governor Nelson had just taken office in 1895 when he chose to seek the seat vacated by William D. Washburn in the United States Senate. Nelson's move to the Senate precipitated criticism in local newspapers and citizens' petitions demanding an election to fill the Senate vacancy, but it did not injure Nelson's popularity. He was reelected to the Senate until his death in 1923.[14] Lieutenant Governor David Clough moved into the governor's chair in 1895.

Governor Knute Nelson

During Nelson's governorship legislation was passed to use state money to improve roads and bridges in the state, to regulate the grain and warehouse industries and to control the rapidly developing iron mines.

The Hinckley Fire was the greatest single disaster during Governor Nelson's term and one of the most devastating forest fires in state history. The Governor appointed a State Fire Relief Commission to supervise distribution of aid to fire sufferers.

In 1894 lumbering and logging dominated Minnesota industry and contributed to the growth of the Twin Cities. Minnesota had become the principal source of the nation's white pine. Along with lumbermen from other states and Canada, Fred Weyerhaeuser had moved from Illinois to Minnesota and had located his home in St. Paul next to James J. Hill on prestigious Summit Avenue.

By 1905 the state's lumber production had reached its all-time high of nearly two billion feet, 98% of which was white pine. But by 1914 Minnesota's lumber production was only half of the 1905 total and by 1921 had fallen to only 20% of the peak year. The supply of white pine had been almost totally depleted.[15]

THE TIMES - 1894

The grain industry had already become an important business in the state and in 1894 was second only to lumbering. The names of Pillsbury and Washburn were well-established in milling circles.

Iron mining was steadily expanding after the first iron ore had been shipped out from the Soudan mine on the Vermilion Range in 1884. Five years later the Merritt brothers discovered iron ore near Mountain Iron on the Mesabi Range, and in 1892 that mine shipped out its first ore. Nearby Duluth was becoming a busy shipping center as well as a flourishing sawmill city.

Railroads were vital to the growth of the state, and business men and settlers alike welcomed the iron rails which forecast progress. Trains carried lumber, grain, iron ore, general freight and passengers across the state and connected Minnesota to the east and west coasts. The name of James J. Hill had become synonymous with railroading genius in the state. In June, 1893, St. Paul citizens celebrated for an entire week their Great Northern connection to Seattle.

During the Panic of 1893 Hill's Great Northern lines remained financially sound while other railroads were going bankrupt. In 1893 the Great Northern Railway Company netted over $5 million, an increase of $700,000 profit over the previous year. Yet despite this, Hill ordered a reduction in wages for section hands to $1.00 a day on eastern roads and $1.25 a day on the western lines. On April 13, 1894, Great Northern employees walked off their jobs. A defiant Hill sent a freight train through from West Superior and when mobs threatened to shut down all operations, he demanded that President Cleveland send in troops to assist the local authorities. Nothing that drastic was necessary as the dispute was brought to an arbitration board of non-railroad men and was settled by May 2. Hill had agreed to pay railroad workers from $1.25 to $1.50 a day, a settlement which amounted to more of a moral than a monetary victory for Eugene Debs and his American Railway Union.[16]

J. J. Hill

When the Northern Pacific announced bankruptcy after the crash, Hill shrewdly proceeded to negotiate for the purchase of their stock. He was stopped temporarily by a Supreme Court decision upholding a ruling preventing the merger of the two railroad companies in what was viewed as a monopoly, but by 1896 Hill and his friends had privately purchased the stock of their arch rival.

Unemployment plagued the cities and villages of Minnesota as it did the workers of the nation. On September 3, 1894, when Labor Day was celebrated for the first time in Minnesota, St. Paul observed the day with a two-mile parade of festive military bands, drum corps, fire wagons, mounted horses and fashionable ladies in carriages. But at the rear 500 unemployed workers marched with a sign saying, "Labor Day, 1894. We are idle."[17]

1894 was a year of contrasts in the state. But despite unemployment, strikes, financial panics and fires, Minnesotans generally had confidence that the state was embarked on a dynamic course toward identity and achievement.

THE TIMES - 1894

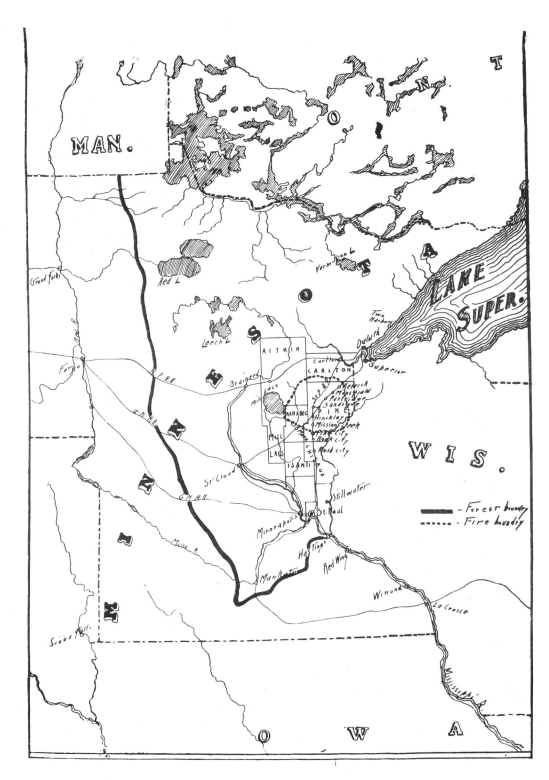

FROM THE ASHES

18

The Fire

IN JULY and August Minnesota newspapers indicated that the summer of 1894 was not an ordinary one. On July 18 and 19 *The Duluth News Tribune* reported that fires were burning along the St. Paul and Duluth tracks from Pine City to Carlton and threatening Hinckley. In July fires were causing great suffering and loss in Wisconsin, where the town of Phillips was said to be destroyed, and communities around Ashland burned. In the latter part of August, fires were reported in Alcona County, Michigan, with heavy losses around Ludington. The papers also noted that temperatures at Duluth in mid-July had exceeded 90° F. for several days. On July 25 Mankato reported 102° F. and Faribault 108° F. Crops through the state were said to be suffering, and some were near ruin from drought and heat.

The dry weather moved a worried farmer near St. Cloud to place the following notice to hunters in the local paper on August 31, one day before the fire:

> Owing to the dry conditions of my meadows, they (hunters) must not hunt on my lands, and hunters found thereon will be prosecuted to the full extent of the law. I have heretofore made no objection to hunters on my premises, but the very dry conditions of everything places me in a position where I must take this action. [1]

On September 1, the same paper noted that fires were burning north of St. Cloud and announced prophetically: "Settlers are about playing out fighting the fire, and unless we get rain within a short time, there is no telling where the devastation will stop." [2]

The Hinckley Enterprise on July 18 said that the "same old foe" was keeping the area well-smoked and residents were complaining of sore eyes and headaches. *The Enterprise* continued to report each week through July and August that fires were burning near Pine City, Mission Creek, Brook Park (Pokegama), Partridge, Sandstone and Willow River as well as in northwestern Wisconsin. On August 29, in its last issue before the fire, *The Enterprise* told of timber and hay burning along the Government Road and smoke again blanketing the town of Hinckley.

BROOK PARK

On September 1, farms surrounding the town of Milaca, thirty miles south-west of Brook Park, were burning, but fire fighters had saved Milaca itself. Near Milaca were forty small farm homes built by James J. Hill on his own land for persecuted Russian Jews, who had earlier fled to New York from Czarist Russia. The homes, never occupied by the Jews, were burned in the fire along with farms of several settlers.

At the Quamba station on the Great Northern railroad five miles south-west of Brook Park, the fire gathered strength and advanced northeast in an uncontrollable blaze. When it reached Brook Park, it had been fanned by an increasing southwest wind into a front three miles wide.

The village of Brook Park, or Pokegama as the railroad station was called, was a new town developed in 1893 when the Kelsey and Markham Land Company, owned by two Kelsey and two Markham brothers, began to sell its 15,000 acres to settlers. At the time of the fire there were from 135 to 150 people living in the village including Scandinavians, Germans, Irish and five families of Russian Jews who had come from Chicago. The Baty and Seymour sawmill processed from 25,000 to 30,000 feet of lumber daily and employed most of the men in town. In the company yards were stock piles of 500,000 feet of lumber. Twenty-five homes, a post office, hotel, general store, boarding house and a newly-built schoolhouse costing $1,000 comprised the town. The school, the pride of the village, had just been accepted from the builder the day of the fire.

Brook Park was described by its residents as a thriving community of contented people who had all the necessities of life and who were happy in their natural surroundings. It was a village not plagued by the vices and "abominations known in modern crowded city life."3

Although fires had been common throughout the hot, dry summer, the men of the town had been able to control them. As an extra precaution many had burned brush or had plowed fields around their homes.

On the day of the fire the lumber mill was closed while the men put up winter hay. At noon the sun appeared blood-red as though there were an eclipse. Fire, eating at the southwestern edge of the village, gained on the men who had abandoned their haying to fight the blaze. Smoke-laden clouds rolled over the town. At 2:00 p.m. a strong southwest wind blew a wave of fire in through an old logging dam on Pokegama Creek. The fire burned fiercely in piles of wood cuttings and slashings dumped by the lumber company. Villagers fled in terror from their homes, and some gathered at the millpond just below the dam. When the fire struck they waded into the deep water as far as they dared and splashed it on themselves. The intense heat from the burning piles of wood drove them to the opposite side of the pond where they tore off their clothing to use for protection over their heads. Bursts of sparks burned their faces and hands.

J. D. Markham
of Rush City

The fire hurdled the pond to the opposite side and began to consume the section house and the lumber yard, adding more heat and smoke to the air. Next, the railroad bridge above the pond began to burn and was in danger of collapsing on the people below. An overdue southbound train going to St. Cloud was expected, and people feared it would crash through the bridge, destroying both them and the crew. They did not know until later that the train had become derailed and lay in the ditch one mile northeast of Brook Park. When the bridge collapsed, it fortunately fell in the opposite direction. In the meantime the fire burned the entire town and raced on toward Hinckley eight miles north.

At about 6:00 p.m. after four hours in the pond, the burned and partially-clothed survivors climbed out of the water and viewed the smoldering desolation of their once-ideal community. Some suffered from severe burns, many had swollen eyes, injured lungs and blistered hands and faces, but all of those in the pond had survived, including a three-week old baby. Two unburned boxcars were discovered in a clearing about a mile southwest of town and forty people took shelter there through the chilly night. They lay on the lath and bricks piled in the cars and used raw potatoes to ease their burns. For breakfast Sunday morning they had partly burned cabbages and potatoes found in a nearby field, roasted eggs from two burned crates and a little water to drink.

Some of the survivors had remained at the pond and were found by railroad men who arrived from the wrecked St. Cloud and Hinckley train. Twenty-three survivors followed the men back to the ditched train and spent

*Brook Park. Pool in which
more than thirty people were saved*

the night in an unburned coach. The crewmen attended to them as best they could, tearing up their shirts to use as wet cloths to ease scorched faces, burned eyes, hands and feet. After an agonizing night the Sunday morning dawn brought no consolation or relief. Trees, still smoldering, lay pell-mell about them. The ground still smoked from burning coals under the black crust, and tree stumps glowed as fire tunneled down to the roots. With no food or medicine the sufferers awaited rescue from the outside world.

Pokegama Creek proved to be the salvation of many who sought refuge in occasional pools of water along the nearly dry creek bed. A group of seventeen survived in a small water hole near the Nelson home. As neighbors ran for shelter in the pool, the Nelsons watched anxiously for their two daughters, Alice and Mabel, who had gone cranberry picking for the day south of Brook Park. As the fire swept over them, the people in the pool covered themselves with wet blankets. After the fury had subsided and the survivors pulled themselves out to the shore, two begrimed, sooty figures came stumbling toward them from the railroad tracks. The two Nelson girls had found shelter in an embankment along the tracks. The parents, though overjoyed to find their daughters had survived, discovered their home and livestock, as well as those of their neighbors, had been swept away. Only blackened ruins of buildings and scorched animal carcasses remained.

Some people of Brook Park sought shelter in wells and a few, such as the C. W. Kelsey family, were fortunate enough to survive. When the Kelseys could not save their home, they ran to the well and lowered a ladder. By keeping themselves and the well opening covered with wet blankets, they all survived despite the suffocating, cinder-laden air. To pacify the terrified children Mrs. Kelsey sang hymns and prayed.

Others were not as fortunate. Joseph Gonyea survived but suffered from severely burned hands and feet. Shortly after the fire eleven people were found dead in a tamarack swamp. Fred Molander's wife and two children were found burned near their farm, but he was missing. His body was discovered in a well on his farm in the middle of October.

After the fire it was officially reported that twenty-six people had lost their lives at Brook Park, but in June, 1895, a local paper claimed that with the recovery of yet another body, the total had risen to twenty-eight.[4] In addition to relatives and friends who were victims of the fire, the citizens of Brook Park had lost all of their possessions, none of which was insured. Their homes, livestock, the town business establishments, places of employment, the new school and their entire model community had been annihilated.

As soon as the villages to the south heard of the devastation, relief and rescue crews began to search the burned area for survivors. Most of the people from Brook Park were brought to Mora, eleven miles to the southwest, where they were given shelter, food and clothing.

THE CHIPPEWA BAND

Another disaster of equal dimension to that of Brook Park, but little reported, befell a band of Chippewa Indians under Chief Wacouta. The band had left the reservation on the eastern shores of Mille Lacs Lake in early July to set up a hunting lodge. They had located on Shadridge Creek halfway between Brook Park and Opstead, a little town on the eastern shore of Mille Lacs Lake. The hunting camp was found in ashes, and half a dozen birchbark dwellings were in ruins. Only one shriveled rawhide tepee remained along with a few melted rifles and shotguns. Twenty-three bodies, among them Chief Wacouta's, were found scattered through the woods for ten miles around the camp.[5] These fatalities were not included in the official death count.

MISSION CREEK

At almost the same time that fire consumed Brook Park, another was burning its way toward a neighboring village lying six miles to the east on the other railroad.

Mission Creek, a small sawmill town three miles south of Hinckley on the St. Paul and Duluth Railroad, was supported by the Laird and Boyle Company which operated the sawmill, ran the general store, hotel and blacksmith shop. In 1894 there were seventy-three inhabitants, predominantly Swedes, twenty-six homes and a public school. At the time of the fire many employees of the mill had left town to work in the Dakota harvest fields. The

Laird and Boyle Company was negotiating an exchange of their Mission Creek sawmill for one owned by the Wisdom and Cannon Company of a neighboring town. Much of the mill equipment had been loaded on flat cars and stood on a side track ready to be transported to Arkansas. In the yards 500,000 feet of lumber awaited shipment to St. Paul.

Men had fought fires around the settlement through much of July and August, and the citizens had been apprehensive. The town itself stood on a cut-over area, and fire had not threatened their dwellings although some of the wood piles and hay meadows farther out had burned. There had been burns along the railroad tracks, smoldering fires in the bogs and marshes and active fires throughout the woods to the south.

On Saturday morning, September 1, the usual smoky yellow-gray haze lay over the town. It appeared to be another day similar to others just past with no signs of rain in sight. Some of the men had been out fighting fires through the morning and had just returned to their homes for noon dinner when great clouds of smoke billowed into the sky to the southwest. This was no ordinary fire. By 2:00 p.m. the wind had reached gale force. At 2:30 a southbound train went through town, but no one boarded it. By 3:00 the sky had darkened to the blackness of night. Terrified people rushed to the company store and begged Ed Boyle to telegraph for an emergency train to take them out of the village. But before anything could be done, the fire had broken through the edge of the woods, and the wind was fanning columns of fire toward the town.

The cool-headed Mr. Boyle ordered everyone to the potato patch back of his store and had men bring two barrels of water into the patch. The people lay on the ground in the furrows covering their faces. Mothers and fathers sheltered their crying children as the fire roared and exploded over them. Fire brands hurled through the air blown by the fierce wind, and soot and cinders rained down on them. The heat was intense, and the smoke and ashes blinded their eyes. Some uttered prayers which they thought to be their last, others clutched each other to face the impending death together. One man lost his senses in delirium.

In two hours, when the fire had blown over, a count showed that every-one was saved. Fortunately the immediate area had been cleared of trees and brush. There in the middle of the patch in a rocker, where her parents had placed her under blankets, sat young Jenny Johnson (Jackson), unharmed, still clutching her doll.*

All the buildings in the town had burned except one, a rough-hewn log cabin owned by David Hedman, which stood on the southwest corner of the potato patch. At about 6:00 p.m. the women and children were brought to this remaining house where they washed themselves as best they could while the men guarded the house outside from flying sparks.

*The doll and rocker are on display at the Hinckley Fire Museum.

*Young Jenny Johnson and her doll
sat in this rocker under blankets
in a potato patch at Mission Creek.
Rocker and doll are on exhibit
at Hinckley Fire Museum.*

A deer, which had become trapped in a wire fence, was brought to the cabin, dressed and cooked, potatoes were dug and roasted. That night the survivors ate their evening meal in silence amidst the smoking ruins. Some wondered if they should try to get to Hinckley to warn that town of the possible disaster, not knowing that Hinckley had already experienced a more tragic fate.

As they ate, a railroad crewman from Pine City arrived on foot from the south, reporting that a work train had reached a burned bridge two and one-half miles south of Mission Creek. He said the train would arrive to rescue them as soon as the bridge could be repaired, perhaps by 11:00 that night. Most of the survivors decided not to wait for the train, but set out on foot over the burned railroad ties and twisted tracks. It was a desolate group that stumbled through the dark to meet the train that took them to Pine City. They had lost everything but the clothes they wore and the satchels some had packed.

The lumber yards were a complete loss and continued to burn for days after the fire. The dismantled sawmill was totally destroyed. Its loss precipitated a series of suits and counter-suits filed by the two companies involved. In the hearings Wisdom and Cannon claimed that a foreman of the Laird and Boyle Company had foolishly ordered a fire started to burn old stumpage, even though the day was windy and he had been advised against it. This fire, they asserted, could have been the beginning of the fire that burned the sawmill and perhaps even Mission Creek.[6]

Pine City, ten miles south of Mission Creek, had fortunately escaped the fire. The residents of that town immediately martialed all their facilities to give shelter, food, clothing and medical attention to the survivors from Mission Creek and other burned settlements.

THE FIRE

John Craig home in Hinckley before fire. John Craig was the Fire Chief at Hinckley and ran a hotel and a saloon.

HINCKLEY

Saturday, September 1, began like any other summer day in Hinckley with a blast from the Brennan Lumber Company whistle at 7:00 a.m. It signalled the beginning of the ten-hour day shift which would turn out another 200,000 feet of lumber to be added to the 28 million feet piled neatly in the yards. The water barrels atop the roof of the main building had been checked, and the hose connections at the hydrants located throughout the yards had been inspected just in case they might be needed.

The day crew arrived, lunch pails in hand. They had noticed nothing unusual about the early morning except that it was dewless and calm, portending another hot, dry day with no prospects of rain. The usual haze hovered over the town, and the acrid smell of smoke mingled with dust from the dirt streets.

All summer the villagers had fought back the fires that threatened the town. They were secure in the belief that they could hold off any real disaster until the inevitable rains would come to relieve the drought. They had confidence in the well-trained nineteen man volunteer fire department under Fire Chief John Craig which had recently paraded in snappy new dress uniforms. This was the same department which had in 1892 won second place in a fire fighting contest of all fire departments west of Chicago. And the town had recently purchased a new fire engine made by the Waterous Engine Works in St. Paul, an engine especially efficient, with its own hot water boiler and steam-driven pistons which produced greater pressure than previous models. The fire department could surely handle any fire that crept near enough to threaten the town. Besides, the major part of the village lay in the triangle formed by the two railroad tracks and the Grindstone River, and a fire would not be apt to cross the cleared areas along the tracks.

Some farsighted residents had given thought to where they might find shelter if a fire struck. Nearly everyone had water wells deep in the ground, and some had root cellars they used for protection from storms. There was also the new fire-proof brick schoolhouse. Furthermore, trains were leaving several times a day both north and south if one had to make a hasty departure.

The stores and shops opened and conducted their usual brisk Saturday morning business. Women at home fired up their wood cook-stoves for early baking before the heat of the day was upon them. But those out in the streets noticed that the sun was a sullen red, and the air seemed oppressively still and heavy.

Toward noon the wind began to stir from the southwest, and ashes and cinders sifted down. At the Brennan yards sparks from burning stumps blew into the lumber piles and started to burn. Mill hands, who weren't out fighting fires, were quickly dispersed to keep the flames under control and were ordered to distribute extra water barrels throughout the yards. Business

Hinckley Fire Department with
Waterous fire engine before fire

27

*Father E. J. Lawler,
Priest at Hinckley Catholic Church*

men, home for lunch, reported, "It looks bad." They advised their families to leave on the next train. Some prudent folks packed a few belongings, headed for the St. Paul and Duluth station and left town on the noon train to Pine City which arrived one hour late.

Sometime between 1:00 and 2:00 p.m. the fire alarm blew its shrill warning that fire was threatening somewhere in the village. Thick grayish-white smoke rolled in, obscuring the sun and darkening the sky. Briefly the smoke lifted leaving a ghastly yellow pall over the town. Then ashes and smoke, borne on the increasing wind, returned, thick and dense. The sky blackened, and some residents lit lamps and continued to work. Others packed their belongings hoping they could still get out of town on the 4:00 o'clock Limited.

The firemen assembled hastily at the engine house, fired up steam in the Waterous engine and pulled out the hose cart. Father Lawler, local priest, was there as usual. He took a special interest in the fire department and never failed to answer the alarms. Fire Chief Craig sent the men to the southwest end of town where fires had begun to threaten buildings along the tracks. They rolled out the hose, attached it to the pipe in the underground reservoir and began to pump. The strengthening wind showered them with cinders and sparks mixed with spray from the hose. A chicken house burst into flame, soon a home was ablaze. One fireman hurried back to the depot to dispatch a wire to Rush City requesting more hose. The hose never arrived because it was sent on a train which had been stopped at Pine City.

The fire fighters, joined by the mill hands, tried to keep ahead of the spreading flames, but the gale-strength wind hurled airborne firebrands and rolls of flame over them into the town. The Waterous was rendered useless when the hose burned between the nozzle and the engine. After two hours Chief Craig assessed the futility of their situation and ordered the men to

*Model of Thomas Dunn
in depot agent's office
at Hinckley Fire Museum*

*Thomas Dunn
telegraph operator
at Hinckley*

abandon the equipment and tend to the safety of their families. Father Lawler ran back to town shouting, "For heaven's sake, leave all you have! Get to the gravel pit, run to the river. Hinckley will be destroyed."[7]

Over at the Brennan Company, all of the mill hands had left their work to help fight fires. A fifteen-year old orphan boy remained at the mill with instructions to blow the whistle if the buildings and yards were threatened.

Shortly after 3:00 p.m. Thomas Dunn, twenty-five year old telegraph operator at the St. Paul and Duluth depot, was stunned when he received a message that Brook Park had burned and lives had been lost. He passed the information on, hoping to alert the Hinckley people to impending disaster. He also feared for the safety of the many passengers who were gathering at the depot to take the fast Limited south, their trunks piled high along the platform. Then Dunn began to worry that the Limited, coming from Duluth under Engineer Jim Root, would run into trouble as it neared Hinckley. It was due at 4:05 p.m., and Dunn hoped he would get word from a station to the north regarding it. Then someone screamed, "The roof of the depot is on fire!"

The terrified people fled into the street which was quickly becoming a corridor of flame. Some ran to the Eastern Minnesota depot and crowded aboard the combined trains of Engineers Best and Barry waiting there. Some ran to the gravel pit, while others went north on the wagon road hoping to outrun the fire. Still others went up the St. Paul and Duluth tracks hoping to reach the millpond but, finding the Brennan yards aflame, had to go on. Many of them managed to board Root's train which had stopped one mile north of town. But Tom Dunn felt duty-bound to stay at his post in case a message came from the Limited. No message ever arrived, nor did the train ever reach Hinckley. As the depot burned about him, Dunn's last frantic message sent north to Barnum said, "I have stayed too long."[8] A body found later near the Grindstone River was identified by his family as that of Tom Dunn.

The gravel pit at Hinckley where about 100 people were saved

7. HINCKLEY - THE SAND PIT WHERE MANY FOUND SHELTER

Round house and water tank at Hinckley

By 3:30 p.m. the sky had become as black as night, illumined only by the balls of fire carried through the sky on the cyclonic wind and blazing flames from the burning buildings whose outer walls seemed to melt. The heat was intense, and gases exploded overhead in a deafening roar.

When people heard Father Lawler's warning and realized the seriousness of the fire, they abandoned their homes and belongings and fled to find shelter. There was pandemonium in the streets. Families were separated in the confusion, wives from husbands, children from parents, brothers from sisters.

About 100 people managed to reach the gravel pit near the Eastern Minnesota tracks where there was a shallow body of water in the middle of a three-acre excavation. The Great Northern Company had dug gravel from the pit to level its roadbed and had caused the townspeople to complain about the eyesore to the community. It was said that a spring kept water in the hole even in dry weather, and animals had been accustomed to go there to drink. But this eyesore and its three feet of water became a haven for both people and animals. Only one fatality occurred in the pit, a man who was reported to have drowned when he was knocked down by a cow. The whole population of Hinckley probably could have been saved at the gravel pit had they gone there.

*The remains of
the Hinckley School*

As the fire blew in sheets over them, and cinders and sparks showered down, those in the pit splashed water on themselves and covered their eyes and noses with wet clothing. They stayed in the water for about three hours until the fire had subsided and it seemed safe to crawl up the banks. What they saw of the town gave them no solace. The only buildings standing were the Eastern Minnesota roundhouse and the water tank. Here the survivors found water and shelter until a relief train arrived just after midnight to take them south to Pine City.

While many had taken refuge at the gravel pit, others had crowded aboard the train that stood waiting at the Eastern Minnesota depot. Engineer Edward Barry, who had arrived earlier, had coupled his freight to Engineer William Best's passenger train which had just pulled in with a load of passengers going to St. Paul. Since Best's train could not proceed south, the railroad crews prepared for an emergency exit back to Duluth, taking with them as many Hinckley people as possible. In the coaches of Best's train were about 100 terrified passengers who had boarded in Duluth and stations along the way.

The first Hinckley refugee taken on the train was John Hogan, a paralyzed man, whose brother lifted him aboard while his mother carried his wheelchair. Behind him others crowded into day coaches, parlor cars, box-

FROM THE ASHES

32

cars and the caboose. Some had scorched faces and bodies and burned clothing. Almost no one carried any belongings other than what was worn. Some had been separated from members of their families and didn't know if their loved ones were aboard the train or remained in the burning town. Young Dr. Stephan helped about twenty children aboard before he got on. Many husbands and fathers helped their wives and children on to the train, then assisted others. A few of the men stayed too long, missed the train and had to find shelter somewhere in the burning town. Some perished, leaving behind widows and families. Engineer Best reported that not all was gallantry as some "excited men pushed women and children from the coaches in their mad haste to get in themselves."9 When the train left, over 350 refugees had crowded aboard.

Engineer Best and Conductor Powers held the train as long as possible despite Barry's attempts to pull out. But when they saw people begin to fall in the streets and walls of houses burn so fast their interiors were exposed, they dared wait no longer. Best released the air brakes, Barry whistled off and at 4:00 p.m. the heavily-loaded cars lurched forward and headed north. Those who had missed the train were last seen running after it with hair and clothing aflame. Just as the train left, the whistle at the Brennan mill blew a shrill and final shriek announcing that fire had struck the yards. It was too late to save the boy stationed there.

The train moved north through a corridor of burning brush and trees. Just after crossing the Grindstone bridge the train halted long enough to take aboard about forty more people who had fled up the tracks. After a harrowing ride toward Sandstone the train crossed the burning Kettle River high bridge just minutes before it collapsed. Then it headed north on the smoky route to Superior and Duluth.

When the train reached Superior, a few people got off, the rest continued on to the Union Station in Duluth. Between 9:00 and 9:30 that night a desolate human cargo was unloaded at the depot. Many sympathetic and anxious Duluth residents were there to meet them, to search for familiar faces among the 475 disheveled passengers that disembarked and to inquire about others still remaining at Hinckley. The refugees, who had no relatives or friends with whom they could stay, were taken to hotels and homes or given hastily prepared temporary quarters at the Armory.

People who had missed the Eastern Minnesota train and those who had run north on the wagon road sought refuge in a swamp near the Grindstone River. There they huddled together in the center of the marsh along with terrified animals that ran out from the burning woods. Flames burned hungrily in the dry grasses, and fireballs rolled overhead in the crowns of the trees. It is believed that death came instantaneously by suffocation to the 127 people who perished there. Bodies were badly burned and charred, many were frozen in postures of motion, some in prayer, some kneeling, some clasping each other.

Al Fraser heard their last cries as he sheltered his family in water barrels nearby. He said, "When the fire wave hit that swamp, there was one piercing cry of mortal anguish; then everything was still except for the howling of the wind."10

About one-third of the town's population lived near the Brennan mill in the northwest section of town, most of them the families of mill workers. When fire swept the town, many of the men were fighting flames at the south side of the village and were cut off from their homes by a wall of fire. Their wives and children sought shelter in several places. Some ran to the Grindstone River where a few were saved, but others died of drowning. Some went to wells and root cellars, but most of them died of suffocation. Others tried to outrun the fire by going north on the St. Paul and Duluth tracks, but some were overtaken by flames or fell asphyxiated along the tracks. Those who succeeded in staying ahead of the fire had gone about one mile when they heard a sound unlike the roar of the fire behind them. A light broke through the blackness, and a train engine appeared on the tracks ahead. It was the southbound Limited passenger train from Duluth engineered by Jim Root.

The people at the head of the group flagged the train with cries of, "For God's sake save us!" Root brought the train to a halt. As the frantic refugees crowded aboard, they poured out the tragedy of Hinckley. More came running from other directions. Altogether about 150 to 160 people managed to reach the train.

By that time Root could see the flames advancing towards them, and there was no alternative but to put his engine in reverse and back up. He remembered a marshy spot near the tracks six miles north of Hinckley, which had been appropriately named Skunk Lake.

It was a fiery trip back to the lake with the flames gaining on them toward the engine which was now at the rear of the train. Some passengers were hysterical and had to be pacified by the crew. Root, himself, passed out at the throttle and was revived when Fireman McGowan threw a pail of water on him. By the heroic efforts of the train crew, all 300 passengers and refugees were delivered to the foul, but life-saving waters of Skunk Lake.

As people rushed off the train, a few were separated from the others and did not reach the water. One man in confusion ran off into a ditch where he perished. Five others were saved in a nearby potato patch, three others in a culvert. Several others, including Conductor Sullivan, continued to run north on the tracks for ten miles with the fire at their heels. They stopped at Miller but were driven out, then went on to Finlayson where the fire still pursued them. Two miles farther they stopped at a gravel pit and waited for a relief train which brought them to Willow River.

Kettle River at Sandstone before fire

Those who stayed at Skunk Lake survived by immersing themselves in the muddy water and covering their heads with wet clothing while the fire burned furiously near the edges of the marsh and above them. When the fire abated, they crawled up to the edges of the swamp and waited through the chill of the night.

The first rescue party to reach Skunk Lake came at midnight from Duluth on hand cars. Two doctors remained while the rest of the party went back to continue repairing burned bridges and tracks so a relief train could get through. At 3:00 Sunday morning another party arrived from Hinckley and took forty survivors back to Hinckley, where they were put on a relief train to Pine City. The remaining people at Skunk Lake were rescued later Sunday morning by the relief train from the north which brought them to Duluth.

When the final tally was made, Hinckley's losses were enormous. The corridors of fire, which had raced to Hinckley from Brook Park and Mission Creek along the two railroad lines, had converged into one "cyclone of fire" that literally consumed the town in a matter of minutes. Two hundred and forty-eight citizens, or more, had perished. The town's property, estimated conservatively to be somewhat over one million dollars, lay in total ruin. Only a few householders could afford the costly insurance assessed on property in a lumber town built of wood. The fire left a devastated Hinckley and surged northward.

THE FIRE

35

SANDSTONE

The second greatest loss of life from the fire was sustained by Sandstone, a village eight miles north of Hinckley. Most accounts state that sixty-three people perished in the village. One report, claiming to be an accurate count of the bodies interred at Sandstone, set the figure at sixty-seven, including a few from outside the village.[11] On September 9 Coroner Cowan reported the final interment of eighty people from Sandstone and the surrounding area.[12] Most of the Sandstone deaths could have been prevented, since the citizens had ample warning to seek shelter in the Kettle River or to board the crowded Eastern Minnesota train to Duluth.

In the early afternoon on September 1 the people of Sandstone were given their first indication that something uncommon was occurring to the south. At 2:15 p.m. M. W. Jesmer, at his watchman's post atop the Kettle River high bridge 150 feet in the air, looked south and saw a red reflection in the sky which appeared to be fire burning in the vicinity of Hinckley. He heard a disturbing rumble, perhaps a strong wind. A few minutes after 3:00 Engineer William Best eased the southbound Eastern Minnesota passenger train across the narrow trestled structure, his headlight burning in the unusual afternoon darkness. Jesmer used his lantern to see and record the number of the engine.

At 4:00 p.m. a fire had started in the woods on the west side of the tracks, and Jesmer sent for help in case the bridge would be threatened. He got word from Mr. Bullis, the railway agent, that Best's train had been halted by the fire at Hinckley and was backing north with a load of survivors. Then the combined train, loaded with passengers and refugees, appeared and was given the signal to cross the bridge. The heavy vehicle lumbered slowly across the structure, which Jesmer reported was burning in twenty or thirty places. The train had gone about 2,000 feet beyond the bridge when the wooden supports gave way and collapsed, leaving the steel span in the center isolated.

Despite the warning from the Eastern train crew that fire had burned Hinckley and was moving toward Sandstone, the people made little preparation for their own safety. No one thought it necessary to leave town on the train, and very few prepared to take shelter until the fire was upon them.

The settlement of Sandstone, located on the Eastern Minnesota railroad, was especially vulnerable as it sat high on the west bluff overlooking the scenic Kettle River. The Kettle flows south through deep ragged gorges and sandstone cliffs to join the Grindstone and ultimately the St. Croix at what is now the Chengwatana State Forest. Sandstone bluffs extend along the Kettle for ten miles, and in 1894 the rock quarries along the river provided the main support of the town. Lumbering was the village's second most important industry.

Quarry at Sandstone before fire

Sandstone was a relatively prosperous community with a population reported to be somewhere between 300 and 600 people, depending upon how many hands had been hired to work the quarries and operate the sawmills and logging camps. The 1890 census indicated there were 517 people living in the incorporated village. At the time of the fire, it was said, the quarry had just received orders for a large amount of work, and in two more days there would have been 600 additional men at work. [13]

When fire struck, Sandstone seemed to be heading toward a promising future. Seventy-five to eighty homes, a newly-built school, a post office, two churches, a hotel, two boarding houses, a bank, four saloons and several stores, sawmills and business establishments comprised the town. Down at the riverside were the quarries, the company buildings and makeshift shanties. Two or three miles north on the Kettle River were the upper quarries at Hell's Gate. Numerous logging camps run by the O'Neill brothers and other loggers dotted the surrounding woods.

The most awesome structure in Sandstone was the high bridge over the Kettle River built by the Great Northern Company in 1889. Two threads of track suspended 150 feet in the air on a fragile cross-beamed steel framework spanned the river for 850 feet. From a distance the bridge seemed too frail to support the heavy freights and passenger trains that crawled across at four miles an hour several times a day.

Kettle River high bridge

On the Saturday of the fire Peter Peterson, superintendent of the Minneapolis Trust Company Quarries, had sent the men home early. It was only 2:00 p.m., but the sky was dark and ominous. Peterson lit the lamps in the company store, ordered some barrels filled with water and had his horses let out of the barns.

At 4:00 p.m. when the town's fire apparatus was taken out, the citizens began to fear that Sandstone was in danger. But those who had the opportunity did not squeeze aboard the Barry-Best train that came through a few minutes later.

As the fire appeared in flashes through the woods at the edge of town, the Rev. Emil Anderson, a twenty-four year old student minister serving the Swedish Congregational Church, ran from house to house, as did Father Lawler in Hinckley, telling people to run to the river. Even then some ignored his warning and assumed their rainbarrels, washtubs, wells and cellars would provide adequate protection should the fire get serious.

Then the wind swept in with a thunderous roar. Anderson, who had rescued a six-month old baby from a cornfield, was propelled by the wind 1,000 feet and set down unharmed with the child near the river. The child's mother was close by, and they all sought refuge in the Kettle River.

FROM THE ASHES

38

*The Rev. Emil Anderson,
student pastor at the Swedish
Congregational Church,
Sandstone*

At 5:30 p.m. the black sky was aflame with balls of fire that burst like rockets, showering sparks and cinders to the ground. The flames bore down with a fury, made one sweep of the town high atop the bluff and reduced it to ashes in minutes. People and animals were trapped in the streets and were overtaken as they tried belatedly to reach the river. Some hid in wells and died of suffocation. A few days after the fire eighteen decomposed bodies were found in one well, twelve of them children.

Some sought shelter in corn fields or potato patches and perished, while others managed to survive under wet coats and blankets. On a farm four miles from Sandstone, Mrs. Bilado saved herself and three of her five children under a wet blanket in a turnip patch. But a fourteen-year old daughter was burned as she chased a blanket that had blown away. In town another daughter perished and Mr. Bilado was badly burned.

The eighteen-year old daughter of Postmaster Erickson fled through the streets clutching a cigar box holding $36.00 of stamp money. She saved herself and the cigar box in the river, but lost everything else. Miss Erickson zealously guarded the postal funds until she could turn them over to Duluth postal authorities to send to Washington D.C.

Watchman Jesmer's dog, stranded on the middle section of the high bridge, howled piteously until he was rescued Monday morning, alive but severely burned.

Most of the people who survived were saved in the Kettle River. Many of them were reluctant to go into the water, and they lined the shores waiting until the fire forced them to plunge in up to their necks. One frightened THE FIRE child was pulled into the water by the family dog and held there until the father came. Those at the river heard the shrieks and cries of their friends and neighbors trapped on the streets above. At one spot in the river, when the fire had subsided, 100 people climbed on a large rock and held a prayer meeting and hymn sing.

At 8:00 p.m. after three hours in the cold water, people began to drag themselves out to the shore. They were chilled, wet and hungry, and some were suffering from burned lungs and eyes. Near the quarry they discovered that the small company office had not burned. Twenty-eight of the weakest and most seriously injured spent the night there jammed together on the floor. The rest stayed outside on the sand or among the rocks. A few found shelter from the flying cinders and ashes under a half-burned boat. Farther along the river another group found refuge in an old house used to store gunpowder. Four unexpended powder kegs were thrown into the river, and the house became a shelter for as many as could squeeze inside.

The Sunday morning sun revealed a desolate sight in the village above. Charred bodies of humans and animals littered the streets. Groups of families were found clustered together short distances from their homes where the fire had overtaken them. Although the clothes on most of the bodies had been burned completely away, it was assumed that many died of suffocation before burning.

No buildings remained standing in the entire village except the quarry office and a shanty by the river. The new school, though built of stone, had been reduced to a bare skeleton. Tree stumps still smoldered, and mounds of glowing coals marked what had once been buildings. Even the outer layer of rock on the cliffs had curled and flaked off in the intense heat. The logging camps in the woods were completely destroyed, but most of the men had escaped.

On Sunday morning partially-burned potatoes were dug up from the ground, and half-burned pig was roasted on a piece of sheet iron. Three cows, found wandering about, were caught and milked. The food was welcome since none had eaten since Saturday noon.

Because of its location Sandstone was literally isolated. The Kettle River bridge and other bridges to the north were burned, and the railroad south to Hinckley was impassable. On Sunday some survivors walked along the river three miles north to the Hell's Gate quarry, then five miles west over a spur track to a relief train waiting at the Miller station (now Groningen) on the St. Paul and Duluth tracks. Others remained in Sandstone and were rescued Monday by handcars that came down to the Kettle River bridge on the burned Eastern Minnesota tracks from Partridge (now Askov). Some Sandstone survivors were brought to Duluth, others stayed at West Superior, Wisconsin, and were transferred to Duluth after a few days.

PARTRIDGE

Small communities, both north and south of Hinckley, suffered partial or complete devastation. Some of them were merely clusters of a few buildings around railroad stations on either the St. Paul and Duluth line or the Eastern Minnesota railroad. They were not large enough to be incorporated as villages.

One such settlement with about fifty people was Partridge (later named Askov) on the Eastern Minnesota, six miles northeast of Sandstone. At the time of the fire a few lumber companies, several homes, a hotel, two stores, a freight and passenger depot with a telegraph station, a section house and a water tank made up the town. Logging camps and homesteads lay scattered about the surrounding area.

Twenty-eight year old Mary Boyington had managed the Partridge railway and telegraph station for five years and was proficient and conscientious in her job. Her husband, Dana, ran the hotel. On the day of the fire Mrs. Boyington noted that the southbound Eastern passenger train engineered by William Best was on schedule in spite of the threatening sky. Best's headlight was on and cut a narrow shaft of light through the murky blackness. Mrs. Boyington checked the time — it was then exactly 2:56 p.m.

Mary went about her usual duties, but felt uneasy about the looks of the weather. She kept close to her telegraph key in case there were some urgent messages. Two hours later the Barry-Best train pulled in from the south loaded with 500 distraught passengers. She heard the woeful story of Hinckley's destruction, but she and the other Partridge people who gathered at the depot did not board the train. They hoped the fire would burn itself out before reaching their community.

Barry took on more water and coal, and some of the trainmen went to the O'Neill logging camp nearby to get tin cups and pails for distributing water to the passengers. Then they were on their way to Superior and Duluth.

Soon after the train had left, conditions worsened until it became apparent that the fire was still advancing and would soon raze their settlement. Mrs. Boyington lingered until the very last moment, then scooped up the company records and valuables and fled. The hotel and all of their personal belongings were destroyed, as was everything else in town but the water tank.

Some people fled north on handcars and pushcars, others headed up a logging road to a small lake in a cut-over area about one-quarter of a mile from the railroad. They plunged into the water and stayed there immersing and covering themselves with wet garments until 1:00 Sunday morning.

Then came the shrill whistle of a train close by, a welcome sound. The survivors stumbled down the logging road, which was lit up by the trees still burning on both sides. Cold, wet and partially-clad, the survivors climbed aboard the boxcars of the freight which had come from West Superior. Other survivors were picked up along the tracks, and the train headed to Superior. Here the refugees were sheltered for a few days before being transferred to Duluth.

Only one Partridge resident, Robert Burns, was known to have perished, although another body which was not identified was reported to have been buried there by the Bailey search party.[14] Except for the Eastern Minnesota water tank, the entire settlement of Partridge was destroyed, but a few homesteads in the surrounding area were spared. Following the fire thirty-nine people in the community were given relief.[15] Although scattered fires were reported farther north, Partridge was on the northeastern edge of the area that sustained total destruction.

FINLAYSON

Seven miles west of Partridge on the other railroad lay the small village of Finlayson, a settlement maintained almost exclusively by railroad and lumber interests. Finlayson was on the St. Paul and Duluth tracks thirteen miles north of Hinckley, seven miles north of the famed Skunk Lake and on the northernmost fringe of the fire zone.

Although Finlayson was not included among the six communities (Brook Park, Mission Creek, Hinckley, Sandstone, Miller and Partridge) reported to have been totally destroyed by the fire, the State Commission Report indicates that eighty-five people were in the village on the day of the fire. All eighty-five claimed relief, and fourteen houses were provided by the Commission for those whose homes had burned.[16]

On the day of the fire the citizens of the town experienced the same anxiety as their neighbors when they witnessed the darkening afternoon sky. It was reassuring to hear the whistle of Engineer Root's southbound Limited as it rumbled through town without stopping. Those who were close enough saw that the train's headlight was on, which was unusual for mid-afternoon.

As the day wore on, conditions grew more distressing. Mrs. A. G. Crocker, a slight, delicate woman, assuming her home on a small pond was one of the safest places in town, had invited her neighbors to gather at her house if they were forced to evacuate theirs. At 5:00 p.m. the fire thundered in from the south. Neighbors rushed to the Crocker house, then to the pond. Children were wrapped in wet blankets, and they dashed water on themselves and covered their heads. At midnight, after seven hours in the pond, it appeared to be safe to leave the water. They were chilled and suffering from smoke and heat.

On Sunday morning the Crocker home was still standing, but fire burned dangerously close. All day adults took turns extinguishing sparks that fell on the roof while the children stayed by the pond. Mrs. Crocker rationed out her remaining supply of food, and everyone received adequate nourishment. Late Sunday night they were picked up by a relief train that brought them to Duluth.

A few miles away the Cheney family had taken shelter in an underground root cellar. As the fire burned, the supply of oxygen in the cellar became depleted, and everyone would have suffocated had it not been for a hapless donkey which crashed through the roof as it tried to escape. The opening let in the necessary ventilation, and all survived, even the donkey.

Some of the Finlayson residents who had been sheltered in other places were rescued by Roper's relief train earlier Sunday, but twenty-nine survivors, among them Mrs. Crocker and her neighbors, boarded a train which returned from a second search for victims at Skunk Lake. At Duluth they were given a meal at the Armory and assigned to places of shelter.

On Wednesday the undaunted Mrs. Crocker was back at her home in Finlayson with a supply of relief provisions. Her home became the mess hall and dormitory for homeless ones returning to town to rebuild.

W. D. Campbell, Conductor

Barry's engine No. 105

44

CHAPTER 3

Trains to the Rescue

THE EASTERN RAILWAY OF MINNESOTA

O N SATURDAY, September 1, Engineer Edward Barry, at the controls of engine No. 105 pulling train No. 24, left the Eastern Minnesota station at West Superior at 7:00 a.m. His freight was making its usual trip to Hinckley and back. As was the policy of the day, each run was given a number. His southbound freight was assigned No. 24, the returning northbound, even though it was the same train, was No. 23. W. D. Campbell, the conductor, headed a crew manned by Fireman Alex Thistle and Brakemen George Gilham, Peter McLaughlin and Charles Freeman.

As the train moved southward, there seemed to be nothing extraordinary about the trip. The woods as usual was hazy from summer fires. But when they reached the Partridge station, fifteen miles northeast of Hinckley, the air thickened with dense smoke, and the sky darkened. The crewmen lit the engine headlight and cab lights.

Ordinarily the train would have reached Hinckley at 11:45 a.m., but Barry had reduced his speed and proceeded slowly through the unnatural blackness. When they arrived in Hinckley at 2:45 p.m., they found firemen fighting a hopeless battle against the fires that were sweeping into the town.

Barry pulled off on the side-tracks. At the south end of the yards the railroad ties were beginning to burn, the rails had started to warp and the boxcars standing to the side were on fire. The heat was so intense the trainmen could not get on the turntable to reverse the engine. Flames were shooting skyward, and the smoke was blinding. But the freight could not leave and make the return trip north since the Eastern passenger train was expected at 3:25 p.m. and had the right-of-way on the single track. So the crew waited nervously for the passenger to arrive.

George Gilham, Brakeman

George Ford, Fireman

F. A. Thistle, Fireman

In Duluth the Eastern passenger train No. 4, engineered by William Best, had loaded for its daily run from Duluth to St. Paul. This was a fast train that ran every day but Sunday. It did not stop at some of the small stations and stopped at others only on signal. Passengers could make the 185 mile trip to St. Paul in six hours, and those riding first class were served a meal en route in the buffet parlor car. A first-class ticket from St. Paul to Duluth cost $4.30.[1]

Passenger train No. 4 pulled out of the Duluth station at 1:00 p.m. with Engineer Best at the throttle and Conductor Harry Powers in charge of the cars. The crewmen were Porter George Goodin, Brakeman O. L. Beach, Baggageman Massey Baker and Firemen George Ford and J. Kellock. There were two parlor cars, two day coaches, one combination smoking car and a coal car. Many people had boarded the train at Duluth, some of them being passengers from the steamship *Northwest,* owned by James J. Hill, which had just docked at Duluth. More people were taken aboard the train at West and South Superior, adding up to a total of about 100 passengers.

Harry Powers, Conductor

William Best, Engineer

Edward Barry, Engineer

The train travelled south into Wisconsin and, as was the case in Minnesota, a smoky haze filled the air. Thirty miles south of Superior, darkness closed in, and the engine headlight and cab lamps were lit. The crew expected to get emergency instructions by telegraph from West Superior somewhere along the line, but none arrived, and the train continued on into increasing smoke and heat. As they approached Hinckley, the sky lightened, but clouds of smoke and flame appeared to be shooting upwards from the south end of town.

When the train arrived at Hinckley at 3:25 p.m. with an apprehensive load of passengers, the town had begun to burn and the wind was whipping flames into the sky. The crew did its usual switching and moved to the water tank in the freight yard. Fireman George Ford managed to get water aboard but was driven away from the spout three times. The freight station, boxcars and railroad ties were burning, and it was evident that the train could not proceed southward.

Best's engine No. 125
of the Eastern Railway of Minnesota

Engineer Best backed the train away from the water tank and stopped near Barry's engine waiting on the side track. The conductors and engineers conferred hurriedly and decided to couple the trains together and make a hasty retreat north bringing out as many Hinckley people as possible. Neither engineer had been able to reach the turntable to change direction.

The Eastern Minnesota railroad had established the rules that when trains were coupled and two crews were on duty, the conductor of senior rank would assume charge and take responsibility. In this case, Conductor Powers was in authority. Powers immediately ordered the freight engine to connect to three empty boxcars and couple to the end of the passenger train. The passenger train was not officially allowed to go north without orders, but the freight in the lead had the right-of-way to return to West Superior. Barry's engine was first, followed by his coal car, the three boxcars, a caboose, the five coaches of the passenger train, another coal car and at the end Best's engine. Both engines were in reverse, Barry's engine pulling at the front and Best's engine pushing and applying the air brakes from the rear.

The two trains waited at the depot while frenzied Hinckley residents came on foot or by wagon from all directions. The trainmen assisted people aboard and occasionally had to restrain men from shoving ahead of women and children.

While Best and Powers were deciding how long it was safe to stay, they heard two sharp blasts from Engineer Barry's whistle, signaling that the train was leaving. The cars began to move. Best jumped into his engine at the rear, applied the air brakes and stopped the train. People continued to rush aboard. Conductor Campbell and a brakeman from the freight came back to Best's engine and threatened that Barry was going to disconnect his engine and pull out if the train did not leave immediately. Passengers who had boarded the train at Duluth were also pleading to go, but Best and Powers thought they could stay a few minutes longer and save a few more people. Several times Barry whistled and attempted to leave, but Best kept a firm hand on the brakes.

The tempo of the fire increased rapidly, houses vanished in minutes and the heat was unbearable. As flames threatened the coaches and ignited the ties underneath, Best worried that perhaps he had held the train too long and had sacrificed everyone. By this time the flames were overtaking people in the streets, and Best could see that very few would be able to reach the train any longer. So he released the brakes, and the train lumbered out of the doomed town with about 350 Hinckley refugees aboard. As the train pulled out, a man on a horse came galloping after it. Passengers reached to pull him aboard, but the horse bolted and both disappeared in the fire. The last forlorn sound people heard was the blast from the Brennan Lumber Company whistle indicating that the lumber yard was burning. It was then 4:00 p.m.

On the way out of town more people were seen running toward the train, but it was impossible to stop for them. Best turned his head so he wouldn't have to witness the pathetic sight.

Just across the Grindstone River about forty people had gathered on a high spot not yet overtaken by fire. The train halted for a few minutes and took them aboard. Douglas Greeley, proprietor of the Morrison Hotel in Hinckley, was the last person to be rescued. There were then about 500 people on the train.

Because Barry was backing his engine, there was no headlight to illumine the track ahead. Two brakemen, Beach and McLaughlin, volunteered to ride on the outside of Barry's engine and serve as outlooks. They carried lanterns and at every bridge signalled Barry to cross. Barry would then whistle to start, Best would release the brakes and the train would proceed over the burning bridge. The brakemen were blinded and scorched, but they survived by dousing themselves with water from the engine tank. Engineer Best said of the two men, "Better grit never was put in man than was in those two fellows."[2] He described the discipline of the train crew as "perfect" with each member functioning efficiently at his job.[3]

As the train pressed northward, trees on both sides of the tracks were burning and falling. Flaming branches and debris hurled by the wind bombarded from all sides. The railroad ties were afire, and the engineers feared that the train would be derailed if the tracks would spread.

O. L. Beach,
Brakeman

Peter McLaughlin, Brakeman

Inside the coaches and boxcars, people were jammed tightly together in the stifling heat. One of the boxcars had been used to carry coal, so the people occupying it were blackened from coal dust. They had to open the door for ventilation despite the flames and smoke. Some of the coach windows shattered, and waves of searing heat blew through the cars. Some people fainted, others screamed hysterically, a few remained calm and tried to pacify those who were frightened. The conductors circulated through the cars, consoling and assuring passengers and caring for the refugees who were injured. One man from Minneapolis begged for morphine to end it all. A group of men had their revolvers ready to use on themselves rather than burn to death. Women prayed, children cried and men cursed. In one coach a father and mother grieved for a lost child, while in another a stranger took care of their child who later was reunited with them.

A passenger, Mrs. Flora Davey of Duluth, secretary of the National Ladies of the Grand Army of the Republic, was concerned because all the society's records were in a trunk she had to abandon back at the burning St. Paul and Duluth depot in Hinckley. Another passenger, H. B. Hansen, a Chicago bicyclist on tour through the northwest, wondered how he would continue his engagements without his bicycle and gear which he had to leave at the same depot.

The eight miles northeast to Sandstone were sheer hell, but when the train stopped at Sandstone they had moved ahead of the flames into dark, thick smoke. The two conductors thought it would be best to stop at Sand-

FROM THE ASHES

50

stone, but Barry and Best urged them to go on, fearing that the fire would soon overtake them. The residents of Sandstone were told of the disaster at Hinckley and were alerted to the catastrophe coming their way, but none chose to leave on the train. Within an hour the fire had burned all of Sandstone.

But the danger for those aboard the train was not yet over. Just out of Sandstone was the famous Kettle River high bridge crossing the river 150 feet in the air. All trains had standing orders to wait for the signal from the watchman, then to proceed across at four miles per hour. Although the wooden supports at each end of the bridge were beginning to burn, Barry got the signal from the watchman to cross. As the train crawled across the bridge, anxious crewmen worried that the weight of the combined trains would be too much for the trestled structure, and they would all be dashed to the river far below. But they reached the other side safely just minutes before the wooden supports collapsed.

Along the route north the train experienced no further difficulties other than the great distress and suffering of the passengers. Along the way Dr. Stephan of Hinckley went through the cars uniting members of families who had become separated.

At the Partridge station six miles northeast of Sandstone, the train stopped while Barry took on more coal and water for his engine. Some of the train crew secured water pails and cups to carry water to suffering passengers in the boxcars. By this time Engineer Barry's eyes were burned, and he had difficulty seeing.

After stopping at every station along the way to inform the residents of the disaster, the train reached West Superior. Some passengers wanted to stay in Superior and left the train. Barry's and Best's engines were retired, and a switch engine brought the cars and coaches to Duluth. Both engineers, who lived in Superior, went home to treat their burns and rest from the ordeal. The remaining load of 475 passengers and refugees arrived at the Duluth station between 9:00 and 9:30 p.m. Anxious and curious crowds had gathered, and Duluth police kept the throngs back while the Mayor and Chief of Police tended to the immediate needs of the sufferers. Those who had no place to go were given lunch, then assigned to temporary quarters where they received food, clothing and shelter.

THE ST. PAUL AND DULUTH RAILROAD

At the same time that the two coupled Eastern Minnesota trains were leaving Hinckley, another passenger train, the Limited No. 4 on the other railroad, the St. Paul and Duluth line, was coming to an abrupt halt one mile north of Hinckley. The train was stopped by a group of frenzied people who were running up the tracks trying to escape the burning town.

Thomas Sullivan, Conductor

John Blair, Porter

*James Root,
Engineer*

The Limited was a fast passenger train on the Northern Pacific's St. Paul and Duluth road and was affectionately known as the "Skalley."* It provided stiff competition for the Eastern Minnesota. In fact it was the most popular passenger train going to the Twin Cities because it could make the run between Duluth and St. Paul in five hours, one hour less than the Eastern. Just as with other railroads this line also numbered its trains — the southbound Limited being No. 4, the northbound was No. 3.

On Saturday, September 1, Engineer James Root of White Bear Lake was at the throttle of engine 69 of the southbound Limited No. 4. He was a veteran of Civil War railroading and gained more fame after the fire, when his name was splashed on the front pages of newspapers across the country.

*A local citizen of Hinckley is positive the name "Skalley" originated among Scandinavians who said, "Aye *skal* go" as they boarded the train.

Root's engine

With Root were Conductor Thomas Sullivan, Fireman John McGowan, Porter John Blair, Brakeman John Monahan (Moynihan or Monihan) and Baggageman George Morris, all residents of St. Paul. Their train consisted of the engine, a coal car, two coaches, two chair cars, a smoking car and a baggage car.

The train left Duluth at 1:55 p.m., the appointed time, with from 110 to 115 passengers. Another 25 boarded at Carlton. The day was cloudy and sultry, and Engineer Root thought a storm was approaching.

As the train neared Carlton, fifteen miles out of Duluth, the sky became so dark that the headlight, cab lamp and coach lights were lit. For forty miles they ran through almost total darkness. The passengers were nervous, and some thought Root should have turned back. Root, however, assumed they would out-run the smoke. As they neared Hinckley the sky turned lighter with the yellowish cast of unnatural twilight. Cinders and black soot were flying in the air. From the top of the hill just north of Hinckley, Root could see men and women running on the tracks towards the train. He turned to Fireman McGowan and said, "There is something wrong!"[4]

One mile from Hinckley the people running up the tracks flagged the train. Root stopped and dismounted. An old lady and her two daughters were the first to reach the train. "For God's sake, will you save us?" they gasped.[5] The time was then a few minutes after 4:00 p.m.

When from 150 to 160 refugees had boarded, Root threw his engine into reverse to try to reach Skunk Lake, a shallow marshy body of water, six miles north of Hinckley. Conductor Sullivan was sure they would not make it, because a cyclonic wind was already blowing flames on all sides of them, and

RESCUE TRAINS

53

the railroad ties beneath them were burning. Some distance down the track three men tried to catch the train, but Root dared not stop. Two of the men grabbed on to the pilot of the train, but one fell off and was burned. The other managed to hang on until the train reached Skunk Lake.

As Root backed the train, a fierce explosion shattered the plate glass cab window and showered him with fragments of glass. The side of his head was injured, and a gash in his neck bled profusely. In a short time Root slumped, his hand still on the throttle. When he revived he was shocked to discover he had unconsciously turned down the steam, and the pressure had fallen to ninety-five pounds. By that time the train had slackened its speed to a crawl, and the fire was gaining. Root immediately opened the throttle but again began to faint. Fireman McGowan entered the cab, and seeing Root's condition, kept him from falling and revived him with a pail of water. Both men dipped their swollen, blistered hands into the water.

While this was happening in the cab, the passengers were experiencing another crisis. Fire had enveloped all of the cars, and the coaches were burning from underneath as well as from the roof. The windows on the west side had broken, and flames were licking at the curtains and upholstery. Smoke poured into the cars through the open windows and from the burning transoms above. Terrified passengers crowded to the opposite side of the aisles away from the fire as far as possible. Each breath was torture. In the smoking car one man jumped out a broken window to instant death. Conductor Sullivan restrained a second man from doing the same.

Some of the passengers stared mutely into space in shock, others recoiled at each wave of flame with shrieks and cries. One passenger said afterwards, "Such praying I have never heard in my life."[6] A religious fanatic ran through one car shouting. "We are all going to heaven together,"[7] upsetting others who tried to remain calm.

In the midst of the bedlam some acts of heroism were performed. Porter Blair, with a quiet reassuring manner, passed out water to passengers and allayed their fears. One lady moistened towels in a washstand for Conductor Sullivan as he tried to keep the end of the car from burning. Several men wet cloths and towels in the chair car lavatory to revive fainting passengers. Mrs. E. N. Saunders of St. Paul, with seven children in her care, remained calm and composed as she consoled her frightened charges.

Back in the cab the injured Engineer Root had been trying to see some sign of Skunk Lake through the smoke and flames. When he saw water in a ditch along the tracks, he assumed he must have reached the lake. He stopped the train and maneuvered it so the passengers could disembark, then fell exhausted to the floor of the cab. McGowan began to carry Root outside, but Root said, "Leave me alone and go help the passengers into the water."[8] McGowan did so, but returned shortly with another man who helped carry Root to safety. As people crowded off the train, Sullivan threw pails of water on the platform while Blair and McGowan helped them exit.

Painting by Bruce Bomberger for True Magazine,
December 1950, in article, "The Suicide Express."

When the railroad company had built the trestle across Skunk Lake, they had divided the lake so that the smaller body of water was on the west side of the tracks. It was here that the passengers fortunately sought refuge. After the fire the east side was found completely burned, and three victims perished. [9]

As the people left the train, they had to climb across a barbed wire fence and wade through the coarse swale growing along the edge of the marsh. They reached the water, eighteen inches of mud and slime. Here they sat or lay, covering themselves with the foul water while sheets of flame swept over them. Porter Blair used a fire extinguisher he had taken from the train to put out flames that ignited clothing.

One survivor counted three waves of fire, each accompanied by tremendous heat and showers of sparks and cinders. Each wave was carried on a roaring blast of wind, and people screamed as burning torches struck them. If such a wave had hit as they left the train, none could have survived its onslaught. After the third wave of fire had passed and the wind had abated, a strange phenomenon occurred — a shower of black "snowflakes" sifted down, almost beautiful in the tragic setting. The time was then about 5:00 p.m.

RESCUE TRAINS

A few people had become separated from the others as they left the train and did not reach the waters of Skunk Lake. Senator Frank Daugherty, his ten-year old son, two women and a six-month old baby survived in a potato patch on high ground near the lake. Another party of three found shelter first in a culvert, then moved to a bare spot of ground where they covered themselves with coats while the flames burned overhead. After the fire these three found two dugouts, each sheltering about a dozen people. Here they spent the night.

Conductor Sullivan, Brakeman Monahan and others from the train ran north on the burning tracks. Sullivan was anxious to get word of the train's fate to railroad officials and to order a relief train to rescue the survivors at Skunk Lake. As they ran, some in the group were overcome by the smoke and fell. Later eighteen dead bodies were found along the tracks by a rescue crew, some of the dead presumably from Root's train.

After great difficulty Sullivan reached the Miller station where he sent a message to Duluth telling of the wreck and ordering a relief train to be sent to Skunk Lake. Then he and several others ran on, keeping just ahead of the fire until they reached a gravel pit north of Finlayson. For several miles Brakeman Monahan carried fifteen-year old May Wellman, saving her life. All the survivors in this group were picked up by a relief train that brought them to Willow River, where they were transferred to another train which took them to Duluth.

Back at Skunk Lake Engineer Root had stayed in the water with the others for three or four hours. When he felt his limbs grow numb from cold, he asked for help to get to the engine for shelter. The men advised Root that the coal car was still burning and the engine was not safe, but Root ordered McGowan to disconnect the engine and move it down the track. Here he spent the remainder of the night, lying on the floor of the cab.

During the night when the fire had abated, the others who had been in the water thought it safe to move to higher ground. Earlier they had been subjected to oppressive heat from the fire, but as the cool night air moved in

Skunk Lake

they became severely chilled in their wet, muddy clothes. Sometime through the night James Lobdell of St. Paul and two other men went on foot to Hinckley. From there they went by handcar to meet a work train that brought them to Pine City. They were the first to carry the news of the burned Limited to the residents of Pine City.[10]

It was not until midnight that handcars from the Williams and Roper relief train reached Skunk Lake from the north. Williams left two doctors and some supplies, then returned to the work train which was repairing tracks and bridges. At about 3:00 a.m. another crew under Dr. Barnum of Pine City and Conductor Buckley of the Limited No. 3 arrived at Skunk Lake on handcars and pushcars from Hinckley. They took forty survivors, among them Jim Root, back to Hinckley where they were moved to a relief train to Pine City. The remaining survivors were rescued and brought to Duluth later Sunday morning when the relief train from the north was able to reach Skunk Lake over the repaired tracks.

Reports differed about the Skunk Lake episode. First of all, sources did not agree on how many passengers boarded the Limited at Duluth. Figures varied from 100 to 200. Conflicting reports were also given for the number of refugees that climbed aboard Root's train near Hinckley. Some indicated 150 to 160, others claimed as many as 300. There were confusing accounts about the numbers saved at Skunk Lake. Assistant General Manager L. J. Miller of the St. Paul and Duluth Railroad issued a report saying that all passengers who had boarded the Limited in Duluth on that fateful day had been saved with the exception of one man. He was O. W. Rowley, general passenger agent of the Winnipeg and Duluth road, who had left the others and had burned several hundred feet from the tracks. He was identified later by a laundry mark on the collar of his shirt. However, other accounts, among them Root's own story, mentioned two Chinese men who were in the train and refused to leave at Skunk Lake. They hid under their seats and were burned. This is partially verified by reports from a search party which later found human ashes inside a burned coach of the train. In addition it was known that several people ran north on the tracks, and some of them were among the eighteen whose bodies were found along the railroad north of Skunk Lake.

One thing is certain — all of those who reached Skunk Lake and remained there were saved. Nelly Bly, after her visit on September 8, wrote in the *New York World:*

It is not a pretty name, Skunk Lake, but it is one that hundreds of people will reverence forever. It is not a pretty lake, either. It is not a lake at all. It is a wide hole filled with black, ill-smelling mud into which one would sink knee-deep at the edge and to the neck in the central depths. Skunk Lake is just as ugly and black today and is burnt clean down to the edge of the mud, except on the north side, where a border of green grass is left untouched. That green grass is all that is left in the blackened mass of ruins that stretches in every direction as far as one can see.[11]

THE ST. CLOUD AND HINCKLEY TRAIN

The St. Cloud and Hinckley Accommodation train, operated by the Great Northern Company, had a short run of sixty-seven miles between St. Cloud and Hinckley and back again. Its usual schedule, every day but Sunday, was to leave St. Cloud at 6:50 a.m. and arrive in Hinckley at 12:05 noon with northbound train No. 45. The crew would then take on whatever freight and passengers awaited them in Hinckley and make the return trip to St. Cloud. The southbound train, No. 46, would leave Hinckley at 1:00 p.m. and arrive back in St. Cloud at 6:15 p.m.

On Saturday, September 1, No. 46 was forced to depart from its usual schedule. When the seven man crew left St. Cloud in the morning, young Engineer William Vogel was at the controls of engine No. 315 with Conductor Edward Parr and Fireman Joseph Lacher, Brakemen John Delaney, B. S. Carrier and M. J. Whalen, and Express Messenger John Vandersluis.*

The morning was sunny and bright and seemed to be the start of another scorching day. The crew was in good spirits anticipating a light Saturday of work and a day off on Sunday. As they neared Brook Park, eight miles southwest of Hinckley, the air was heavy with smoke. Engineer Vogel slowed the train, and the crewmen closed the doors of the cars to keep out the heat and fumes.

When they arrived at Hinckley at 2:00 p.m. they were two hours late and conditions looked threatening. A crew of fire fighters was out trying to control a small blaze near the Eastern Minnesota roundhouse. Since there was no load of freight waiting for them, Conductor Parr and Engineer Vogel thought it wise to leave town as soon as possible. They quickly coupled on a coach and a baggage car, adjusted their air brakes and left. Only two passengers boarded the train — D. A. Kingsley, an advance agent for the Wells Theater Company, and sixty-five year old Mr. Carver, who was going to his home in Brook Park. The crew hoped to have a fast ride back to St. Cloud with their light load.

When they were only a mile out of Hinckley, small fires were burning in the woods along the tracks. Suddenly the air exploded into a mass of flames on all sides, and the wind blew furiously toward them. Engineer Vogel kept thundering ahead for three more miles until he stopped at what he feared was a burned bridge over the Mission Creek. But he could still see the tracks across the bridge, and since they did not appear to be warped, he opened the throttle and took the train across. The bridge swayed and sagged, but held. For the next three miles the train slashed through an inferno of falling trees, flying torches, burning railroad ties and warping tracks. About one mile

*There were three spellings of this name: Vandersluis (Brown), Sanderluis (Wilkinson) and Van Dersluiz (*The Minneapolis Journal,* September 3, 1894).

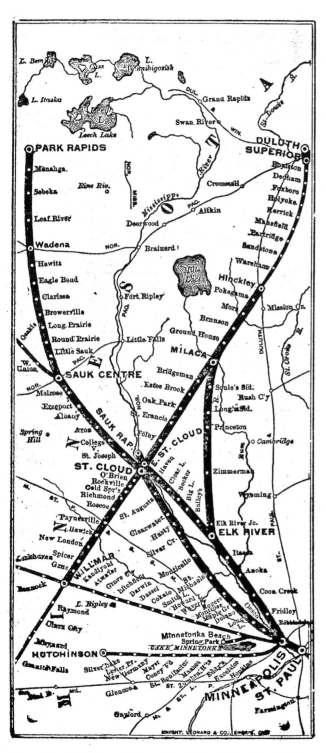

From Great Northern Railway timetable, September 1894,
showing route and schedule of St. Cloud and Hinckley Line

OSSEO AND ST. CLOUD LINE.

No. 1 Ex. Sun.	Daily Ex. Sun.	Miles	STATIONS	Daily Ex. Sun.	No. 2 Ex. Sun.
8.30 AM	3 30 PM	00	Lv..ST. PAUL...Ar	11.55 AM	6.05 PM
8.55 AM	4.05 PM	10	....Minneapolis..Ar	11.10 AM	5.30 PM
9.00 AM	4.12 PM	..	..Clearwater Junc..	10.55 AM	5.20 PM
9.10 AM	4.30 PM	17	....Robinsdale.....	10.35 AM	5.11 PM
9.22 AM	4.59 PM	24	.......Osseo.....	10.13 AM	4.59 PM
.... x	5.22 PM	29	..Maple Grove.....	x 9.53 AM	x
9.43 AM	5.37 PM	36	......Rogers.....	9.43 AM	4.42 PM
9.56 AM	6.02 PM	41	...St. Michaels....	9.10 AM	4.31 PM
10.15 AM	6.36 PM	46	.....Monticello....	8.34 AM	4.16 PM
x 10.32 AM	x 7.05 PM	50	...Silver Creek....	x 8.02 AM	x 4.03 PM
10.37 AM	7.15 PM	58	......Hasty......	7.53 AM	3.59 PM
10.48 AM	7.35 PM	65	....Clearwater....	7.32 AM	3.50 PM
x 11.05 AM	x 8.05 PM	71	...St. Augusta....	x 7.00 AM	x 3.36 PM
11.25 AM	8.30 PM	76	Ar..ST. CLOUD. Lv	6.35 AM	3.25 PM

See also Trains 3 and 4 between St. Paul, Minneapolis and St. Cloud.

ANOKA, ELK RIVER, MILACA AND HINCKLEY.

No. 19 Ex. Sun.	No. 5 Daily Ex. Sun.	Miles	STATIONS	No. 6 Daily Ex. Sun.	No. 20 Ex. Sun.
1.05 PM	3.30 PM	00	Lv ..ST. PAUL ..Ar	10.55 AM	6.55 PM
1.30 PM	4.00 PM	10	....Minneapolis..Ar	10.25 AM	6.25 PM
1.40 PM	4.10 PM	12	. Minneapolis Junc .	10.17 AM	6.15 PM
1.48 PM	4.20 PM	14	. Northtown Junct ..	10.07 AM	6.07 PM
1.54 PM	4.28 PM	18	......Fridley.....	10.00 AM	6.00 PM
1.56 PM	4.30 PM	19	...Brighton Junc...	9.58 AM	5.58 PM
2.03 PM x	4.41 PM	25	Coon Creek Siding..	x 9.49 AM	5.49 PM
2.10 PM	4.50 PM	29	......Anoka......	9.42 AM	5.41 PM
x 2.21 PM	5.05 PM	36	......Itasca......	9.29 AM	x 5.28 PM
2.30 PM	5.40 PM	41	....Elk River.....	9.21 AM	5.20 PM
2.33 PM	5.45 PM	42	..Elk River Junc ..	8.45 AM	5.15 PM
2.48 PM	6.30 PM	51	....Zimmerman....	8.05 AM	5.01 PM
3.03 PM	7.10 PM	60	....Princeton.....	7.25 AM	4.47 PM
3.10 PM	7.33 PM	64	...Long's Siding...	6.45 AM	4.40 PM
3.19 PM	8.02 PM	69	...Soule's Siding...	6.22 AM	4.33 PM
3.27 PM	8.25 PM	73	...Milaca Junc....	6.05 AM	4.27 PM
3.30 PM	8.30 PM	74	.....Milaca.....	6.00 AM	4.25 PM
3.38 PM	....	79	......Tosca......	....	4.16 PM
3.49 PM	....	86	...Ground House...	....	4.06 PM
3.58 PM	....	91	......Brunson.....	....	3.58 PM
4.03 PM	....	94	.......Mora......	....	3.54 PM
4.12 PM	....	100	......Quamba.....	....	3.44 PM
4.21 PM	....	105	.....Pokegama....	....	3.37 PM
4.35 PM	....	113	Ar . HINCKLEY . Lv	....	3.25 PM

ST. CLOUD AND HINCKLEY LINE.

	No. 45	Miles	STATIONS	No. 46	
	6.50 AM	76	Lv ..ST. CLOUD..Ar	6.15 PM	
	7.28 AM	86	.....Parent......	5.23 PM	
	7.44 AM	90	.....Foley......	5.02 PM	
	7.53 AM	92	...St. Francis....	4.49 PM	
	8.01 AM	95	....Oak Park.....	4.40 PM	
	8.19 AM	98	...Estes Brook....	4.19 PM	
Daily Ex. Sunday.	8.31 AM	101	...Bridgman.....	4.04 PM	Daily Ex. Sunday.
	9.40 AM	104	.....Milaca.....	3.45 PM	
	10.01 AM	109	......Tosca......	3.00 PM	
	10.26 AM	116	..Ground House...	2.37 PM	
	10.45 AM	121	....Brunson.....	2.19 PM	
	10.55 AM	124	......Mora......	2.09 PM	
	11.16 AM	130	.....Quamba.....	1.48 PM	
	11.36 AM	135	....Pokegama....	1.29 PM	
	12.05 PM	143	Ar HINCKLEY . Lv	1.00 PM	

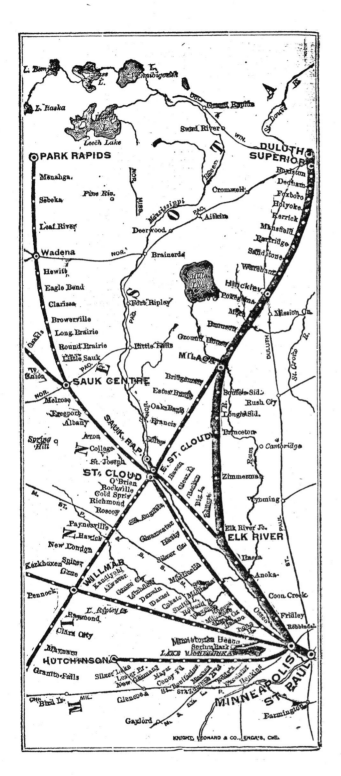

EASTERN MINNESOTA RAILWAY.
West Superior and Duluth.

No. 23 Ex. Sun.	No. 3 Ex. Sun.	Miles	STATIONS	No. 4 Ex. Sun.	No. 24 Ex. Sun.
......	1.05 PM	00	Lv ..ST. PAUL.. Ar	6.55 PM	......
......	1.30 PM	10	....Minneapolis..Ar	6.25 PM	......
......	1.40 PM	12	.Minneapolis Junc.	6.15 PM	......
......	1.48 PM	14	..Northtown Junc..	6.07 PM	......
......	1.54 PM	18	.....Fridley......	6.00 PM	......
......	1.56 PM	19	..Brighton Junc...	5.58 PM	......
......	2.03 PM	25	....Coon Creek.....	5.49 PM	......
......	2.10 PM	29	.....Anoka.....	5.41 PM	......
......	2.21 PM	36	....Itasca.....	5.28 PM	......
......	2.30 PM	41	....Elk River.....	5.20 PM	......
......	2.33 PM	42	.Elk River Junc..	5.15 PM	......
......	2.48 PM	51	...Zimmerman...	5.01 PM	......
......	3.03 PM	60	...Princeton...	4.47 PM	......
......	3.10 PM	64	..Long's Siding..	4.40 PM	......
......	3.19 PM	69	..Soule's Siding..	4.33 PM	......
......	3.27 PM	73	..Milaca Junc....	4.27 PM	......
9.40 AM	3.30 PM	74	....Milaca....	4.25 PM	3.30 PM
10.01 AM	3.38 PM	79	....Tosca....	4.16 PM	3.00 PM
10.26 AM	3.49 PM	86	...Ground House..	4.06 PM	2.37 PM
10.45 AM	3.58 PM	91	....Brunson.....	3.58 PM	2.19 PM
10.55 AM	4.03 PM	94	.....Mora.....	3.54 PM	2.09 PM
11.16 AM	4.12 PM	100	...Quamba....	3.44 PM	1.48 PM
11.36 AM	4.21 PM	105	...Pokegama..	3.37 PM	1.29 PM
1.20 PM	4.37 PM	113	...Hinckley....	3.25 PM	11.45 AM
1.50 PM	4.48 PM	119	...Wareham.....	3.11 PM	11.20 AM
2.00 PM	4.51 PM	121	...Sandstone..	3.08 PM	11.15 AM
2.56 PM	5.03 PM	127	...Partridge....	2.56 PM	10.20 AM
3.30 PM	5.16 PM	136	...Mansfield...	2.42 PM	9.45 AM
4.00 PM	5.29 PM	144	...Kerrick.....	2.28 PM	9.15 AM
4.30 PM	5.43 PM	152	...Holyoke.....	2.13 PM	8.40 AM
5.00 PM	5.57 PM	159	...Foxboro.....	1.59 PM	8.10 AM
5.30 PM	6.10 PM	166	...Dedham....	1.46 PM	7.35 AM
6.00 PM	6.25 PM	173	...Boylston..	1.31 PM	7.05 AM
......	6.34 PM	......	..South Superior..	1.25 PM	......
6.40 PM	6.45 PM	181	..WEST SUPERIOR.	1.15 PM	6.30 AM
......	7.00 PM	185	Ar ...DULUTH...Lv	1.00 PM	......

Train No. 4 connects at Elk River for Northern Minnesota points, and at Minneapolis with Manitoba Express 7:10 P. M. Washington and Montana Express 8:20 P. M.

* Flag station—train stops only on signal. ‡ Trains do not stop.

Trains Nos. 3 and 4 have Buffet Parlor Cars, serving dinner and supper en route.

W. C. FARRINGTON, Gen. Manager, Duluth, Minn.

From Great Northern Railway timetable, September 1894, showing route and schedule of the Eastern Minnesota Railway

northeast of Brook Park the engine hit a twisted rail and plunged off the embankment into the ditch, partially overturning the baggage car and pulling the coach crosswise on the tracks.

The situation appeared utterly hopeless. The fire had surrounded them, and if Best's passenger train, which was expected soon, would arrive, it would crash into them from the rear.

Conductor Parr and Expressman Vandersluis left the baggage car and made a dash through the flames for the coach to join the brakemen and the two passengers. The flames were burning through the cracks to the inside of the coach, and the cushions caught fire. They threw the burning seats outside, said their farewells to each other and lay down on the floor assuming this was the end.

But Brakeman Whalen was not ready to give up so easily. He thought of the water tank in the engine and devised a plan where two men at a time would dash outside to get pails of water to throw on the burning coach, then run back inside while another pair went for two more pails. They continued this for about an hour and were able to save the coach. In the meantime Engineer Vogel and Fireman Lacher had stayed alive on the floor of the engine with water from the tank turned on them.

When the fire had subsided, two men came down the tracks through the smoke, one dragging the other. They were two railroad section men, Thomas Gorman and his son, who had taken shelter under a railroad bridge a mile away. Young Gorman carried his father to the coach, left him there and started back on the tracks to find the rest of his family.

By 5:00 p.m. the fire was subdued enough for the crewmen to walk to Brook Park hoping to get word out about their wrecked train and secure some aid. What they found were charred bodies lying in smoldering ruins and twenty-three suffering people in the pond near the still-burning lumber mill. The men helped the survivors out of the water and led them back to the wrecked train. It was about 7:00 p.m. when they reached the coach of the train.

Throughout the long night the trainmen administered to the suffering, partially-clothed refugees. The men used their own shirts for cloths to apply water to burned faces, mouths and eyes. Moans and cries of pain were heard through the night.

At daybreak Sunday morning four trainmen and passenger Kingsley walked on the twisted tracks back to Hinckley finding several burned bodies along the way. At Hinckley they discovered the town had been totally destroyed except for the Eastern Minnesota roundhouse and water tank. One-hundred fifty cars of grain were still burning intensely in the yards. The men drank water from the tank and found some crackers and bread to eat in the roundhouse. One Hinckley survivor was leading a cow along the tracks and gave them permission to milk it. They sent the milk in a pail together with the crackers to the survivors with a six-man rescue team which went on a handcar back to the wrecked train.

Skunk Lake
as it appeared in 1976

A relief train arrived in Hinckley from Pine City on the St. Paul and Duluth railroad. The trainmen and Kingsley boarded it and were taken to Pine City where they received food and care. Before he left with the others for St. Paul, Conductor Parr sent a message back to St. Cloud telling of the wrecked train.

On Sunday Theater Agent Kingsley related the dramatic story of the wrecked train and told of his own heroic deeds. When the trainmen heard Kingsley's account, they sent a letter to the editor of *The St. Cloud Daily Times* pointing out Kingsley's actual behavior. In their opinion the agent was anything but a hero since all he did was lie down and cry, "Boys help me! I am smothering; get me a drink; I am choking; put wet cloths over my face to keep me from smothering."[12] They said the only aid Kingsley rendered was to give the other passenger, old Mr. Carver, a handkerchief to put over his face. Furthermore, the crewmen observed, Kingsley himself would not be living if they had not helped him survive.

The survivors at the wreck were rescued through the day Sunday. Sixteen of them were brought to Hinckley on handcars and put aboard a relief train to Pine City. The others were brought out by a crew that arrived from Mora Sunday afternoon.

CHAPTER **4**

Aid for Survivors

DULUTH

ON THE MORNING of September 1 Duluth citizens noted it was another sultry, dirty day. By 10:00 a.m. the air was heavy with smoke and cinders which increased in density as the day progressed. At the Union depot Conductor Powers loaded his passengers aboard the Eastern Minnesota train and Engineer Best pulled it out on schedule at 1:00 p.m. Seasoned passengers had seen small fires along the tracks all summer and weren't particularly concerned. At 1:55 p.m. when Conductor Sullivan and Engineer Root left the depot with their Limited passenger No. 4 on the St. Paul and Duluth line, the weather was overcast and sultry with the appearance of an approaching storm.

During the afternoon a southwest wind began to blow clouds of smoke over the town. By 4:00 p.m. the street lights were turned on, and lamps were lit in offices and homes. About half an hour later the sky lightened with an unhealthy dull red glow, and the people in the streets began to speculate as to the cause. Some thought it was a "monstrous, unnatural phenomena, [sic] while others of the superstitious class began to advance the theory that it was the beginning of the end of the world."[1] Others who were less imaginative assumed it was a fire somewhere, but they were uncertain as to its location and extent. People who had sent family members on the trains began to crowd the telegraph offices to see if there was word from stations down the line, but one by one the wires went dead until there were only two lines out of town.

At 6:00 p.m. Saturday the electrifying wire came in to C. M. Phillips, telegraph operator of the St. Paul and Duluth Railroad, from A. I. Thompson, agent at Miller, saying: "The country is all burning up. No. 4 is burned up. Send relief."[2] Then the line went dead. This was the message delivered

63

by Conductor Sullivan as he staggered into the Miller station after his harrowing flight up the tracks from the burned Limited at Skunk Lake.

In Duluth the news of the Limited spread rapidly. Frantic people swarmed to the telegraph stations for further word about kinsfolk who had been aboard the train and relatives who lived in the burned area. Incoherent and incomplete telegraph messages made the situation more confusing.

At 7:00 p.m. another shocking wire arrived. Mayor Ray T. Lewis received the message that about 500 people from the burned town of Hinckley were arriving in Duluth at about 9:00 p.m. on the Eastern Minnesota emergency train engineered by Barry and Best. Mayor Lewis lost no time in alerting Chief of Police Armstrong and the police department to help arrange food and temporary lodging.

Between 9:00 and 9:30 the train arrived with 475 passengers. Some had left the train in Superior. Mayor Lewis and Chief Armstrong were at the depot to meet them. While the police kept back the crowds, the mayor assured the refugees that they would all be given care and shelter. The Ideal and Zenith restaurants provided food for everyone, and the refugees were escorted by police to various places of shelter about town. Some of the refugees were bedded down at the Armory where cots and mattresses had been put out on the floor; others were sent to hotels, hospitals, public buildings and private homes.

When Agent Thompson's startling wire telling of the burning of Root's train arrived at the St. Paul and Duluth telegraph office at 6:00 p.m. Saturday, railroad officials were alerted immediately. General Yardmaster Dave Williams jumped into action. First he wired Conductor Roper at Willow River to take his "way" freight and rescue the passengers of Root's train as quickly as possible. Then Williams sent wires to all trains south to pull in at the nearest side tracks so emergency trains could get through. In an hour a relief train under Williams and Conductor Wellmann was ready to leave. On the train were Drs. Magie, Codding, McCormick and Gilbert of Duluth, General Agent C. M. Vance and two newspaper reporters together with supplies, medicines, blankets, food and other emergency provisions.

As the Williams-Wellman train went southward, there was dense smoke in the air, but they reached Willow River without difficulty. At Willow River they met Conductor Roper, who, by that time, had made two unsuccessful attempts to reach Skunk Lake. Roper had been stopped by burned bridges and culverts but had managed to rescue a young woman and a baby who were close to drowning in a burned culvert south of Miller. He had also taken on the refugees who had fled up the tracks from Miller and Finlayson. In this group were 21 persons, including Conductor Sullivan, Brakeman Monahan and others from the burned train at Skunk Lake. Williams inquired about the fate of the Limited, but Sullivan was so distraught and in such excruciating pain from his burned eyes that he could give no coherent answer.

Among the other refugees were R. M. Bell, superintendent of the Union depot at Duluth, and his fifteen-year old daughter, who had also been on the Limited and had escaped up the tracks from Skunk Lake. Bell gave Williams the hopeless reply, "Everything is burned and everybody is dead."[3] He advised Williams that it was useless to attempt to reach the Limited.

But Williams felt compelled to continue his rescue efforts. He transferred the survivors to his relief train to be brought back to Duluth. General Agent Vance and Conductor Wellman were put in charge of the train, and Drs. McCormick and Gilbert were assigned to administer medical care to the refugees on the way. This train reached Duluth at 2:45 Sunday morning with 125 passengers aboard.

In the meantime Williams and the other men climbed aboard Roper's train, by then blistered from the heat, to make a third attempt to reach Skunk Lake. Engineer Kelly was at the throttle with Drs. Magie and Codding aboard. They went as far as possible but had to stop at a burned bridge south of Miller. After transferring emergency supplies to a handcar, Williams, Roper and the two doctors continued over the badly-warped tracks, all the while protecting their faces with wet handkerchiefs. At times they had to lift the handcar manually across a burned trestle or culvert. Along the tracks they found eighteen burned bodies; some presumably were people from Root's train.

At midnight the four men reached Skunk Lake. There in the darkness they saw the fire still smoldering in the coal car, and by lantern light they could make out piles of smoking rubble which had once been the coaches. The scene bore a foreboding spectre of death. But they decided to call out in hopes that somewhere in the blackness there were still a few souls alive. In answer to their shouts came a chorus of human voices. It is hard to surmise which group was more joyful at the sound, the rescuers or the rescued.

When Dave Williams saw the large group of survivors at the edge of the swamp, he decided it was best to leave the two doctors to treat the sufferers, while he and Roper returned to Miller on the handcar to begin an all-out effort to repair the tracks so a relief train could reach Skunk Lake as soon as possible. Williams immediately summoned all available crews to work through the night on the damaged railroad and sent another handcar back to Skunk Lake with more supplies. Early Sunday morning he sent the comforting message to Duluth from the Rutledge station saying, "Have been to wreck with handcar — could only get to Miller by train. Wreck is one and one-half miles south of Sandstone [Sandstone Junction] and all burned up — passengers all right but exhausted — they are in a marsh — we go with timber to build bridge — tell everyone all are alive and well as can be expected — will arrive in Duluth at 9 a.m."[4]

After the railroad crews had worked all night, Roper's train was able to reach Skunk Lake at about 8:00 Sunday morning. There they found that a party under Dr. Barnum and Conductor Buckley had been to Skunk Lake at

3:00 a.m. with handcars and pushcars and had brought forty survivors to Hinckley where they boarded a relief train south to Pine City. The rest of the survivors wanted to go to Duluth, so had waited at Skunk Lake for Roper's train. They were taken north out of the fire zone, then transferred to another relief train which arrived in Duluth at 12:00 Sunday noon. Hordes of people were on hand to greet them, many overjoyed to find relatives and friends among the living. Police and volunteer workers tended to the refugees who had no place to stay. *The Duluth News Tribune* wrote the following account of their arrival:

> The appearance of the people was more than motley. Begrimed with dust and smoke, suffering with injuries from the fires, wound in dirty, wet blankets and clothes and huddled together in fear and anguish, the sight they presented was more than pitiable. They tumbled off the trains like flocks of sheep and followed closely and quietly the directions of the police and relief authorities. [5]

PINE CITY

During the afternoon of September 1 citizens of Pine City, fourteen miles south of Hinckley, watched the black smoke to the north in the vicinity of Brown's Hill, a siding on the railroad mid-way between the two towns. The telegraph lines had been burned out at Brown's Hill so there had been no communication with Hinckley during the afternoon. Railroad crews had been out trying to keep culverts and bridges repaired for the passage of trains. It was assumed that the Brown's Hill fire was localized, and there was no indication then that the towns to the north were in peril. But the Brown's Hill fire was the beginning of the conflagration that raced down the St. Paul and Duluth tracks to Mission Creek.

Some Pine City residents reported hearing a weird rumble like the sound of explosions to the north in mid-afternoon, but no one knew the cause. When the northbound Limited No. 3, with Conductor John Buckley and Engineer James Sargent, came to Pine City on its way to Duluth, the train was stopped since the condition of the track north was uncertain. This was the train carrying the fire hose from Rush City which had been requested by the Hinckley Fire Department.

John F. Stone, proprietor of the Pine City Pioneer House and local correspondent for *The St. Paul Pioneer Press*, had been concerned about the fires for some time. At 10:30 Saturday evening he sent a descriptive report to St. Paul saying:

The forest fires north of the town are raging with savage fury, the high winds through the day have fanned every spark into a flame and it has been traveling over the country, sweeping everything before it. Settlers are being driven from their homes to seek shelter in the marshes; hay and buildings are consumed, and the air in suffocating condition from heat and smoke. The north bound Limited train with all the passengers, is now laid up at this place waiting to get through to Duluth. Crews are out working on burnt culverts and repairing bent rails to get the trains through if possible, tonight. There is no communication with Hinckley, but it is feared here that the town is in imminent danger. Relief crews are being sent out from town as rapidly as possible to aid the distressed settlers. At this writing (10:30 p.m.) the wind has died away and hope has correspondingly increased. No danger to this town at present. STONE[6]

One-half hour after he had dispatched the message, a party of seven begrimed men arrived from Hinckley on a construction train which had been repairing bridges, rails and culverts through the night. One of the men was Angus Hay, editor of *The Hinckley Enterprise,* who had survived at the gravel pit in Hinckley, and with him were three passengers from Root's train who had walked to Hinckley during the night. At Hinckley the men had found an abandoned handcar which they had taken over the burned tracks to meet the work train south of Mission Creek. This was the same train which took out some of the Mission Creek survivors. When the train arrived in Pine City, residents heard for the first time the shocking news of the destruction of Mission Creek and Hinckley and the burning of the Limited at Skunk Lake.

John Stone's next communique to St. Paul read:

Hinckley burned to ashes; many people lost their lives in the fire, balance are homeless and destitute; send relief if possible at once. The little town of Mission Creek entirely wiped out. Engineer Jim Root probably fatally burned. Situation appalling and heart-rending in the extreme. STONE[7]

Pine City people hastily mobilized all their resources. Mayor A. G. Perkins called for immediate aid to be sent to Hinckley. Young men went from door to door awakening people, relating the shocking news and asking for supplies to be brought at once to the Pine City depot. In half an hour an engine and two coaches were ready to leave with Dr. E. E. Barnum of Pine City, Engineer Sargent and Conductor Buckley of the Limited No. 3, two other doctors and about seventy-five volunteers aboard. They carried with them medical supplies, drugs, clothing, food and other necessary items.

The route to Mission Creek and Hinckley was hazardous. Trees were still smoldering, culverts and trestles were perilous and rails were twisted. The train arrived in Hinckley just after midnight. There some 200 people were found sheltered in the Eastern Minnesota roundhouse. The doctors treated those who were most severely burned while the rescue party helped escort the others to the train. Searching parties went out in the dark with lanterns to

AID FOR SURVIVORS

67

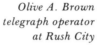

Mayor S. C. Johnson
Rush City

Olive A. Brown
telegraph operator
at Rush City

find other survivors among the dead. Some people were still at the gravel pit. Those who were able walked to the train; others were so weak they had to be carried. Shortly the train left for Pine City with its first load from Hinckley. Along the way they picked up Mission Creek survivors who had not reached the work train earlier.

Dr. Barnum stayed on at Hinckley and went with Buckley and Sargent on handcars and pushcars up the St. Paul and Duluth tracks to Skunk Lake.

Back at Pine City very few people had returned to their beds. There was a frenzy of activity preparing emergency quarters for the expected refugees. The skating rink was converted into a temporary hospital where the most seriously injured and burned were treated. The town hall became the eating house, and the school, churches, hotel and stores were used for shelters. The women of the town prepared food, gathered clothing, bedding and supplies. By the time the first trainload of refugees arrived from Hinckley about 2:00 a.m. Sunday, Pine City was ready.

RUSH CITY

Rush City, lying ten miles south of Pine City, had been alerted to Hinckley's severe fire condition Saturday afternoon when Olive Brown, Rush City telegraph operator, had received a request from Hinckley to send as much fire hose as the village could spare. Mayor S. C. Johnson quickly rounded up the hose and put it aboard the northbound St. Paul and Duluth Limited No. 3 leaving Rush City at 4:00 p.m. The hose never arrived at Hinckley, nor did train No. 3 since it was held at Pine City.

FROM THE ASHES

68

Dr. A. J. Stowe
Rush City

Dr. J. E. Gemmel
Rush City

At 11:30 Saturday night Operator Brown was still at her depot office. With her was Mrs. James Root, wife of Engineer Root of the St. Paul and Duluth Limited No. 4. Root's train should have arrived in Rush City at 5:12 p.m. and the two women, fearing there had been trouble, anxiously waited for some word to arrive.

Their worst premonitions were realized when a paralyzing message came along the wires from Pine City to be relayed to the dispatcher at St. Paul. It said:

> Hinckley, Mission Creek and No. 4 train are all burned up, except the engine. The passengers on No. 4 are in Skunk Lake, about six miles north of Hinckley, and about half the people in Hinckley are dead. We want all the assistance possible. Notify both doctors at Rush City, and any others that can be got here at once. [8]

Miss Brown acted instantly. She first ran to the homes of the two local doctors, J. E. Gemmel and A. J. Stowe. As the doctors gathered their equipment and medical supplies, Miss Brown and Mrs. Stowe ran from house to house rousing people from their sleep, asking for provisions and help. Soon the mill whistle blasted a shrill fire alarm awakening the rest of the village and calling the citizens together.

AID FOR SURVIVORS

Mayor D. W. Bruckart,
St. Cloud

In less than an hour 300 townspeople had gathered at the depot bearing an assortment of hastily-gathered clothing, food and supplies. A light engine was commandeered into service from the railroad, with an engineer and a fireman to run it. Clothing, food, blankets, bolts of cloth for bandages and 130 gallons of milk were loaded aboard. Many citizens volunteered to go along, but since space was limited, only the two doctors, Rush City Mayor S. C. Johnson, Editor C. E. Elmquist and three others boarded the engine. The rest of the volunteers and supplies were to follow on a special train.

The engine sped up the tracks to Pine City. But there they were halted. The relief train which had been sent earlier to Hinckley was expected back shortly, and the Rush City engine had to wait its return. In the meantime the second contingent arrived from Rush City on the special train, carrying Drs. Kronstadt of North Branch, Dr. Tictin of Harris, more Rush City citizens, supplies and several handcars.

The Rush City crews were anxious to be on their way, so despite the danger of collision with the relief train, ten men climbed on two handcars and set out toward Hinckley. Their night ride was perilous, but fortunately just beyond Mission Creek they sighted the train in time to flag it. Dr. Stowe and Dr. Kronstadt boarded the train and returned to Pine City while the other two doctors continued on with the crew to Hinckley.

At Hinckley six men from this party under Rush City Marshall George Knight set out to rescue the survivors at the wrecked St. Cloud and Hinckley train, while the others stayed at Hinckley to search for more survivors among the ruins. As they walked through the desolate town, searching for the living, their lanterns illumined scenes of indescribable horror. Distorted, charred bodies of men, women, children and animals were scattered about indiscriminately. Homes and buildings were heaps of black rubble, and trails of gray ash marked where village sidewalks had once been. Black smoke still belched from the Brennan lumber yards at the north end of town.

Early Sunday morning the second relief train arrived at Hinckley carrying doctors, volunteer workers and supplies from Pine City, Rush City and other towns to the south. Crews were organized to cover the area in search of the living and the dead. Hinckley survivors and passengers from Root's train were put aboard the train, given food and medical care and brought to Pine City.

Back at Rush City Olive Brown had stayed faithfully at her telegraph, receiving and sending messages through the entire weekend. Monday she was exhausted and was forced to rest. The Rush City station was flooded with communications going to and coming from all parts of the country. There were news items for papers, death lists, inquiries from worried relatives and messages from stranded passengers. Miss Brown performed admirably without sleep, recognition or reward.

ST. CLOUD

Although St. Cloud was situated outside the immediate fire zone sixty-seven miles southwest of Hinckley, it was connected directly to some of the burned villages by the St. Cloud and Hinckley line of the Great Northern system. Trains made daily runs, except on Sundays, between St. Cloud and Hinckley.

Early Saturday afternoon St. Cloud residents had received news that the towns of Foreston and Milaca to the north of them were in danger. A train carrying water and a crew of forty men went north, but stopped at a burning bridge near Foreston. The train returned to St. Cloud bringing reports of the terrible conditions.

Later Saturday afternoon communications between St. Cloud and Hinckley were cut off, so no news arrived from the north. Confusing messages came from St. Paul, leading to rumors which seemed too incredible to believe. Early Sunday morning a telegram arrived saying Hinckley was burned and 30 lives lost. At noon another message arrived stating that 200 people were dead, followed by another reporting that 300 had perished. Another wire arrived from Conductor Parr saying the St. Cloud and Hinckley train was in the ditch just north of Brook Park, but the crew was safe, and twenty-five people were sheltered in the coach of the train.

Sunday morning a railroad work train was sent out from St. Cloud with a crew of men, equipment and building supplies. They proceeded north, repairing burned bridges and culverts as they went, working their way slowly through Milaca and Mora. When they reached a point four miles northeast of Mora, they stopped at a burned bridge. Here they met the Mora rescue crews that had picked up Brook Park survivors on handcars. The survivors were taken aboard the train and brought back to Mora where they were given shelter.

Sunday afternoon Mayor D. W. Bruckart called a meeting of St. Cloud citizens at the Grand Central Hotel. A decision was made to send a relief train to Brook Park as soon as possible. By Monday noon the train was ready to leave. It carried a committee of St. Cloud people, two doctors, two nurses and work crew as well as provisions, horses, a wagon and lumber for 75 coffins. On Monday afternoon teams of volunteers went from door to door collecting clothing, bedding and other donations. The following day another trainload was sent to Mora, where most of the Brook Park refugees were sheltered.

Through the succeeding weeks and months St. Cloud proved to be a most generous benefactor to the neighboring villages to the north. The town "adopted" 77 homeless families around Milaca and helped them rebuild. They also gave donations directly to the citizens of Brook Park. Altogether St. Cloud cared for 377 fire victims. [9]

HELP FOR BROOK PARK

Rescue work at Brook Park was especially difficult since all communication to that town had been cut off in mid-afternoon the day of the fire. Until Monday afternoon there was no access to the town from the north or south except by handcars over the damaged railroad tracks. No buildings remained in the town for shelter, so survivors had scattered to unlikely places such as the two unburned boxcars and the wrecked train, further complicating the job of locating them. Reports were confused and often in disagreement as to how and when various groups of survivors were rescued and brought out of Brook Park. However, most accounts indicated that the first party to reach that town came from Mora, eleven miles south. Mora generously offered sanctuary to about 100 survivors from Brook Park and the surrounding area.

The town of Mora lay on the southern edge of the burned area on the Great Northern tracks. The Quamba station, where the fire supposedly began, was mid-way between Mora and Brook Park. When communication between Mora and villages to the north had been cut off Saturday afternoon, townspeople suspected that conditions were serious. But no one knew the extent of the fire until word was brought to them by Anton Smith of Pine City.

Ole Nelson, Great Northern section foreman, immediately took a crew on a handcar and headed north from Mora. They were the first ones to reach Brook Park, arriving sometime Sunday morning. There they found sixty

The Rev. James Thompson
of Mora

homeless, suffering people. After giving the survivors their lunches, the crewmen returned to Mora carrying with them only three refugees. One of them was Joseph Gonyea, who was severely burned and in need of medical attention. At Mora Gonyea was given a cot in the town hall until the quarters in the local church were ready. The other two survivors requested transportation to Minneapolis.

Foreman Nelson and Depot Agent W. Long organized a larger rescue team that went back to Brook Park on two handcars and a pushcar, taking with them a two-day supply of provisions. Dr. Cowan of Hinckley was ahead on a velocipede with medical supplies. They arrived at Brook Park Sunday afternoon and gave the survivors medical care and food. In the town they found several burned bodies which they covered temporarily to await burial.

Then the crew pushed on northeast of Brook Park to the wrecked St. Cloud and Hinckley train. Here they found only two families remaining, the others having been rescued Sunday morning by a crew arriving from Hinckley. The Mora team then returned to Brook Park with the two families from the train, loaded up as many other Brook Park survivors as they could carry and headed south toward Mora. Waiting at a burned bridge four miles north of Mora was a work train from St. Cloud which brought the survivors back to Mora.

At 9:00 Sunday night the work train arrived in Mora. The survivors were taken to the Methodist Church which by that time had been converted into a temporary hospital under the direction of its energetic pastor, the Rev. James Thompson. Generous amounts of bedding, blankets, clothing and food were donated by the citizens of Mora and more supplies came later from St. Cloud and towns to the south. Dr. J. A. Lewis, local physician, was on duty to give medical aid, and volunteers worked long hours attending to the needs of the sufferers. Joseph Gonyea, who needed special care for his burns, was sent to a hospital in St. Cloud.

The twenty-three people who had found shelter in the wrecked St. Cloud and Hinckley train one mile northeast of Brook Park were first reached by the rescue team that arrived by handcar from Hinckley sometime Sunday morning. The rescuers were a party of men who had come to Hinckley from Rush City on handcars. When the men first reached Hinckley, they headed to the Eastern Minnesota roundhouse where they found the four trainmen and passenger Kingsley, who had walked in from the wrecked train. One of the trainmen asked, "Has anybody gone to Pokegama [Brook Park]?...Our train was wrecked there. The people of Pokegama are in the cars, for God's sake go up!"[10]

George Knight, marshall of Rush City, and five other men volunteered to attempt the rescue and climbed aboard one handcar and were off to Brook Park. The trainmen sent with them the pail of milk they had secured from the surviving cow at Hinckley and the crackers they had found in the roundhouse.

Since no railroad work crews had repaired the damaged tracks between Hinckley and Brook Park, the route was beset with obstacles — fallen trees, twisted rails, burned bridges, culverts and trestles. On the way three of the six men wanted to abandon the rescue attempt, the other three favored continuing. Two miles from the wrecked train they were forced to stop at a long trestle which was badly gutted. Instead of carrying the handcar around the trestle through a smoldering marsh, they decided that the three discouraged men would wait at the handcar while the other three would walk to the ditched train. Marshall Knight was one of the men who continued. When they arrived at the wreck, they found the hungry, suffering survivors and gave them the milk and crackers, their first taste of food since the fire struck.

Because the handcar could not carry all of the people, sixteen were chosen to go back with the three men, each of whom carried a child on his shoulders. They walked back to the waiting handcar and improvised a platform from rails and partly-burned boards salvaged from the railroad bed. On the trip back to Hinckley the car had to be unloaded and lifted around burned culverts and twisted rails fifteen times.

At Hinckley the Brook Park survivors were put aboard a relief train and brought to Pine City. The six men who had rescued them unanimously agreed to return to Brook Park to get the remaining survivors. However, when they arrived back at the wreck, they found only one man and his wife, the rest having been found by the team from Mora. The six exhausted rescuers returned to Hinckley after working non-stop for twenty hours.

On the following days rescue crews returned to Brook Park to bring out the remaining survivors. The 32 Russian Jews, who had taken shelter in the unburned boxcars, were among the last to be brought out on Tuesday. In the group were 15 young children, some suffering from painful burns. Their desolate parents were so terror-stricken by the events of the preceding days, they wanted nothing more than to get out of the burned area, and they vowed never to return. They were brought first to Mora, then sent to St. Paul, where they arrived still carrying their only belongings, three bundles of sooty bedding they had used in the boxcars. In St. Paul two Jewish benevolent societies cared for them until October when they were sent back to Chicago.

Throughout the week following the fire search parties from Mora, St. Cloud and other towns combed the area from Brook Park to Hinckley in search of more survivors and bodies of those who perished in remote places. J. D. Markham of Rush City, one of the partners in the land company which owned the town site, worked tirelessly in rescue operations.

AID FOR SANDSTONE

Of all the railroad personnel who figured prominently in rescue operations, few worked harder or longer hours without rest than did General Yardmaster David Williams of the St. Paul and Duluth Railroad. It was Williams who first responded to the emergency message from the Miller station that came to Duluth at 6:00 p.m. Saturday saying that Root's train had burned. Williams was in the first party that reached the burned train from the north, and he spent the rest of the night organizing work crews to repair tracks, culverts and bridges so Roper's train could reach the survivors as soon as possible. After the Skunk Lake rescue was completed and fire sufferers safely delivered to Duluth Sunday noon, Williams still could not afford to rest.

Sunday evening another emergency message arrived from Miller saying, "There are 150 people at Sandstone without food or shelter. For God's sake get them out of there."[11] So Williams organized another relief train which was soon on its way to rescue the Sandstone survivors. The train, under the supervision of O. D. Kinney, had on board several doctors, nurses, news reporters and a crew of volunteers. With them they carried supplies of food, clothing, coffee, liquor, tools and lumber for coffins.

It was dark when the train stopped at Miller. Out of the blackness came a pathetic figure, a survivor from Sandstone who had first fled north to the Hell's Gate quarry, then walked west on the spur track which went cross-country to Miller. He told them of Sandstone's destruction and of the survivors who had fled with him to Hell's Gate. Two men of the relief party went back to Hell's Gate to lead the people sheltered there to the waiting train. After walking five difficult miles on the burned spur track the survivors arrived at Miller in the early morning darkness. They were a disheveled, pitiful group, many shoeless and partially clothed.

The rest of the rescue crew who had gone on to Sandstone arrived there in the middle of the night. After walking cross-country they came to the Government Road, the Eastern Minnesota tracks and the site on the bluff where the village of Sandstone had once stood. Their lanterns lit up sights of human carnage which had to be tended to when daylight permitted the work of burial to begin.

The searchers slowly made their way down the sandstone cliffs to the river bottom where they discovered signs of life. Several people were sheltered among the rocks, others in the sand. In the small quarry office, the only remaining building, were twenty-eight sick and ailing people lying crowded together on the floor, many suffering from agonizing burns. The men gave the injured as much aid and comfort as possible, but attempts to move them had to wait until morning. Those who were able followed the rescue party back to the train waiting at Miller. It was a difficult journey, and weary children had to be carried. The Kinney train, filled with 247 Sandstone survivors, arrived at Duluth at 7:25 Monday morning. They were fed breakfast at the Armory, then assigned to quarters by the relief committee. Others in Kinney's rescue party had stayed back at Sandstone to begin the unpleasant task of searching for and burying the dead.

At the Eastern Minnesota office at West Superior word had reached the railroad officials Sunday that Sandstone had been completely wiped out and people were trapped in the Sandstone river bottoms. William C. Farrington, General Manager, wired Samuel Hill advising him of the conditions. The message read:

> Four-hundred people in Sandstone alive but absolutely destitute of food or help of any kind. Forty-six dead in streets which people there are unable to bury. I leave about two o'clock Monday morning with special relief train of six cars containing men, doctors, groceries, provisions, teams and will go as far as Partridge packing and teaming supplies seven miles to Kettle River in order to reach people at Sandstone. [12]

Farrington's train left at 4:45 Monday morning. As they approached the burned area, they made frequent stops to check on the welfare of settlements and lumber camps along the way. Everything appeared to be normal until they reached the station at Partridge. There they found nothing but a stark water tank standing guard over piles of ashes and rubble. The train stopped because the tracks ahead were impassable.

The party broke into two groups with one crew going toward the Hell's Gate quarries, the other going southwest to Sandstone on handcars. It was a slow ride since rails were twisted, and culverts, trestles and bridges were damaged. Each man carried food, supplies, axes, shovels and as much lumber for coffins as possible.

The air was stifling with smoke from the smoldering peat fires, and the heat was oppressive. By mid-morning they had reached the north end of the Kettle River bridge. They could see the 300 foot steel span in the center still standing, but the wooden bridges at both ends had burned and collapsed. In the distance on the opposite bluff was what remained of Sandstone.

The party crawled down the steep rocky cliffs to the river. They hailed a survivor on the opposite shore who managed to cross in an old flat-bottomed boat. After several trips the rescuers had ferried to the other side of the river.

At the quarry office they found the remaining survivors lying prostrate on the floor, suffering from swollen faces and burned bodies. They were given food and medical care. Then members of the rescue team began to make plans to move the injured across the river to the handcars. Meanwhile the rest of the party climbed up the ravine to the burned town site. There they joined the party from the St. Paul and Duluth train and the crew of Sandstone survivors who had begun to bury the dead.

Toward evening the Eastern rescue crews descended again to the river flats. They found that the injured sufferers from the quarry office had been moved on two improvised stretchers, a bed spring and a piece of canvas, down to the river side and had been ferried one at a time across the river. Each had then been carried up the 135 foot embankment to the railroad tracks and the awaiting handcars.

While the rescue and burial crews had been working at Sandstone, twenty-four year old James Norman Hill, eldest son of James J. Hill, had made several trips back to the train waiting at Partridge to get materials with which to improvise slings to extend between handcars to transport the injured.

At 8:00 p.m. Monday the train left Partridge with a total of 91 survivors from Sandstone and surrounding areas. When they arrived at West Superior at midnight, there were just a few people at the depot to meet them. The Superior relief committee had been wired about their arrival so had quarters prepared for them. Seven of the injured were taken to a hospital. After a few days most of the refugees were transferred to Duluth.

On succeeding days other search parties returned to the Sandstone area to rescue the living and bury the dead, but it wasn't until September 18 that trains were able to cross the Kettle River bridge to reach the town.

AID FOR SURVIVORS

Hinckley amidst the ruins

CHAPTER 5

The Dead and the Missing

BURIAL AROUND HINCKLEY

AFTER THE FIRE had swept across Pine County and parts of adjoining counties, the first imperative task was to give immediate aid to the living. When all the survivors had been rescued and given shelter, there came the grievous job of searching for the dead, identifying and burying the bodies.

As dawn broke Sunday morning, the survivors who remained in the ravaged towns picked their way through the smoking rubble and came face to face with the appalling reality of the fire. They saw a sickening litter of human bodies intermingled with dead animals. Some human corpses were recognizable, others were shapeless, charred forms.

The survivors set about doing what was necessary. Those who were able joined the parties that came from neighboring towns, Duluth and the Twin Cities to search for and bury the dead. Doctors and morticians offered to help identify the bodies and assist with interment. Caskets and lumber to build boxes for burial arrived from neighboring towns along with horses and wagons to transport the dead.

Dr. D. W. Cowan of Hinckley, coroner of Pine County, was one of the first on the scene. After rescuing survivors and administering temporary medical care to those who needed it, he turned his attention to his official duties as coroner. One of his most difficult tasks was identifying the dead, some burned beyond recognition. Information similar to the registration for refugees was recorded for each of the deceased, with the name, address, where and how the body was found, by whom, where buried, what valuables were on the person, in whose custody the valuables were left and the name and addresses of friends or relatives.

Editor Angus Hay was also concerned with identification of the dead, DEAD AND MISSING

79

and he kept records of witnesses who had knowledge of the deceased. For those who carried life insurance, positive identification was necessary to avoid contested claims later.

Although every effort was made to identify the dead, badly-burned bodies were sometimes mistakenly identified, and a person reported as dead was later happily found alive. Such was the case with Dr. Ernest Stephan of Hinckley, whose brother identified a corpse at Hinckley as that of the doctor. Said Dr. Stephan, "When my brother saw me in the flesh, he shook for an hour."[1]

But in many cases there were no remaining items of clothing, pieces of jewelry or marks of identity to indicate who the deceased were. One man reported that of ninety-four bodies found at one place only four could be identified. Coroner Cowan's *Death List* dated November 24, 1894, included ninety-nine "unknown" entries such as the following:

> 323. Unknown — Male; age about 40; found on country road, 1 mile from Hinckley; burned beyond recognition; nothing but shoes left on his body; weight about 150.
> 354. Unknown — Girl; age about 18; found 1 mile north of Hinckley, on railroad track; nothing else to identify; buried in Hinckley.
> 365. Unknown — Nothing but particles of bones left; found in woods north of Hinckley.
> 381. Unknown — Infant; found near baby carriage in swamp, one-half mile north of Hinckley. [2]

Other factors impeded recovery, identification and burial of the dead. First, the bodies were scattered over a large area, and locating them was difficult. Then, the September weather was hot, and decomposition set in rapidly rendering the work of burial particularly distasteful. Undertaker Frank Webber of Pine City, in charge of burial at Hinckley, advised that after a few days the bodies "must be buried where found. It will be impossible to move them as they are literally falling to pieces."[3] Search parties worked from sun-up to dark to inter the dead as quickly as possible, but some bodies were not found until months later. In one case remains were found and identified four years later.

In Hinckley a few horses, wagons and hayracks found unburned, along with others shipped in, were used to transport the dead to the cemetery. Volunteer crews scoured the areas near the town where people might have fled for shelter. In the swamp north of the Grindstone River ninety-six bodies were recovered, piled on the wagons and brought to the cemetery. The procession to the burial ground one mile east of town was a somber one. Here a few "fortunate" deceased were placed in ready-made coffins shipped in, others were given hastily-built wooden boxes, but most were buried en masse in four long trenches. Those deceased who had family members or friends among the living in town were buried in private graves.

*Hinckley searching party
at ruins of cabin in the woods*

*A funeral procession
at Hinckley.
Bringing in the unknown dead.*

81

*Searching party finding
an entire family*

In outlying areas the bodies found near railroad tracks were laid alongside the tracks to await transportation on handcars or relief trains to the nearest towns. St. Paul mortician O'Halloran came to Hinckley on a work train Sunday evening with a load of 32 caskets. On the way he filled all of them with bodies found beside the tracks. O'Halloran kept descriptions of each of the deceased, saving fragments of clothing and items of jewelry for later identification. The coffins were brought back to Pine City to await burial.

On Sunday James Sargent of the Limited No. 3, which had been stopped at Pine City Saturday afternoon, organized a burial crew that went on handcars north on the St. Paul and Duluth tracks from Hinckley to Skunk Lake. Along the way they recovered thirty-one bodies which were wrapped in blankets and whatever available cloth could be found. They brought them to Hinckley and laid them beside the tracks for burial.

When rescue teams found bodies in remote areas, they buried them where they were found, marking the graves with plain wooden stakes bearing the names of the victims if they were known. Personal effects were collected and marked for later identification.

As the burial crews worked, a few unscrupulous individuals seized the opportunity to profit from the tragedy. An occasional shadowy figure was seen lurking over dead bodies in the streets and at the cemeteries. Jewelry and other valuables had been quickly snatched, and if the clothes on the

Dr. D. W. Cowan
of Hinckley,
coroner of Pine County

bodies were still intact, occasional pockets were found turned inside-out and empty. In Hinckley local vigilantes patrolled the streets until county officials took over.

Frank G. Webber left his own business in Pine City to supervise the burial at Hinckley. Men worked in relays, some with kerchiefs over their noses, others smoking cigars to cover the stench. A few stalwart individuals persevered, but some sickened and were forced to quit the disagreeable work. Webber described the procedure:

> We started in Monday morning with 21 men; we found 96 bodies at the cemetery ready for interment; they were all burned beyond recognition. We dug a trench 60 feet long, 6 feet wide, and 4 feet deep, and in this trench these 96 unidentified bodies were buried. Sixty-five of these bodies were buried without even a box for a coffin, and the balance were furnished this dignity. I went back Tuesday morning with the same men and finished the work Wednesday, burying in all 233 bodies. [4]

A news reporter from *The St. Cloud Daily Times* visited the cemetery and wrote a more graphic description of the burial:

> The scene at the . . . cemetery, on the raised ground back of where Hinckley stood, was a sight to craze stout hearts. . . . Here 20 men were busy with picks and shovels digging trenches for the dead and covering them up as the naked bodies or those in boxes were deposited. . . . In several places hands and feet protrude out of the thin covering of earth. . . . From the boxes and uncovered dead bodies the black blood and discolored fluids had dripped from the bodies until it stood in great puddles on the ground and filled the air with a stifling stench. Numerous parties were about the cemetery hunting for lost relatives. Sightseers came only to take a hasty glance at the scene of horror and walked quickly away, unable to look upon the scene. About the burying ground were pieces of clothing, pieces of hats, shoes and bunches of hair. [5]

DEAD AND MISSING

*Searching party
gathering up remains
at Hinckley*

While Webber's crew worked grimly at the trenches, over at the side of the cemetery mourner John Best Jr., with the help of two neighbors, was digging one large grave to be the final resting place for his loved ones. Of fourteen members of the Best family, spanning three generations, there remained only John, his wife and child, and an older brother, Christian. Christ had found and positively identified three members of the family, but the rest were presumed to be among the unidentified dead. The entries in Coroner Cowan's *Death List* for this one family were as follows:

41. Best, John — Age 63; residence, 2 miles south-east of Hinckley; found on road, 60 rods west of his house; identified by his son Christian; buried at Hinckley; identified by a jack knife which he carried.
42. Best, Eva — Age 60, married, wife of John Best; found with John Best in the road west of the house; identified by Christ Best.
43. Best, Bertha — Age 18, single, daughter of John and Eva Best; identified by Christ Best.
44. Best, William — Age 21, single, son of John and Eva Best; not identified.
45. Best, Fred — Age 23, single, son of John and Eva Best; not identified.
46. Best, George — Age 25, single, son of John and Eva Best; not identified.
47. Best, Victor — Age 8; son of John and Eva Best.
269. Weigle, Anton — Age 33, married; residence, Hinckley; not found, but supposed to be among the unidentified bodies taken from the swamp, one-half mile north of Hinckley; reported by Christ Best.
270. Weigle, Eva — Age 22, wife of Anton Weigle; was burned with her parent, John Best, was not found.
271. Weigle, Winnie — Age 4, daughter of Anton Weigle; not identified. [6]

FROM THE ASHES

In December it was reported in *The Hinckley Enterprise* that a local boy, while searching for a Christmas tree, had found the body of George Best near the old home a mile east of town. No inquest was held, as it was assumed he died on September 1 in the fire. The two surviving brothers buried another member of their family.

As rescue and burial work continued in Hinckley, one of the last places to be searched was the millpond at the Brennan Lumber yards. Fire had continued to smolder around the pond in piles of slashings and sawdust for days and had prevented crews from reaching the water to search for possible dead. Numerous rumors circulated that scores of people had perished there although the foreman of the Brennan Company insisted that no one could have gone through the yards after he left.

Angus Hay reported to *The Duluth News Tribune* on Tuesday, September 4, that a search party had attempted to reach the millpond. The fire was still burning fiercely and sending up blinding smoke, but the men, protected by canvas, had managed to get within fifty feet of the pond. They came back with the grim news that the pond was covered with bodies floating on the water.

Searching for relatives in the death trench

Burying the dead at Hinckley.
90 unidentified bodies in one trench.

The next day Hay filed the report that it was "impossible to see all the bodies, but the pond is covered with faces of those who are floating.... Dynamite is being used and every effort made to secure the bodies."[7] But dynamite was not used. Instead it was decided to remove one board at a time on the holding gate so the pond would drain gradually. When the water level had fallen three feet, a crew again searched the pond site. They reported finding only a man's hat and shirt. On September 7, when the draining was completed, the final search was made. To everyone's relief, the only corpse found was that of an unfortunate cow.

BURIAL AT BROOK PARK

On Monday evening, September 3, a crew of nine men loaded a handcar with two army tents, thirty blankets, food, tools and supplies and left Hinckley to go to Brook Park. In the party were the Reverend William Wilkinson of Minneapolis, together with J. D. Markham of Rush City and B. J. Kelsey of Kenyon, two of the four owners of the Kelsey and Markham Land Company. The trip was perilous as the dim light from their lanterns did not penetrate the blackness to warn of dangers ahead. After stopping several times to carry their handcar and supplies around impassable sections of track, they arrived at the burned bridge over Pokegama Creek. Leaving their handcar, they walked on to the two unburned boxcars at Brook Park

*Bodies brought in
from the outskirts
near Hinckley*

where they found the remaining survivors and a work crew from St. Cloud. It was then after midnight. They distributed the blankets to the survivors and bedded down until dawn.

The St. Cloud crew had brought cooking utensils and food. Wilkinson's party pitched their tents and set up a temporary camp where they cooked over an open fire and ate on the ground. Through the succeeding days Wilkinson's party with the other search crews scoured the area to locate those who had perished. They recovered nineteen dead, all of them naked and so grossly disfigured that only one was positively identified. The bodies were placed in wooden boxes and buried temporarily on the Fred Molander farm. Wilkinson conducted a burial service, and each grave was marked with a wooden cross and the name if identity could be established.

It wasn't until October 17 that Fred Molander's name was moved from the "missing" to the "deceased" list. His body was found in a well by a neighbor and recovered by Dr. Kelsey. Molander was buried in a wooden coffin on his own land. On that same day the body of Jay Braman, a favorite young man of the town, was disinterred from the Molander farm and was the first to be buried in the new cemetery. Services were conducted by the Rev. Wilkinson at both burials. The other deceased which had been interred at the Molander farm were later moved to the cemetery, and some were sent to other towns for burial.

There were twenty-six reported deaths in Brook Park, twenty-three of them lie buried in two trenches at the Brook Park cemetery. However, on June 26, 1895, *The Hinckley Enterprise* reported that the recovery of yet another body, supposedly that of Charles Anderson, brought the total to twenty-eight victims of the fire in the Brook Park area.

DEAD AND MISSING

BURIAL AROUND SANDSTONE

Early Sunday morning Peter Peterson, quarry superintendent, organized parties of survivors to begin the search for the dead in Sandstone. In the first hour forty victims were found, many of whom were in family groups no farther than 100 feet from their homes. The bodies were charred and fleshless and indicated they had been overcome in flight. Whole families had burned together in cellars and wells. Since there were no coffins or lumber for boxes, bodies were temporarily covered where they were found.

On Monday the local crews were joined by search teams which walked in from Kinney's train at the Miller station on the St. Paul and Duluth tracks and the Farrington party which arrived from Partridge by handcars over the Eastern Minnesota tracks. Since the bodies had already begun to decompose through the heat of Sunday, it was imperative that the men temporarily bury the dead, even though Dr. Cowan, the county coroner, was not there to record the deaths. Through all of Monday the men worked digging shallow two-foot trenches, placing bodies in them and marking each grave for later identification.

On Monday another search crew under Judge J. C. Nethaway of Stillwater rode on a handcar from Hinckley to the Miller station. For two days this party conducted a search from Miller west to Grindstone Lake, and in that area discovered several families who had suffered horrible deaths. This crew then worked down to Hinckley where Judge Nethaway continued to help with burial throughout the following week.

Early Tuesday at 3:00 a.m. a relief train left Duluth on the Eastern Minnesota road with a burial party assigned to comb the outlying territory for six to eight miles around Sandstone. William T. Bailey, veteran lumberman, and George E. Ash, surveyor general, were in charge of the party, and with them were thirty experienced woodsmen and three clergymen.

They arrived at Partridge at 6:00 a.m. where they dismounted and continued on foot to Sandstone. Peat was still burning and smoking, and the bent rails formed grotesque shapes over the track bed. At the Kettle River high bridge they crawled down the embankment and ferried across the river, where they discovered a few more survivors who had taken shelter in the quarry office. They left clothes and food with the sufferers, then proceeded up to the top of the west bluff. As they walked through the ruins of the town, their feet would occasionally break through the black crust to the hot coals still burning beneath the surface.

The party split into two groups. One group went to the Bilado farm four miles from Sandstone where they found the blackened, bare body of fourteen-year old Flora Bilado, who during the fire had left her mother's side to retrieve a blanket that blew away. Her body was lying about 400 feet from the turnip patch where her mother and three other children had survived. The men nailed together a crude, wooden box, dug a grave and the clergymen said the last rites. Flora was temporarily buried on the family farm.

Judge J. C. Nethaway
of Stillwater

The second group of searchers discovered an old dried-up well near the Peter Englund home which appeared to have been used for a shelter, but the heat was so intense around the structure, the men decided to leave the excavation until the following day. Wednesday they returned and began to dig. After they had cleared away the debris, one by one, bodies of men, women and children in a horrible state of decomposition were discovered. When the bottom of the hole was finally reached, eighteen deteriorated bodies had been recovered. The odor was nauseating and the bodies were said to be "decapitated, dismembered and fairly cooked in the vapor from their own bodies."8 As best they could, the men removed the disintegrating corpses, laid them out on the ground and examined them for marks of identification. Among the dead were Mr. and Mrs. Englund and their seven children. All of the deceased were put in boxes and brought to the Sandstone cemetery for burial.

In the same vicinity another family had perished in a cellar. They were found leaning against a wall with arms clasped around each other. Before the Bailey party left Sandstone Wednesday night, they had buried twenty-three more citizens of the Sandstone area.

On September 9 Coroner Cowan and a crew of workers arrived at Sandstone to register and bury the dead. Since no clergyman was present, no burial rites were performed at the final interment. Eighty bodies from Sandstone and the surrounding area were buried, but Cowan reported there were still one-hundred persons not accounted for in the vicinity.

DEAD AND MISSING

MEMORIAL SERVICE

Many of the dead were buried without benefit of a clergyman performing the last rites of the church. However, on Monday evening, September 3, six ministers and priests of different faiths met at the common grave in Hinckley and conducted a simple ecumenical burial service.

Survivors felt that there should be a public expression of homage paid to the deceased. Since Pine City was the town closest to the scene of the fire, it was selected as the place to hold a Memorial Service on Sunday, September 9. Original plans called for the ceremony to be held in the afternoon at Robinson Park. A trainload of people was scheduled to arrive from Rush City and towns to the south to attend the service.

But during the afternoon the all-too-familiar sight of a crimson glow appeared in the sky, and rolls of smoke billowed over the town. The train at Rush City was detained, as were the regular passenger trains. At Pine City terrified citizens and refugees fled from their homes, tents and temporary quarters and crowded aboard boxcars and coaches made ready for an emergency evacuation. Finally the smoke cleared, the people returned to their dwellings, and the trains were on their way. The cause of the scare appeared to be revived fires flaring near Mora and Milaca. Farther north the communities of Carlton, Barnum, Mahtowa and the west end of Duluth were threatened.

The Memorial Service was rescheduled for the evening at Tierney's Hall. Clergymen and civic leaders conducted the program while a heavyhearted audience sat silently listening and grieving. Passages from the Bible and names of the deceased were read, vocal solos were sung, acts of heroism recounted and words of comfort and encouragement offered. The Rev. Mahlon Gilbert, assistant Bishop of the Episcopal Church of the Minnesota Diocese, gave an emotional main address to a moist-eyed audience.

When the ceremony was over, survivors felt a small degree of consolation in having publicly honored their departed relatives, friends and neighbors.

MISSING PERSONS

One of the great difficulties during the chaotic days following the fire was the task of reuniting separated family members. Lists were posted daily at the relief centers, and newspapers issued rosters telling where people were staying. But many refugees searched in vain for the names of missing relatives. Some in desperation resorted to placing notices in newspapers such as:

The mother of John, Hans and Ole Hanson, boys 13, 15 and 17 years old, has not been heard of. The father has been reported alive, but no one here has seen him yet. [9]

Mrs. Gorman of Hinckley is sick at the Coulson house and is very anxious about her six children. [10]

Mrs. John Sletten lost a 4-year old child. When last seen the child was in the care of one Andrew Newson, near Hinckley. [11]

In some cases children, who were assumed to be orphaned, were "adopted" by well-meaning people, leaving desperate parents trying to locate them. Ten-year old Selma Johnson was taken from the Pilgrim Congregational Church by a woman who said she was a member of the church and was taking Selma to wash, dress and care for her. It was found that the lady did not belong to the church, but it was believed that the girl was found. Little Hilda Peterson was taken from the Bethel in Duluth by a lady who thought she was to be adopted. In the meantime the mother, who could talk little English, was beside herself with worry in Pine City.

Some happy families were united during the week following the fire, but Mrs. Otto Olson's experience was not so fortunate. During the fire Mrs. Olson, Hinckley, had become separated from her husband and children when she ran back to their home for blankets. Mrs. Olson found shelter somewhere in Hinckley but was badly burned. She was brought to Pine City, then sent to the Asbury Hospital in Minneapolis for treatment, where she was out of her mind with worry. On September 18, with her face still swathed in bandages, she made her way to the mayor's office to plead for help in finding her family. Three children answering the description of her own were reported to be in Duluth, and Mrs. Olson was overjoyed. But upon being discharged from the hospital, she discovered that she had been given false information and she alone survived. Coroner Cowan made the following entries for the Olson family:

186. Olson, Otto — Age 38, married; residence, Hinckley; not identified; supposed to have burned in the swamp, one-half mile north of Hinckley; has wife left.

187. Olson, _____ Age 1, son of Otto Olson; found in the river.

188. Olson, _____ Age 9, daughter of Otto Olson.

189. Olson, _____ Age 4, son of Otto Olson. [12]

The Duluth News Tribune described the hope turned to despair of the survivors during the week after the fire:

Many of the Hinckley survivors had hoped that friends and relatives left behind might have reached a place of safety. But as the relief parties worked down into the stricken territory and the extent of death's havoc gradually became known, hope is given up and family reunions have been few and far between. In one case a bereaved mother and children had still hopes that their bread winner was safe, while the committee had yet to break the sad news that he is among the dead. [13]

As grievous as was the news of verified deaths of loved ones, at least there was a finality about knowing for certain the fate of missing family members. There were some survivors who were not granted even that consolation. In some cases it was months before bodies were found, and some were never located. Survivors could only assume that a missing relative lay among the unidentified dead.

Just after the fire Lee Webster, mayor of Hinckley, searched in vain for his young wife at relief shelters in Duluth and Superior. On Wednesday after giving up hope of finding her alive, he returned to Hinckley to conduct another futile search for her body among the unidentified dead.

On October 16 Fred Molander's body was finally found at the bottom of a well and was buried beside his wife and children at Brook Park. John and

"Suffering Endured"
charcoal sketch done in 1895
by Nicholas R. Brewer
[to be used in mural]

92

"Suffering Endured"
charcoal sketch done in 1895
by Nicholas R. Brewer
[to be used in mural]

Christian Best did not learn the fate of their brother George until December when George's body was found by a lad searching for a Christmas tree. Mrs. John Nelson of Hinckley had to wait four years to positively identify the body of her husband found one mile west of town. She recognized the watch, chain and rifle as belonging to her husband.

Among other missing persons were seasonal laborers whose families lived elsewhere, immigrants with families in the "old country", visitors who happened to be in the area on the day of the fire or those who were passing through. A St. Paul paper expressed the fear that a large number of St. Paul hunters who had gone to hunt prairie chickens near Hinckley, Mora and Sandstone may have perished because they had not been heard from since the fire. In Minneapolis relatives worried about Mrs. Haley who, with six children and two men, was on her way to Canada by wagon. By mid-September she still had not been heard from, and all were thought to be victims of the fire.

In early November an old man, William Goodsell of Butternut Lake, Wisconsin, arrived in Hinckley to determine the fate of his son, believed to have perished there. With help he disinterred the bodies of the unidentified DEAD AND MISSING dead at the Hinckley cemetery but found no evidence of his son. Then he went to the area near Skunk Lake where more unidentified graves were scattered about. There he found one that appeared to be his son's charred body, the only identifying mark being a fragment of a shirt with his son's laundry mark. Mr. Goodsell was satisfied and brought his son's remains back to Wisconsin.

For months after the fire local newspapers continued to publish notices which began with the familiar phrase, "Another body was found at...." In June 26, 1895, *The Hinckley Enterprise* noted:

> While travelling through the woods near the Grt. Northern tracks two miles north of town last Sat., Mike Lynch discovered the bones of a human being — another victim of the forest fire of last Sept. Deputy Coroner Stephan was notified and at once attended to the burial of the unknown person. This makes two bodies found within the past week. When will this end? [14]

Among the deceased in Hinckley were two young Swedish sisters who had worked for three months in the kitchen at Bartlett's lunchroom at the St. Paul and Duluth depot. Their parents, recent immigrants, lived in Illinois. When the fire struck the depot, the Bartletts and their employees fled north on the tracks and met Root's train which backed up to Skunk Lake. All of the Bartlett workers survived except the two girls who could not endure the strain and fell along the tracks and perished. When the sisters first arrived in Hinckley, they wrote home faithfully every week, but when their letters stopped abruptly, relatives in Illinois assumed some tragedy had befallen them. Long after the parents of the two girls had passed away, two relatives visited Hinckley in the early 1970's and inquired about them. Only then did they learn from an elderly survivor of the fire that the two girls had been victims of the fire. Said one man, "Thank God, now we know." [15]

ANIMALS, A PROBLEM

The fire took a heavy toll of domestic animals and wildlife, which created another problem. The burned forests were littered with dead birds, deer and hosts of small animals. Carcasses of cows, horses, oxen, dogs, cats, hogs and chickens were strewn about streets and farms. And as with the human dead,

Death on the road

the animal bodies quickly decomposed in the unseasonally warm weather. An unbearable stench arose from decaying bodies, and doctors warned against an outbreak of disease if the animals were not tended to.

But disposing of animal carcasses was not simple. Burying was not feasible since there were great numbers of dead animals strewn everywhere, and burning could not be done without kerosene. Hasty requests were sent to the Relief Commission for oil for burning and chloride of lime to sprinkle over the rotting remains, but the problem persisted throughout the summer and fall of 1895.

The animals that survived the fire created no less of a problem than did those which died. Some suffered intensely from burns and starvation. Squads of soldiers from Fort Snelling were sent out to shoot them and salvage the meat if possible. Wild and domestic animals, which had not been burned, searched in vain for blades of grass and clean water. Most grazing meadows were burned black, haystacks had turned to mounds of ashes, and ponds and streams were thick with soot and cinders. The Duluth Humane Society offered to care for and help feed some of the animals, and the Relief Commission sent hay and feed to the villages, but animals in outlying areas could not be reached.

A few home owners were fortunate enough to find their own milk cows and horses alive. If hay and feed could be secured, the cows gave welcome fresh milk, and horses were invaluable for transportation and work. At Hinckley attempts were made to corral the stray animals so they could be fed until the owners could identify and claim them.

DEAD AND MISSING

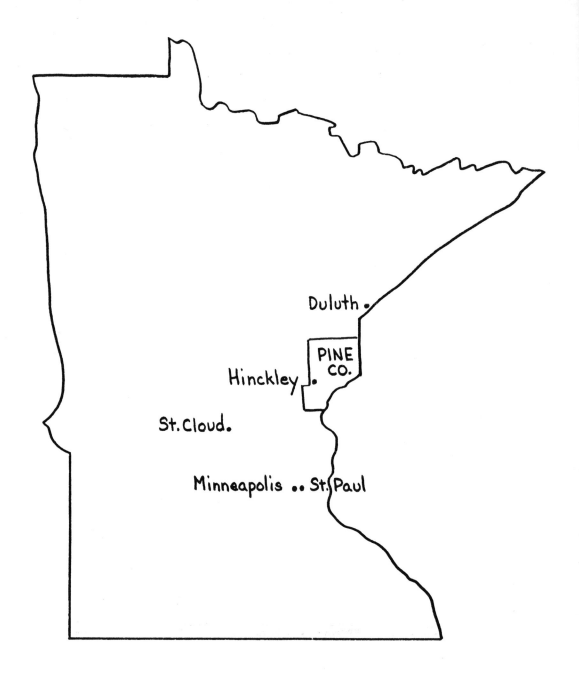

Duluth .

PINE
CO.

Hinckley .

St. Cloud .

Minneapolis .. St. Paul

MINNESOTA

CHAPTER 6

Relief

S TRAINS evacuated hundreds of fire survivors from the burned area and brought them to nearby towns and cities, there was an immediate outpouring of compassion and generosity. Citizens of neighboring towns not only donated money, supplies, clothes, food, furniture and numerous miscellaneous items but offered their services to assist in every possible capacity. Men joined search and burial crews and helped with rebuilding. Women volunteered to feed, clothe, shelter and nurse scores of the destitute. But as the total number of sufferers swelled to an estimated 1,500, the problem of administering relief was compounded into a formidable task.

On September 3 Governor Knute Nelson issued a Relief Proclamation and appointed a State Relief Commission to receive and disburse contributions of money and supplies. On September 5 the State Commission elected Charles A. Pillsbury chairman, and the Commission began to organize permanent relief measures. Local relief agents were appointed to work at relief centers to register all survivors, determine their needs and supervise the distribution of money and supplies. But before the machinery of the State Commission could be set in motion, each local community had rallied its citizens in an all-out effort to give temporary aid and comfort to their destitute neighbors.

PINE CITY

In Pine City Mayor A. G. Perkins called together all residents at a meeting at Robinson Park early Sunday morning for the purpose of organizing immediate relief measures. He appointed an official relief committee under the chairmanship of James Hurley and assigned duties to each member of the committee. Within two hours the town had been completely organized.

	1	2	3		1	2	3		1	2	3	

GOOD FOR 21 MEALS
TO

STATE RELIEF COMMISSION.

NOT GOOD UNLESS COUNTERSIGNED.

J. F. JACKSON, Agent, Pine City.

Countersigned.

	1	2	3		1	2	3		1	2	3	

Meal ticket
used at Pine City

Every available facility was pressed into service. The old skating rink became an improvised hospital for the most seriously injured, the town hall was turned into the clothing headquarters, the lodge hall served meals, the courthouse, churches, school, hotel and private homes provided lodging. Fifty army tents were pitched in the city park as quarters for workers and refugees, with four or five people assigned to each tent. When the trains began to bring in sufferers, Pine City was prepared.

As each train arrived with its cargo of bereft survivors, Pine City citizens soon realized the magnitude of the job confronting them. The first immediate needs of the sufferers had to be tended to at once — medical care for the injured together with food, clothing and shelter for everyone. Donations of supplies were welcome, but they had to be sorted, stored and distributed where needed. Meals had to be provided at all hours for refugees and workers. Doctors, nurses and volunteer aids worked around the clock caring for the suffering, but drugs and medical supplies were in short supply. On following days large numbers of reenforcements and provisions arrived from other towns.

Since Pine City was the village closest to the burned area which still had telegraph service to the south, it immediately became the communication center for outgoing messages. Just after the fire wires were jammed with news reports, inquiries about survivors and stranded passengers, messages of sympathy, offers of assistance and business transactions concerning relief. And as soon as the railroads resumed their regular schedules, Pine City was overrun by visitors, some searching for family members, some visiting refugees and some coming out of curiosity. On September 5 *The Duluth News Tribune* reported that a "large number of toughs and bums flocked into Pine City and their conduct became so boisterous that all saloons were ordered closed and additional police protection secured."[1]

On September 3 Pine City welcomed the arrival of H. H. Hart of the State Commission who set up headquarters and took over the job of coordi-

Ray T. Lewis,
Mayor of Duluth

nating relief activities. He devised meal tickets which entitled refugees to free meals, issued transportation passes and approved requisitions for clothing and supplies. A systematic registration of all survivors was established which included complete information on each individual or family. This registration provided the basis for determining both temporary and permanent relief. Hart maintained his headquarters at Pine City for one month, then moved to Hinckley to be closer to the center of the actual relief work.

Among the fire sufferers were those not seriously burned or injured who were encouraged to resume a normal life as soon as possible. Those who had relatives or friends with whom to stay were provided free transportation to their destination. Single men and women who could find employment elsewhere were given an outfit of clothing, a small amount of money (usually from $5.00 to $15.00) and sent on their way with a railroad pass. Men with families or businesses went back to their communities to rebuild as soon as lumber and materials were available. But those who had no other place to go, or who needed limited medical care, stayed on at the relief centers for several weeks. The ones who were severely burned were sent to hospitals in the Twin Cities, St. Cloud or Duluth. On September 4 ten seriously injured people were moved from Pine City to Minneapolis hospitals. Among them were Mrs. Otto Olson, who had lost her husband and three children in the fire; Mrs. M. E. Greenfield, who grieved the loss of five children; and Emma Hammond, who, though not expected to live, considered herself more fortunate than her "sisters" who had died near their "house of entertainment" at Hinckley.

Many Pine City citizens gave unselfishly of their goods and time, but few served more heroically than did Dr. E. E. Barnum who, just after the fire, worked for 72 hours without sleep. Dr. Barnum was on the first relief train that went to Hinckley from Pine City. He went with the crew on handcars to rescue the survivors at Skunk Lake, then returned to Hinckley to assist there. Following that, he returned to Pine City and was in charge of the improvised hospital where he labored night and day. When medicines and hospital supplies were short, he bought them with his own money. And all the while he was helping others, Dr. Barnum was worried about his own thirteen-year old daughter, Kate, who had been visiting in Hinckley on the day of the fire. Kate was planning to return to Pine City on the 4:00 o'clock Limited, but when the train did not arrive and fire struck the St. Paul and Duluth depot, Kate ran through the burning streets and caught the Barry-Best train at the Eastern Minnesota depot. Dr. Barnum did not know of his daughter's safety until he got word that she was in Duluth at the home of a friend.

In the Report of the State Commission, Chairman Pillsbury commended the Pine City citizens as follows:

> The highest praise is due to the citizens of Pine City for the promptness and efficiency with which they met the emergency. On Sunday morning, September 2d, without any previous warning, nearly five-hundred refugees poured into Pine City, a village of a thousand inhabitants. A relief committee was immediately organized and systematic plans were adopted. When the relief train from St. Paul, Minneapolis, Stillwater, White Bear and Rush City arrived at seven o'clock Sunday evening, with blankets, clothing, provisions, hospital supplies and a military guard, they found literally nothing to be done; all of the sufferers had been fed, an eating house had been established, sleeping quarters had been provided in the courthouse, schoolhouse, and private families, and a hospital had been organized for the sick. Considering the resources of the village of Pine City, this was in our judgment the most extraordinary achievement in the history of this calamity. [2]

By the middle of October most of the fire sufferers had left Pine City, returned to their communities or had found lodging or work elsewhere. The survivors were loud in their praise of the generosity and kindness extended to them by the sister village. Altogether about 500 refugees had been sheltered in this town with a total population only twice that number.

E. C. Gridley,
Chairman of the Duluth
Relief Committee

DULUTH

On Sunday at 11:00 a.m. Ray T. Lewis, mayor of Duluth, called a meeting of Duluth business men and citizens at the council chambers. To an overflow crowd he stated the magnitude of the task facing Duluth people in providing relief for hundreds of impoverished refugees coming in by the trainload. He reported the arrival of the Barry-Best train at 9:30 Saturday night carrying 475 people, including about 375 fire sufferers from Hinckley who owned nothing more than the clothes they wore. Then early Sunday morning at 2:45 General Agent Vance and Conductor Wellman had delivered another 125 survivors from the Finlayson area and those who had fled up the tracks from Root's train at Skunk Lake. Mayor Lewis also reported that another trainload of survivors was expected shortly from Root's train. The Duluth citizens responded to their mayor's appeal and promptly pledged $3,000 to start a relief fund. A relief committee was appointed with E. C. Gridley as chairman.

At noon, as expected, the trainload of begrimed, half-clothed survivors from the burned Limited arrived. The police and women volunteers escorted those who had no relatives or friends with whom to stay to various quarters about town where they were fed, washed, clothed and given lodging.

With the arrival of nearly 1,000 refugees in less than 24 hours, it soon became evident that the job of relief needed to be coordinated and systematically operated. On Monday the relief headquarters opened in the Herald building. Subcommittees were assigned to specific functions. The auditing and finance committee paid all bills, the transportation committee issued RELIEF

Mrs. A. M. Miller,
President of the Ladies' Relief Society
of Duluth

free passes to fire sufferers on any railroad in the country (one man applied for a pass to Liverpool, England), the supply committee outfitted and equipped the sufferers with necessities, the purchasing committee handled all necessary purchases that were not donated, the information bureau secured personal data on each refugee and the registration committee handled each request for relief. Clearly the relief headquarters became a busy place.

One group which mobilized immediately was the Ladies' Relief Society. This group had provided aid one year previous to the victims of a fire at Virginia, Minnesota, and was able to swing into action quickly. At 6:00 o'clock Sunday morning they opened a clothing collection depot in their headquarters at the Lyceum building but soon had to move to larger quarters when the citizens of Duluth responded during the first day with thirty to forty wagons full of clothing. Some of the apparel was sturdy and serviceable, some was dainty and impractical, but all was welcome.

By 9:00 a.m. Sunday Mrs. A. M. Miller, president of the Society, had a large crew of workers distributing clothing to the refugees who had arrived the previous night. Other women were at the Union depot to meet and assign quarters to the refugees who came in through the day. The Ladies' Society also stocked the relief trains that left Duluth through the succeeding days. They sent clothing, blankets, medicines and supplies back to survivors remaining in the burned areas and provisions for crews working in search and burial parties. It was reported that the sixty-eight women in the Society distributed 22,591 garments, 1,500 pairs of shoes, hundreds of yards of cloth and innumerable pieces of household equipment to the sufferers.

The Rev. C. C. Salter,
Chaplain at the Bethel,
Duluth

The churches of Duluth responded quickly to the call for aid. Many of them disbanded their usual Sunday morning worship to organize relief efforts. At the Pilgrim Congregational Church the people who had assembled for the 11:00 a.m. service forsook their usual worship to begin turning their quarters into dormitories and a dining hall. When M. W. Bates, an old war veteran, took charge of securing donations, few could refuse and the contributions flowed in. By 5:00 p.m. the church was ready to take in 98 women and children from the Barry-Best train which had arrived in Duluth the night before. By 9:00 o'clock Sunday evening all the children had been fed, bathed and put to bed. A professional nurse was on duty every night, a doctor attended those who were ill and an interpreter was called in since some of the children did not speak English.

The church, usually quiet on weekdays, became alive with activity. Monday morning all the clothing of the sufferers which could be salvaged was sent to the laundry to be washed. A tent was set up outside in the yard for the children's playground. The church kitchens bustled with food preparations, but on Monday night worried cooks reported that the milk supply had run out. Tuesday morning seven large cans of milk were found on the church doorstep. On Monday so many people crowded into the church to find relatives and to offer help that guards had to be stationed at the doors and lists of sufferers posted on an outside bulletin board.

Other churches and organizations also offered help. The First Presbyterian Church cared for those needing special medical attention in dormitories set up in their basement classrooms. About 150 refugees were sheltered there, among them Mr. and Mrs. Stephen O'Neil of Sandstone with twelve of

RELIEF

103

their fourteen children. Miss Erickson of Sandstone was there also, still clutching the cigar box holding $36.00 of stamp money which she later turned over to the United States postal authorities. The St. Paul's Episcopal Church maintained dormitories in the upper floors of the Berkelman Block, where they cared for the more seriously injured. By mid-week they took charge of 150 refugees who were transferred from Superior. The Odd Fellows turned their office rooms into a hotel where they sheltered 50 members and their relatives. They also organized relief crews to return to the burned area to help their suffering brothers.

The Duluth Woman's Home Society took in orphans and lost children, and a few overjoyed parents were able to find their children there. But others were never claimed, and newspapers soon let it be known that there were homeless children who needed permanent care and homes. The orphans who were not placed elsewhere were eventually sent to the Forest Lake Children's Aid Society where they awaited adoption.

Those who were most critically ill were sent to Duluth hospitals. Peter Bilado of Sandstone, who had been severely burned, was treated at St. Luke's, while Conductor Sullivan of the Limited which burned at Skunk Lake and Father Lawler of Hinckley were given care at St. Mary's. At Maternity Hospital three children were born to women who had fled from the fire. Mrs. C. A. Crocker of Finlayson named her son born Sunday, September 2, James Paul Duluth Crocker in honor of the city which offered her shelter. Mrs. John Turnquist of Hinckley named her infant daughter Mary Addie Amerit in recognition of the three nurses who tended her at the birth. Mrs. Julia Stewart of Sandstone named her newly-born daughter Jessie Francis Maud in honor of her three nurses.

The Armory which was the headquarters of Company "C" of the Third Infantry was one of the busiest places in Duluth. It was designated as the central office of the relief committee, and from there all relief efforts were coordinated. On Saturday night temporary sleeping quarters were set up on the Armory floor for many who came in on the first train, but on Monday it was converted into a mess hall. Three long dining tables were made of pine boards, several stoves, cooking utensils and supplies were brought in and set up in one corner to serve as a kitchen. An old piano case became an ice-box to store milk, butter and meat. Dishes and cups were borrowed from crockery stores in town.

Three cooks worked from morning to night preparing up to 1,500 meals a day. Twenty-five "pretty girls not accustomed to handling heavy trays of dishes"[3] were supervised and kept in line by older women, while Major Braden and twelve militia men stood guard to see that nothing unruly occurred.

The serving of meals was a model of organization. Three meals a day were served to as many as 500 people. All the single men sat at one table, the family groups, including one cat, sat at another and at the third was an assortment of miscellaneous diners. The food was placed on the tables before the people were called, and coffee and tea were served after they were seated. In twenty minutes all had been amply fed. It was reported that the refugees were amazed and delighted with the food, some no doubt eating better fare than they were accustomed to.

Dr. C. C. Salter, chaplain at the Bethel, a shelter for homeless men, offered the entire Bethel building to be used for fire survivors. Superintendent C. F. Robel began immediately to arrange sleeping quarters and eating facilities. Volunteers brought in cots, bedding, provisions and food and offered their services. By Sunday night nearly 200 refugees had been lodged there. Women from the Ladies' Relief Society supervised bathing and distributed clean clothes, while a Pennsylvania doctor, who happened to be visiting in town, volunteered to attend the sick. Families were assigned to sleeping quarters in the large lecture room, single men were bedded down in the bowling alley and single women in the gymnasium. Everyone ate in the Bethel dining hall where volunteers served as many as 900 meals a day.

On succeeding days after their physical needs were met and the trauma of the fire had lessened, the refugees at Bethel and elsewhere had time to contemplate their plight. Although they still considered themselves fortunate to be alive, they began to ponder the hopelessness of their future. Some huddled together in small groups talking in hushed tones of the loss of loved ones or of burned homes and possessions. Some thought they might return and begin to reconstruct their lives; others couldn't face such a bleak prospect and wanted to go elsewhere. Still others dejectedly shook their heads and didn't know what they were going to do.

Remains of the Samuelson root cellar near Skunk Lake. Photo by author in 1978.

But the human spirit has a built-in mechanism for hope and continuity. At 5:00 o'clock Sunday afternoon at the Bethel a baby girl was born to a Hinckley woman. The doctor who attended the mother and baby reported both were doing well. In early October a lady from Mississippi read of the birth and sent a donation of money for the baby's care.

On Tuesday, September 4, Minnie Samuelson and John Derosier continued the wedding that had been interrupted by the fire. On that fateful Saturday Minnie, age seventeen, and John, age twenty-eight, their families and guests were assembled at the Samuelson home near Sandstone Junction for the wedding ceremony. When fire surrounded the house everyone scurried for shelter to the stone root cellar where milk was usually stored.* As flames burned at the wooden door they used milk to quench the fire and pour over themselves. The house, belongings and the wedding gifts were all destroyed, but everyone in the wedding party was saved.

At 1:00 p.m. Tuesday in the Bethel assembly hall, Mrs. McKinley began to play "The Wedding March." The radiant bride and groom entered and marched to the front where Dr. Salter awaited them. Minnie was lovely in her donated garb, a pastel dress, a lace veil with orange blossoms and a corsage of roses. The pair was attended by Mrs. J. J. Crowley, member of the Ladies' Relief Society, and Chief of Police Armstrong. After reading the marriage vows Dr. Salter kissed the bride and congratulated the groom. Among those witnessing the ceremony were about a dozen Samuelsons of various ages and the family dog. Following the wedding everyone enjoyed a feast of fruit and dainties prepared by the Duluth ladies. A gift of money was presented to the wedding couple. The newlyweds could not afford a honeymoon, but later settled in Sandstone Junction where John built a home with lumber given him by the Relief Commission. On Sunday, March 10, 1895, Minnie gave birth to a 7½ pound girl in their new relief home.

After a week the Duluth relief committee decided that the sufferers needed to get out for an airing, and the workers needed time to clean and ventilate their quarters. So they arranged for everyone to be brought to a park for an all-day picnic on Sunday, September 9. When the pastors of the churches heard of the plans, they protested saying that such an activity should not be arranged to conflict with their church services. Furthermore, they said, many of the sufferers were "strong believers" and wanted to observe the Sabbath properly. So the plans were altered. The refugees were taken by wagon to Lester Park for their outing in the afternoon.

The spiritual welfare of the refugees was not neglected. At the Bethel, prayer meetings were conducted every evening in the Swedish language, and some of the churches held special Sunday services for the sufferers. The fire provided clergymen with texts for many fervent sermons for some time.

As volunteers of Duluth worked tirelessly to comfort and aid the refugees, another group found the situation inviting and expended efforts in

FROM THE ASHES   *The root cellar still stands in the vicinity of Skunk Lake.

a different direction. On September 8 *The Duluth News Tribune* ran the following item:

> One of the worst features of the late fire is the fact that many of the keepers of the houses of prostitution have been trying to secure the young and pretty girls who have been left fatherless and motherless to come to a life of luxury and ease and at the same time a life of shame and degradation. Yesterday two of the women went to the vestry of the St. Paul's church and talked for quite a while with a number of girls there trying to persuade them to come to their places of sin. Dr. Ryan finally learned of what was going on and immediately reported it to the police. Capt. Thompson said he would look into the matter this morning and if he can learn who these women are, he will make it warm for them. Thus far none of the girls have consented to yield to the offers made by the bagnio proprietors. [4]

The day before, a woman of "questionable appearance" was seen at the Congregational Church trying to hire two sixteen and seventeen-year old girls to "work in a boarding house (so she said)." [5]

On September 10 a letter to the editor appeared in *The Duluth News Tribune* in defense of the accused "landladies from the point." * It read:

> Will the people who enter this charge against us please state the two persons to whom Dr. Ryan has reference? All the landladies and girls have given largely of both money and clothing to fire sufferers. We are human and are willing to do anything in our power to help them.
>
> The idea of landladies from the point trying to get young and innocent girls to lead the live we are leading! There is not a landlady on the point who is as heartless as that. There is not one of them who would not tell a young girl who had never been used to leading this life to find some other way of taking care of herself.
>
> Are we to have no credit for what we have done? If the people who are making these charges would look into the matter a little they would find things greatly misrepresented. No one is ever ready to say a good word for us, but are always ready to talk against us, finding great delight in talking of things they know nothing about. ONE OF THEM. [6]

After the first few days of dispensing temporary relief a delicate situation arose between the city of Duluth and Superior, Wisconsin, the sister city across the bay. On the day of the fire telegraph lines to the south of Duluth were totally destroyed, and it took several days for the wires to be repaired and communication restored. Hence the story of Duluth's supreme effort on behalf of over 1,000 fire sufferers was not told immediately. In the meantime Superior, which was still connected to the outside, was sending wires telling how Minnesota refugees were arriving in that town and were being given relief.

---

*The "point" is a narrow strip of land jutting out into Lake Superior.

During the week following the fire it became apparent that Duluth was being given no credit in newspapers across the country for the work that had been going on day and night since the refugees arrived. It prompted Mayor Lewis of Duluth to comment that he "deplored the fact due to the deranged local telegraphic service, which allowed Superior to send nine-tenths of the press dispatches and take credit to herself for the whole work of relief."[7] An irate Duluth newspaper editor stated it more bluntly:

> People of Duluth have some complaint against newspapers in outside cities over the almost ignoring of the work of relief done here. . . . The St. Paul papers have columns about the relief work done there and the plans for future work, and the Chicago papers devote much space to it also, as they do to that of Superior, almost ignoring the fact that Duluth has been doing scarcely anything else for several days than take care of sufferers and extend aid in every way. . . . It was Duluth which was first on the ground. Duluth homes were filled with women and children almost before the news was known in the Twin Cities. It was Duluth which had a relief fund started at 8 o'clock Saturday night and whose women with her men were at the depot to take charge of the incoming refugees, while other men were working their way down the St. Paul and Duluth tracks to reach the scene of destruction and it was only Duluth which had a general relief committee organized and at work early Sunday morning.[8]

When Governor Nelson and the State Commission visited Duluth the week after the fire, the governor commended the city on its excellent work. He indicated that by the telegrams from West Superior, the State Commission was led to believe that Duluthians were shirking their duty. He added, "We are happy those dispatches are false and incorrect."[9] As the governor spoke to survivors, sometimes in Norwegian, his eyes filled with tears. He said the sufferers were "noble characters. . .hopeful for the future and eager and willing to get started again in providing for themselves."[10]

Throughout the week following the fire the men began to leave the various places of shelter. Some found employment, some returned to their burned homes to begin rebuilding, some went out on the crews to search for bodies and bury the dead. But women and children were not allowed to return to their homes until shelter was available for them. A week after the fire all remaining refugees in Duluth were transferred to the Bethel. As the State Relief Commission began to organize plans for permanent relief, the local committee gradually and willingly relinquished their functions.

Among the Duluth citizens and businesses there had been an outpouring of generosity. People donated their money, clothing, household goods, supplies and volunteered their time to help where necessary. Benefits of all sorts were held by societies and organizations to raise money for the relief fund. Grocers donated all the food, except meat, for the refugees, dairies gave free milk, bakeries turned out hundreds of loaves of free bread. Stores donated percentages of their sales to the fund, and owners of public baths invited refugees to have free Turkish or Russian baths. Doctors and nurses not only aided the sufferers in Duluth, but accompanied the relief trains that went back into the burned areas. Railroads provided free transportation for refugees and shipped all relief supplies free of charge. Telegraph companies sent free messages, and newspapers published free personal communications. Clergymen donated their time liberally wherever needed, whether to dispense comfort, search for missing persons or bury the dead.

The citizens of Duluth were commended for their beneficence and their immediate response to the call for aid. The State Commission reported that about 1,200 people had been given relief at Duluth.

DONATIONS

When the word of the fire first reached the outside world, headlines all over the country screamed the sensational news. The initial reports were sketchy, hysterical and often in error. Reporters from Duluth, St. Paul and Minneapolis were dispatched immediately to the burned area. In many instances news correspondents were among the first to go on relief trains, then by handcar or on foot to the scene of the disaster. Since all telegraph wires were down, emergency wires had to be strung and temporary communication facilities improvised. But in spite of the difficulties the shocking news spread rapidly.

Individuals, businesses and organizations across the country were prompted to donate money and supplies of every sort to aid the sufferers. Cities and towns set up relief funds to collect money. Railroads shipped donated goods free of charge from any place in the country to the fire district. The editor of *The Minneapolis Journal* observed that "beneath the materialistic tendencies and innate selfishness of the average man there is a current of human sympathy that needs only the occasion to call it into play."[11]

When the extent of the devastation became apparent, government officials, civic and religious leaders and newspaper editors urged people to contribute generously to their unfortunate brothers. The editor of *The Duluth News Tribune* stated the case: "Sympathies are much, but they do not repair homes, they do not feed children and they do not clothe. There must be more help to show that our sympathies are genuine and deep."[12]

So donations large and small began to pour in. Kenneth Clark, treasurer of the State Relief Commission, was appointed to receive all cash contributions. Industries set up employee subscriptions, being sure to designate honest persons to collect funds. Musical and cultural organizations gave benefit concerts and programs; theatrical groups sponsored dramas, shows

St. Luke's Hospital, Duluth

and stereopticon displays of fire scenes on large screens. Churches and civic groups had promoted lectures by those who had lived through the fire. Some societies sent funds to help specific nationalities — the Germans, the Swedes or the Norwegians. Lodges and fraternities gave help to their own members. Athletic events such as the baseball game between the fat and lean men of St. Peter and LeSueur were sponsored to raise money.

The wealthy also gave. James J. Hill gave $5,000 and donated 5,000 acres of land to settlers. He also made available his collection of photographs of the fire taken along the Great Northern railroad for benefit exhibits. John D. Rockefeller telegraphed $1,000 from his private funds. From England came donations from James J. Hill's former associates — $5,000 from Lord Mount Stephen and $6,000 from Sir Donald Smith and Lady Smith. From Constantinople came 300 Turkish pounds given by the Sultan of Turkey.

The hearts of children were also touched by the stories they heard of impoverished fire victims. In Duluth the Victoria Club, a group of eight little girls under ten years of age, called a meeting to decide whether to spend their club money on ice cream or give it to relief. They forsook their personal pleasure and voted that their $ .65 should go to the fire sufferers. In the same city eighty-one newsboys donated a total of $18.18 to the relief fund, with Billie Groosky, the mascot of the group, donating $ .03. In Minneapolis five ten-year olds raised $3.60 in pennies and nickels by giving a show, while three others earned $2.25 by selling flowers.

But along with the honest and generous citizens there were those who seized the opportunity to pocket some easy money. A number of individuals

*St. Mary's Hospital
Duluth*

posing as collectors of relief funds went from door to door for donations. In Chicago a man named Schroeder masqueraded as a clergyman, gave lectures on the fire and collected money for fire sufferers at each event. The papers in the Twin Cities, as well as in eastern cities, warned citizens to donate only to those authorized to collect funds.

As soon as refugees arrived in Duluth, Pine City and Mora, there were immediate needs to be met. One of the first was food. Restaurants in Duluth provided the fire sufferers with their first meals as they arrived. Then donations began to come in to the relief centers from all over the state. Bakeries fired up their ovens and shipped out thousands of loaves of bread, meat dealers supplied barrels of pork, bacon and ham, dairies gave milk and butter, the millers gave carloads of flour and grocers offered a variety of foods. One storekeeper in Duluth said to a relief worker, "Our store is at your disposal. Go and get what you want."[13]

The second immediate need was for clothing. At Duluth the Ladies' Relief Society specialized in the collection and distribution of new and used clothes. Clothing manufacturers donated whole outfits or large numbers of jackets, dresses and underwear. The Montgomery Ward Company gave a total of 500 pair of shoes with instructions that a pair be shipped by express to each recipient.

RELIEF

H. H. Hart of St. Paul,
Secretary of the State
Fire Relief Commission

Although appeals were made repeatedly for useful contributions, some donors sent frivolous items such as dancing slippers, silk stockings, feathered opera fans and elegant hats of all descriptions. Refugees were grateful for most any kind of wearing apparel as long as it fit reasonably well and was serviceable. But an occasional person was hard to accommodate. One man at Pine City tried on three or four coats before settling on one that fit but did not quite please him. When asked if the coat was satisfactory, he answered, "Yes, I guess so. It is a pretty good coat, but I never did like a three-button cut-away."[14]

Some contributors ransacked attics and sheds and donated items which should have been discarded — a length of sooty stove pipe or a copper wash boiler full of holes. But most citizens and businesses gave useful items including lumber and building materials, coffins for burial, furniture, household utensils and dishes, stoves, tools and hardware. Grain dealers donated carloads of wheat which could be sold for cash. Items that weren't donated were purchased by the State Commission from the relief fund.

The coordination of collecting and distributing items was a mammoth undertaking. In the Twin Cities the relief committee of each city collected, sorted and stored the items in warehouses and directed shipments to the burned areas as requisitioned by the state agents.

Other needs had to be met by a generous public. The fire left a large number of orphans and widows with children who had no means of support. The Duluth relief committee made appeals to churches to adopt a fatherless family of the same religious faith to become wards of the church. They also requested that anyone wishing to adopt or give employment to children and young or old people should contact them.

FROM THE ASHES

Kenneth Clark of St. Paul
Treasurer of the State
Fire Relief Commission

There were responses to these requests such as the following:

Mrs. R. A. Fuller of Barnum would be willing to take an active boy from 3 to 10 years of age for six months with the understanding that if she liked him she could keep him. [15]

Mrs. Woods of Hunter's Park wants a girl who can work and go to school. [16]

Mayor Eustis of Minneapolis received many offers to help and among them was this letter from a North Dakota man (the original spelling has not been altered):

Mr. Mayor of Mpls.:

I sea by the Papers, that there [is] a grate destres on a count of fire, and lots needs asistence. I wold like to help some and the only way I can sea is to take som widow in my house if there is any that wants to com and can talk English without to many children, you may send one heare. 1 or 2 children I wont mind no more and I will pay her fair wages for the winter. (Unsigned) [17]

A total of $96,458.69 was collected in cash contributions. Of that amount $11,600.00 was donated by foreign countries, $70,147.50 came from Minnesota, and $14,711.19 from other states. [18] When donated goods and services were added, the State Commission estimated that a total of $184,744.00 was spent to furnish relief to over 2,600 fire sufferers. [19]

RELIEF

THE STATE FIRE RELIEF COMMISSION

State officials were first notified of the fire when Tams Bixby, the governor's private secretary, received a telegram at 11:15 a.m. September 2, stating the extent of the fire and asking for aid. Bixby immediately informed Governor Nelson, and they decided a course of action. Bixby then contacted the National Guard and local wholesalers for supplies. At 4:00 Sunday afternoon a loaded train left St. Paul with ten National Guardsmen, a committee, an undertaker and newspaper reporters. On the way north they took on other volunteers and supplies and reached Pine City that evening.

On September 3 Governor Nelson made an official relief proclamation issuing a call to all "liberal and public-spirited citizens, to all municipalities and to all religious and benevolent institutions of this state, to take immediate action toward securing contributions for the relief of the prevailing distress."[20] He appointed C. A. Pillsbury of Minneapolis, Kenneth Clark of St. Paul, Charles H. Graves of Duluth, Matthew Norton of Winona and Hastings H. Hart of St. Paul to the State Relief Commission, authorizing them to receive and disburse contributions of money and supplies.

On September 5 the State Commission held its first meeting in St. Paul and elected Charles Pillsbury as chairman, Kenneth Clark, treasurer, and H. H. Hart, secretary. On September 6 and 7 the Commission visited Duluth, Pine City and Hinckley and found that the local committees in Duluth and Pine City were well-organized and were efficiently handling temporary relief.

Feeding hungry survivors at Hinckley, Tuesday, September 4th

Robert A. Smith,
Mayor of St. Paul

But a systematic method of distributing meals, clothing, supplies and transportation passes had to be adopted at all relief centers, and permanent relief measures had to be formulated. H. H. Hart set up his headquarters at Pine City and devised a uniform system for relief. At first clothing and food were given out to everyone who appeared to be in need, but soon meal tickets were issued entitling each refugee to twenty-one free meals, and extra clothing was given out only by requisition. Local agents were appointed to begin the detailed work of registering refugees at each center. Complete personal information was secured on each individual or family which later became the basis for determining the permanent relief given out by the Commission. As soon as temporary facilities were available in Hinckley, the Commission headquarters was moved there to be closer to the scene of operation.

The local relief committees in the Twin Cities organized by Mayors Robert A. Smith of St. Paul and W. H. Eustis of Minneapolis functioned co-operatively with the State Commission and handled the storage of donated goods that came in from communities in the state and the nation. They kept accurate records and inventories and sent out goods to the burned areas as needed.

One of the first actions of the State Commission was to establish guidelines for dispensing permanent relief. They set up the following policies:

1. Local agents would be appointed and given exclusive power to make decisions on individual cases except when the help of the entire commission was needed;
2. Relief was not to be considered as fire insurance to reimburse individuals or families to the extent of their losses, nor was anyone to be better off after the fire than before as a result of state relief;
3. Local agents should give out aid in a friendly, supportive manner so as not to undermine the self-respect and initiative of fire sufferers;
4. All possible assistance and incentive should be given fire sufferers to become self-supporting and independent as soon as possible;
5. Fire sufferers should be given employment whenever possible in rebuilding and carrying out relief measures;
6. Local agents should adopt a policy of *generous* aid to hasten the rehabilitation of individuals and families before the approach of winter;
7. Fire sufferers should be urged to return to their former locations, but if they want to go elsewhere they should be given from $20 to $25 for each family member. Single men should be given the same amount and outfitted with a suit of clothes;
8. Those who held fire insurance on their property should receive no state relief unless the insurance was far less than the relief they were entitled to receive.[21]

As the work of the Commission continued, the complexities of administering permanent relief multiplied. This was particularly true in working out equitable arrangements for those who held property or were paying on mortgages. The Commission wisely decided that relief houses should not be built on heavily mortgaged land, since the company holding the mortgages would benefit if foreclosure occurred. The Commission appointed R. C. Saunders of Hinckley, Pine County attorney, to investigate all land titles. Saunders tried to secure for each home owner a clear title to a small parcel of land on which the house would be built, or at least induce land companies to extend contracts and liberalize terms of payment. If neither of these was possible, Saunders helped the home owner find a free or cheap piece of land on which the house could be built.

The investigation of land titles was a lengthy process and the Hinckley people became impatient as the days passed. They contemplated their annihilated village and saw the magnitude of the job of rebuilding before winter came. They were understandably concerned with the delays of the State Commission. Their complaints were first aired in the newspapers, to the displeasure of the State Commission. Charges and countercharges were made, and Minnesota newspapers began to take sides. Generally the Twin Cities and Duluth newspapers defended the integrity of the State Commission and its management of relief, while small town papers close to Hinckley rallied behind the cause of the fire sufferers.

On September 19 Chairman Pillsbury and three other members of the Commission went to Hinckley to meet with the local committee to hear their complaints. The meeting was held in a temporary shed. The Hinckley people charged that there was no representation from Pine County on the Commission. Furthermore, they said, the Commission was slow in releasing

W. H. Eustis
Mayor of Minneapolis

materials to rebuild the town, and local residents were becoming discouraged and were talking of leaving. They charged that the local agent, appointed by the Commission, was incompetent and treated those getting relief as "paupers." Also, the agent ignored advice from the residents who knew the situation best and had given aid to those who were undeserving and refused aid to others who were entitled to it. The agent had not hired Hinckley workers for local jobs but had employed workers from other towns.

After listening to the charges Pillsbury defended the work of the Commission and expressed confidence in the competence of the agents in charge. He outlined the work being done, the steps involved in clearing titles to the land and securing more favorable mortgage terms for home owners. He stated that the Commission had tried to dispense aid fairly, considering the need, condition and size of the family, not what individuals or families lost. After the meeting Pillsbury reported that he believed only a small group, perhaps 3%, of the Hinckley people were dissatisfied with the handling of relief. The rest, he said, were content with the work of the Commission.

Twin Cities and Duluth editors rose to the defense of the Commission. The editor of *The Duluth News Tribune* wrote:

> The protest sent out from Hinckley over the work of the state relief commission is in exceedingly bad form....It is entirely likely, too, that the objections are not generally shared by the fire sufferers. [22]

A Minneapolis editor expressed his opinion:

> The trouble with the Hinckley people is that they expected too much to be done
> at once. The commission is attending to its work in a prudent, business manner.
> The money and supplies come from the whole state and it required discretion and
> discrimination in distributing them. The commission have to find out who the
> actual fire sufferers are first, were not this done great injustice would be done
> many needy persons. Immediate necessities must first be supplied. The rehabilita-
> tion of the town comes afterward. It cannot be rebuilt in a day. It will take time,
> and in the meantime the Hinckley people should be patient. The commission is a
> good one, and can be trusted. There is no use for anyone to get ill-natured about
> relief. Substantial relief will be given the real sufferers as far as money will
> permit.[23]

But the feud was just warming up. Charles Elmquist, editor of *The
Rush City Post*, took up the cause of the Hinckley people declaring: "*The
Rush City Post* has made itself the vehicle of complaints of the small minority
who think they were not fairly treated."[24] Elmquist claimed that the State
Commission was dishonest and wasteful in spending relief money, and he
called for a published statement of their expenditures. He wrote:

> There is a wide spread feeling of discontent and that about the only persons who
> were satisfied with the work of the commission were those who were in their
> employ at a fat salary and the ones who lost nothing in the fire but were actual
> gainers thereby. . . . [It was a] unanimous opinion that the commission deserved to
> be fired bodily from the place as it had displayed its incompetency to deal with
> matters which should be left in the hands of a local committee.[25]

In December the State Commission ran out of relief money and threatened to halt operations. This precipitated another rash of protests from
Elmquist. He wrote:

> What a spectacle the state commission had made of itself! The moment a country
> paper inaugurates an investigation, the commission declares it will have no more
> to do with the sufferers at Hinckley and refuses to carry out the work which it
> started.[26]

The Twin Cities papers continued to defend the integrity of the Commission, and other editors joined the dispute. The editor of *The Red Wing
Republican* called Elmquist the "Meanest Man in Minnesota,"[27] an epithet
echoed by Chairman Pillsbury. To this Elmquist replied, "We are rather
proud of the title. . .gained in an honest effort to procure justice for the
suffering."[28]

A more strident voice was raised on behalf of the Commission by Miss
Horace Greeley Perry, editor of *The St. Peter Journal*, who wrote:

Charles Elmquist
Editor of
The Rush City Post

[The commission] has suspended operations because of dissatisfaction and continual howling of not getting enough by the citizens. The task is not pleasant anyway, for the people of Hinckley are as ignorant as ungrateful. They know that a large amount of money had been raised for their assistance, and they imagine that it ought to be turned over to them in cash. . . . Hinckley [can not] be built up as quickly as it was destroyed. [29]

Angus Hay, testy editor of *The Hinckley Enterprise,* took offense at the words of Editor Perry, and as soon as his paper was back in publication, he responded with equally barbed words:

Certainly the author is well and safely located; and while this same author's nether limbs are encased in the trousers of Horace Greeley, her mind is enshrouded in that darkness which is the usual concomitant of residence at or near St. Peter. . . . Her sex prevents *the Enterprise* from allowing "the pen to say what the tongue would speak." [30]

Rush City editor Elmquist, ever anxious for another bout, jumped into this feud of words saying:

Brother Hay is engaged in a pencil fight with the editor of *The St. Peter Journal* — a woman. Of course Brother Hay is badly handicapped. Respect for a woman, even though she is an editor, restrains him from saying what he feels. But when this faraway editor writes about the ignorance of people she has never seen, it is about time she was brought to her bearings. [31]

RELIEF

Alvah Eastman
Editor of
The St. Cloud Journal Press

Despite the threats and the controversies the work of the State Commission continued. Members of the Commission made personal loans amounting to $15,000 to extend the relief work and were reimbursed when the legislature later approved $20,000 from the state coffers. Early in 1895 the Commission released a sixty-page report giving a detailed account of their activities, receipts and disbursements. Editor Elmquist and other critics were apparently satisfied.

Another disagreement arose when St. Cloud decided not to funnel its relief money through the State Commission, but rather chose to give it directly to Milaca and Brook Park. The Rev. William Wilkinson, Rector of St. Andrews Episcopal Church in Minneapolis, had been appointed by the Commission as relief agent in Brook Park, since he had an interest in that community and had given much time to rescue work and burial of the dead. But as St. Cloud became involved with relief work at Brook Park, there arose a head-on confrontation between Alvah Eastman, secretary of the St. Cloud relief committee, and Agent Wilkinson. Eastman, outspoken editor of *The St. Cloud Journal Press,* was the self-appointed watchdog of the local agent and the Kelsey and Markham Land Company, which held large mortgages on homesites at Brook Park, and he used his paper to air the dispute.

Eastman alleged that Wilkinson had made him a questionable proposition regarding the building of relief homes at Brook Park. Eastman reported that when the two had met, Wilkinson had said, "It is all arranged. You and I and Mr. H. (Howard) of Duluth are to have charge of building the houses

*John G. Howard
of Duluth,
Superintendent of Building*

at Pokegama, (Brook Park) and the commission will give us the necessary funds. Then when we get them completed, we will have a grand opening, throw up our hats and claim we were the fellows who did it!"[32] Furthermore, said Eastman, the St. Cloud committee recommended that settlers be given *ten* acres of free land on which to build a relief home, not *two* as agreed upon by Wilkinson and the Kelsey and Markham Company. Eastman also claimed that the land company was charging too much for its land ($8.00 an acre), and if the settlers could not meet the payments, the two free acres would be of little value in supporting themselves.

Several newspapers promptly reported Eastman's allegations, and many rose to the Reverend's defense. The Twin Cities papers asserted that Wilkinson was:

> ...a large-hearted, earnest and useful man...who was one of the first men to offer his services and had the confidence and cooperation of the state and local relief committees. He fed the hungry, comforted the bereaved and the dying, dug graves for the dead, read the services over them, helped build new houses, and did everything that could be done for the comfort of the living and gave Christian burial to the dead. The complaints against him must be based on misinformation.[33]

Wilkinson responded to Eastman's charges by posting $100 with *The Minneapolis Tribune* to be given to the relief fund if Eastman could prove his statements. He threatened, "If Alvah Eastman does not unconditionally retract every allegation in that article, he will stand a suit for libel."[34] But Eastman refused to make "an unconditional retraction of truth to please Mr. Wilkinson or anybody else."[35]

RELIEF

DATE...........

Surname _Queen_   Given Name _Michael_

Born at _Ireland_   Age _67_

Wife's name _Bridget_   Age _64_

Born at _Ireland_

Number of Children _6_ Names, with ages _Margaret (33) married, Mary (33) married, Frank (31)_
Bertha (28) perished, Thomas (24) perished. Last four lived at home.

Are you helping to support others? _Yes_ Whom? _Her daughter family of 6 (11. 41)_

Were any of your family hurt, and how badly? _Yes Bertha & Thomas perished_

Where were your dead found, if any? _Hinckley_ By whom identified? _All the family_

Residence at time of fire _Hinckley_ Post Office address _520 West First Street_

Length of time lived in Minnesota _23 yrs_ HABITS! _Good_

ABLE BODIED? _Too old_
Occupation _Pump man_ Business for himself—Yes or No _No_

Owns his home—Yes or No _No_ If mortgaged, for how much? _____

What property was destroyed by the fire? & v _House furnishing ($300)_

Had Insurance—Fire $ _No_ Life $ _No_ Accident $ _No_

What property left and its value? _Clothing_

Have you property elsewhere? _80 acres at Verndale Minn_

Address of relatives and friends _Mrs McLain, St Paul (912 Fremont St)_

Can you expect help from them? _Yes_ How much? _Simply a home there_

Do you want to go to them? _Yes_ the family want to go there If not there, where? _Stay at Hinckley_

What can you do if we help you to get there? _Run the pump_

HAVE YOU A JOB PROMISED YOU _Yes_ What?
Have you an income of any kind? _Salary_ What? _50 per month_ Pension? _Yes ($6 month)_

Have you any pressing debts? _No_ What?

Needs: Have you received help before (Friends furnished $10)
Transportation for wife Bridget to St Paul —

What do you think you need most? _____

Decision _9/13_ _____

Furnished _____

DATE...........
Register's Signature _____   Applicant's Signature _Michael Queen_

The State Commission mediated the dispute and took over the building of homes at Brook Park. Wilkinson did not press his libel suit, not did Eastman retract his statement. However, Eastman did concede that Wilkinson should be given credit for the good he had done. The Kelsey and Markham Company donated two acres of land to each settler, and the rebuilding of Brook Park was under way.

In spite of the controversies that arose, the members of the State Commission worked arduously at the task of rebuilding the burned communities before the winter season began. H. H. Hart of the State Board of Corrections and Charities, who had been appointed secretary of the Commission, was made the general overseer of all relief work. J. G. Howard of Duluth was in charge of all construction work including the building of homes, purchasing lumber and materials and employing carpenters and workers.

Before permanent relief could be dispensed, detailed information was secured on each refugee including name, birth place, members of family, residence, occupation, losses and property salvaged, status of property ownership, insurance and assets, references, needs and future plans. At one relief center a conscientious agent requested an additional bit of information as to the "habits" of the registrant. This invariably referred to the person's drinking habits and elicited a variety of responses such as "do not touch liquor to my lips", "use no liquor at present", "drink some and have been drunk but not for two years" or "occasionally drink beer but don't get drunk."[36]

On each registration were listed the items of temporary and permanent relief given to each refugee. This information was later transferred to a ledger book which furnished a complete record of all relief given each fire sufferer or family and the total value in dollars of such relief.

The Commission's work was compounded by the complexity of the individual cases. First, the sufferers were scattered over a large territory and were supervised by ten different local agents. Second, each situation was different. Some fire sufferers were residents who wanted to return to the community provided there was work for them. Some had lost everything but did not plan to return since there was no employment available. Some were transient workers who had been living in a community temporarily and had lost personal belongings. Some were farmers who had lost not only property and livestock but their livelihood as well. Some were widows with families with no means of support.

The Commission tried to take into account the needs and circumstances of each sufferer, but there were unavoidable inequities in distributing relief to so many. As rebuilding began, residents complained that hardworking, needy people did not receive what they deserved, while "ne'er-do-wells" were given more than they ever had owned in their lives. The Commission acknowledged this problem in their report, stating:

> It has been a cause of grief. . . to see some of the people. . . gradually lose their spirit of independence and become willing, and even eager, to take all they can get.[37]

Other complaints arose concerning the morals of the recipients of relief. Chairman Pillsbury answered this by saying that it was the intent of the Commission to act on the *needs* of the refugees, not their *morals*. Furthermore, he said, "This money was not all given by saints. Much of it was given by those who do not call themselves over-religious. We shall ask no questions on such matters; we shall try to see that all have a place in which to live and that they have enough to eat, and clothes suitable to wear."[38]

Once again greed surfaced. As soon as money, free goods and services were available, there were opportunists who took advantage of the situation. At Duluth an arrest was made when an individual attempted to duplicate orders to receive additional supplies and clothing. At one relief center a man, probably not a refugee, got in line and demanded a shave and a haircut while women and children waited patiently for clothing to cover themselves. One woman was reported to have collected supplies once at Pine City, twice at Hinckley and asked for more at Duluth. In October three men who returned from productive work in the Dakota harvest fields represented themselves as sufferers and were given clothes and $10.00 in cash.

Before any houses could be built, the Commission had to secure more liberal terms from the land companies that held mortgages on burned properties. If the companies would not comply, the Commission tried to find free or cheap land on which to build. Most of the companies were responsive to the request and made generous offers. Some companies donated two acres, or gave a free lot to home owners. Some extended the time for payment, while others gave credit on the mortgage equal to the value of the building erected by the Commission, which in some cases wiped out nearly all of the home owner's indebtedness. Some companies gave employment to heads of families and provided a free lot for building a house.

122   Mrs Best   Hoof & page 455

Registration Blank.

Enterd.
Ledger Page 455

Name Best, John 38, Birth place

Wifes Name Mary 32, Birth place

Children, Alice 2. Birth place   Men
Baby born 28 Sept   { Mother ill to be
confined
kept with child
to Hosp Hinckly

2 m SE from
Residence ^ Hinckley, How long 4 y, How long in   father, mother
3 brothers + 2 sister
burned

Minnesota 9 m.

Occupation Farmer
Farm 80 acres
Did he own his home
Land 160 Bldg burned 70   If mortgaged, for how much.
$ none. How much insurance $ none

What property left 4 Cows, 2 horses a few potatoes
perhaps 20 bu + Clothing - No coat
Value $:

Address of friends None

Ability of

Needs Clothing for self

Wants to go to back to the farm

RELIEF
125

110

d page 454

Registration Blank Enterd.
Ledger Page 454

Name *West Christean* 32 Birth place *Scandinavia*

Wifes Name _____, Birth place _____

Children, _____ . Birth place _____

Residence 2 m se of *Hinckley* with brother, How long 6 y, How long in

Minnesota 6 y

Occupation *Farmer*

Did he own his home _____ . If mortgaged, for how much.

$ _____ . How much insurance $ _____ .

What property left *Clothing on his back &*
one horse

Value $ _____

Address of friends *None*

Ability of _____

Needs *Clothing (order given to brother)*

_____

_____

Wants to go to _____

When James J. Hill gave his donation of $5,000 and 5,000 acres of land, his motive was not entirely philanthropic. First, he was anxious to see the lands around his railroads populated to insure future business. And he had another consideration. A telegram dated September 5, 1895, from Samuel Hill to James J. Hill included these words:

> Liberal money contributions being made by citizens. Would you feel disposed to give on behalf Company fifty farms, forty acres each, say total two thousand acres, to actual settlers from our lines? Aside from grounds of charity I think this wise in view of the question which must be met *this winter in Legislature* regarding *taxation** of lands. [39]

While land terms were being settled, the fire sufferers were growing increasingly restless and impatient with the delay. Days were becoming noticeably shorter, and the brisk fall air was a constant reminder of approaching winter. Women and children were not allowed to return to their communities until some sort of shelter was provided for them. They were eager to return home, and husbands and fathers wanted to be reunited with their families.

As soon as the terms with the land companies were settled, construction began. The Commission adopted a basic plan for a simple frame house, 16 x 24 feet in size costing from $95 to $150. The houses were one story or one and one-half stories high depending upon the size of the family. A lean-to could be added for exceptionally large families. People who had owned a mere "shack" before the fire were given from $40 to $100 worth of building materials with which to erect their own homes with or without assistance from carpenters. Generally no homes were built for single men unless they had owned a home before the fire, but the Commission waived this restriction if a young man had since married and intended to settle down. In some cases married men who had not owned a home, but intended to stay in a community, were given from $50 to $75 to build a house since there were no homes or rooms to rent. Widows with large families were given larger homes. The average cost of carpentry to erect one home was $35, but those who could do their own work were given that amount in cash.

When the houses were completed, they were equipped with simple furniture, household utensils and dishes, bedding and linens, tools and hardware and a three-month's supply of food. Some who had many children were given a cow, and a few farmers were given a team of horses in lieu of other assistance. But when animals were provided, the Commission also had to supply hay and feed to carry them through the winter. The Commission had wanted to purchase sewing machines for seamstresses and for women with large families, but the relief money did not extend that far.

---

*In the original telegram the five italicized words were written in unintelligible code with the decoded words added above in a different handwriting.

GREAT NORTHERN RAILWAY LINE.

After transmitting telegrams which in their judgment would have served the Company's interest if sent by train mail, or which appear unnecessarily long, operators are required to make a copy of them and forward to Superintendent of Telegraph. Operators will write all telegrams in ink, and enclose those for delivery on trains (except to trainmen) in sealed envelope.

Received From	Time Received	SENDER	RECEIVER	TELEGRAM.	SENT TO	TIME SENT	SENDER	RECEIVER
	1055 A			TIME FILED _____ M.		1110		

FROM _____ 5 _____ Minneapolis 5   TO Mr Jas J Hill

DATED _____ 189_   At _____ Prest G N Ry Co

On Special

Visited Hinckley yesterday, Walking from Duluth track to Sandstone with Engineer Toltz, who assures me iron span over Kettle river substantially uninjured. Newspaper report fail to describe the desolation. Probably over five hundred people burned. Country like an ash-heap. Intense heat melted car-wheels fast to rails. absolutely nothing left standing in Sandstone. Everything in quarry burned, except office. Farrington pushing everything from the east, and McKenna from the west. Trust company

---

GREAT NORTHERN RAILWAY LINE.

After transmitting telegrams which in their judgment would have served the Company's interest if sent by train mail, or which appear unnecessarily long, operators are required to make a copy of them and forward to Superintendent of Telegraph. Operators will write all telegrams in ink, and enclose those for delivery on trains (except to trainmen) in sealed envelope.

Received From	Time Received	SENDER	RECEIVER	TELEGRAM.	SENT TO	TIME SENT	SENDER	RECEIVER
				TIME FILED (25) M.		1110		

FROM _____

DATED _____ 189_   At _____

will probably start Quarries saturday. About fifty farmers tributary to our lines have been burned out. Liberal money contributions being made by citizens. Would you feel disposed to give, on behalf Company fifty farms, forty acres each, say total two thousand acres, to actual settlers from our lines? Aside from grounds of charity I think this wise in view of the Legislature question which must be met tragedy zone indelible linguis

F. 1153.   2-25-94. 1000M. McG.

GREAT NORTHERN RAILWAY LINE.

After transmitting telegrams which in their judgment would have served the Company's interest if sent by train mail, **or which appear unnecessarily long,** operators are required to make a copy of them and forward to Superintendent of Telegraph. Operators will write **all telegrams in ink,** and enclose those for delivery on trains (except to trainmen) in sealed envelope.

Received From	Time Received	SENDER	RECEIVER	TELEGRAM.	SENT TO	TIME SENT	SENDER	RECEIVER
				TIME FILED _____ M				

FROM _____ *taxation* (3)   TO

DATED _____ 189_   AT

regarding Thivies of lands. Please advise, All well here.

Samuel Hill

When sent put on Mr Saml Hills desk

Three-page telegram from Samuel Hill
to James J. Hill, September 5, 1894.
Contains coded message regarding taxation of railroad land.

As families settled in their houses, some items were in short supply and could not be delivered immediately. Items of clothing such as children's and men's underwear were scarce, and the supply of calico and muslin for sewing did not meet the demand. And there were mix-ups. One family received four bed springs, but only one bed, while another family had beds but no springs or mattresses.

Before the winter came the Commission distributed 500 bushels of winter rye for farmers to plant on the burned land for an early spring crop. The following spring, with aid from the Agriculture Department, they gave out grain, vegetable and flower seeds to plant for a summer crop.

By the end of November, 1894, the State Commission had concluded its official functions, but local agents continued to handle the distribution of relief in each community. During this time Hinckley had a turn-over of four local agents in charge of relief, with George Holt from Minneapolis, general agent of the Commission, conducting the final phase. It was the intent of the Commission to terminate all relief by May 1, 1895, but the relief ledgers indicate that it was still distributing seeds until May 30.

RELIEF

45

John Best

38 yrs. near Hinckley.
w/ May 32, 1 ch. 2 yrs. baby born Sep. 28/94. (Parents, 3 brothers & 2 sisters burn...)

1894				
		Furnished at HINCKLEY.		
Sep.	25	6 loaves Bread²⁵ Bacon¹⁰⁰ 2 ℔ Coffee⁵⁰	1 75	
		4 Bales hay¹⁶⁰ 2 sacks feed¹⁵⁰	3 10	
		1 Mattress¹²⁵ 4 Comforts³⁰⁰	4 25	
	29	1 Bale hay⁴⁰ 2 sacks feed¹⁵⁰ 4 loaves bread²⁰	2 10	11 2
		Furnished at HINCKLEY.		
		Nº 2 House ⁺4	1 95	
	"16	Cash, in lieu of Comfo.13d. ⁺673	20	
Oct	3	1 Mens Clo. Outfit⁵⁰⁰ 1 Saw⁵⁰ 1 Square⁵⁰	6	
		4 ℔ Crackers¹⁵ 1 Ham¹²⁵	1 40	
		4 bales hay	1 60	
	6	1 Coffee mill³⁰ Matches¹⁰ 1 Pr. Mitts²⁵	65	
	8	Outfits for 4 of Furniture,		
		Bedding, Hardware & Crockery	48 31	
		Provisions for 4 for 3 mos.	29 73	
	18	1 Pr. Overalls⁵⁰ 2 suits Underwear¹⁰⁰ ⁺122	1 50	
		2 Shirts¹²⁰ 1 Cap⁵⁰ 1 gal oil¹⁰ "	1 80	
		1 Comb¹⁵ 1 Looking Glass⁴⁰ "	55	
		2 Milk Pans³⁰ 5 ℔ Dr. Apples²⁵ "	55	
	29	1 Pr. Rubbers¹²⁵ 2 Pr. Socks⁵⁰ 1 Brush¹⁰ ⁺618	1 85	
		10 bales hay⁴⁰⁰ 5 sacks feed³⁷⁵ ⁺767	7 75	
Nov	6	1 Clock⁷⁵ Cloth line & Pins⁵⁰ ⁺880	1 25	
	10	1 Stable Fork ⁺950	30	
	14	2 suits Underwear¹⁰⁰ 1 Pr. Pants¹⁰⁰ ⁺948	2	
		1 Pr. Suspenders	25	
	15	21 bales hay⁸⁴⁰ 3 sacks Bran¹⁵⁰ ⁺997	9 90	
	16	1 Mens Clo. Outfit⁵⁰⁰ 1 childs D.³⁰⁰ ⁺982	8	
		Baby Clothing¹⁰⁰ 2 Prs Mitts⁵⁰ 2 Cloaks³⁰⁰ "	4 50	
		1 Lamp⁴⁰ 1 Pr. Overshoes⁷⁵ "	1 15	
1894				
Jany	10	Provisions for 5 for 30 days ⁺723	14 38	
Feby	13	" " 5 " 30 " ⁺908	14 38	
Mch	20	1 Lumber wagon	50	
	22	Provisions for 5 for 60 days	28 76	
		8 sacks feed⁶⁰⁰ 1 sck bran⁵⁰	6 50	
Apr	16	300 ℔ Flour & bal Provisions & Pfs.		
		sugar for 5 for 30 days ⁺1335	14 38	
	24	6 sacks feed⁴⁵⁰ 1 sck bran⁵⁰ ⁺1424	5	
May	20	For seed: 20 bu. Pot.⁸ 2 bu. Oats¹ 13 bu. Corn³⁵	⁺7 35 ⁺⁺9 35	48 67
				497 9

Christian Bert
32 yrs.
single.   near Hinckley.

1894			Furnished at PINE CITY.					
Sept.	2		Clothing			5		
	7		Undersuit 50 1 Pr. Pants 100 1 Pr. Socks 25			1 75		6 75

Furnished at HINCKLEY.

	4/7	Building Material $94 48 *169			
	12/17	Cash 5 52 *841	100		
	"	Cash. Bldg. allowance *842	35		
		Cost of hauling lumber	9		
Oct.	1.	1 Sack Feed		75	
	2	2 " " 150 1 Bale Hay 40	1 90		
	19	2 Suits Underwear	1		
Nov.	4	1 Shovel 40 1 Fork 40 *848		80	
	9	35 bales hay 1400 3 sacks bran 150 12 sacks feed 900 *930	24 50		
	15	2 shirts 120 1 Pr. Suspenders 25 *963	1 45		
	24	Provisions for 2 for 3 mos *233	19 03		
		Outfits for 2 of furniture,			
		Bedding, Hardware & Crockery *303	37 70		
1895		10 bales hay 400 8 sacks feed 600 *1278	10		
Apr.	2	Cash (for Plow 15 Harrow 14) *1096	29 13		
May	2	20 bu. Seed Potatos.	8		
	20	6 " " Oats.	3		
		½ " " Corn		55	28 68
					28 8 43

The State Commission kept detailed records of all contributions, expenditures and dispensations of relief. The actual records including registrations, vouchers for payments, receipts, requisitions for supplies, transportation passes issued and ledger books are collected in the Governor's File in the Archives and Manuscripts Division of the Minnesota Historical Society. The ledger books include a summary page for each fire sufferer showing what dispensation was made for each.

Early in 1895 the Commission submitted its official report to Governor Nelson and requested a state audit of their records. In their report the State Commission stated that a total of 2,636 people had been given aid, 2,026 being from Pine County. The largest number was from the village of Hinckley where 921 received aid and 181 were helped in the near vicinity. At Sandstone 420 were given relief, 129 at Brook Park, 67 at Mission Creek, 85 at Finlayson, and 69 at Sandstone Junction and Miller. In the burned area 215 houses were built, 62 of which were erected by the fire sufferers themselves with lumber provided by the Commission. The total money disbursed for aid up to December 31, 1894, amounted to $104,843.95,[40] an amount $45,000 less than the state had spent on a Minnesota exhibit at the Chicago Columbian Exposition in 1893. The estimated grand total of all aid dispersed, including money, donated materials and free transportation was estimated to be $184,744.00. In addition to this was the amount spent later by the state legislature to provide grain and seeds for spring planting and money appropriated to rebuild roads and bridges.

Relief home of Sheriff Hawley in Hinckley

*Relief home
of Seba De Boer
in Hinckley*

133

*George D. Holt
of Minneapolis,
General Agent*

*Relief Home
of the McNeal Family
in Hinckley*

134

CHAPTER *7*

Repairing and Rebuilding

RAILROAD OFFICIALS knew the importance of maintaining uninterrupted freight and passenger service flowing along the steel arteries of the transportation network. Shippers depended upon fast, dependable delivery of grain, lumber and general merchandise, and passengers had become accustomed to hopping the fast expresses that sped between the Twin Cities and Duluth in record time. Fires notwithstanding, the service had to continue.

Both railroad lines maintained work trains and crews that stood ready to be dispatched instantly to trouble spots. Men would work day and night to keep the lines open and operable.

After the devastation of September 1 the sparks had not even died before work crews were out repairing the lines. L. J. Miller, Assistant General Manager of the St. Paul and Duluth Railroad Company, assessed the losses on his road: 22 miles of track, 18 miles of fence, 22,000 ties, a 90 foot bridge over the Grindstone and 3 culverts and trestles. At Miller the station had burned, and in Hinckley the railroad yards and depot were demolished, together with two section houses, a water tank and pump house, coal bin, turn-table and engine house. All coaches of the Limited No. 4 were burned and engine No. 69 was damaged. Thirty-two freight cars standing in yards were also destroyed. Newspapers stated that the St. Paul and Duluth losses were estimated at $57,000.

Reconstruction began immediately. Yardmaster Dave Williams and his crews worked down from Duluth to Skunk Lake, while E. L. Brown, Director of Transportation, had crews coming up from Mission Creek. After rebuilding the bridge over the Grindstone River north of Hinckley, Brown's crew worked north to Skunk Lake, and at 5:25 p.m. on September 3 the two trains met. At 6:00 p.m. the line was declared open from St. Paul to Duluth, and one hour later a train went through Hinckley on its way to Duluth.

REBUILDING

135

Wrecking crews clearing the tracks.

After the line was repaired, the only obstacle to through traffic was the blackened hulk of Root's engine which stood on the track at Skunk Lake, a stark reminder of the grim drama of the past two days. The repair crew shoved the ruined coal tender off the track and left it. Root's engine, sooty but still intact, was pushed down to Hinckley where it was moved to a side track. The engine with its scorched exterior, burned cab, broken windows and missing headlight became an instant tourist attraction. Later the tender was brought in from Skunk Lake and scrapped, but the engine was over-hauled and put back on the road for many more years of service. What happened to No. 69 in intervening years is not known, except that it was sold at one time to the Crookston Lumber Company of Bemidji and was operated at Kellihar, Minnesota, to haul logs from Island Lake to Bemidji.[1]   By 1964 it had been retired, having fulfilled every expectation for engine longevity.

On the Eastern Railway of Minnesota the problems were more acute and losses heavier. By September 3 the line had been opened from Duluth south to Partridge. A day or two later the road was in operation between St. Paul and Hinckley, but the stretch between Hinckley and Partridge, which had sustained heavy damage, and the Kettle River high bridge, which needed extensive repair, remained impassable. James J. Hill had noted that 250 feet of wooden supports on each side of the center steel span had burned and needed to be rebuilt. [2]

During the week following the fire numerous telegrams were dispatched from St. Paul to New York officials of the Great Northern advising them of the condition of the line. On September 3 F. E. Ward wired E. T. Nichols, Secretary and Assistant Treasurer of the Great Northern Company in New York:

> Latest reports indicate that Eastern Minn. Line opened to Partridge. Steel span in Kettle River Bridge apparently uninjured, but wooden bridge burnt out. Probably take two weeks to repair line. Great Northern will be opened to Hinckley in a day or two. About one hundred and fifty loads and sixty empties burned. [3]

On September 4 James J. Hill wired General Manager W. C. Farrington at Duluth to hurry completion of the Sandstone bridge. He said, "Do not hesitate to put on all the men that can work and get the material on the ground from the most convenient places."[4] Farrington acted promptly on Hill's orders, and on September 6 he wired Hill from Partridge saying that the Eastern work train had reached the Kettle River bridge, having repaired everything down to that point. He said rebuilding had begun on the north end of the high bridge, and by burning eight locomotive headlights men could work through the night. In the meantime crews were repairing lines northward from Hinckley to the other side of the Kettle River bridge. On September 10 Farrington reassured Hill that he had 60 men working south of the bridge and 125 men on the north side. He said, "[The] track will be in first-class condition within ten days and in better shape than ever when business begins to move."[5]

But Hill wanted to see for himself and went out to inspect the lines personally. He was not satisfied with the progress. On September 15 he dispatched a sharply-worded wire to Farrington saying:

> Say to Mr. Miller that he must personally see that Bowman's work is pushed. The Great Northern's engineering department with all the Companys [sic] resources behind it have totally failed to do as well as a country crew picked up at random, and he must see that this is remedied. Bowman's work yesterday afternoon was simply disgraceful. [6]

Because of the delay in opening the Eastern road, cargo began piling up at Duluth and the Twin Cities, and clients complained of loss of profits from the halt in shipping. Eastern Minnesota officials negotiated an agreement with the St. Paul and Duluth Railroad Company whereby Eastern could use the St. Paul and Duluth tracks between Hinckley and Duluth until the Kettle River bridge was repaired. On September 6 Eastern began running one freight and one passenger train each way daily on their competitor's road.

Later four Eastern freights and one passenger were running north and south each day, but the extra trains had to accommodate the regular schedule of the St. Paul and Duluth.

One complication arose from this arrangement. On September 13 Assistant General Manager Miller of the St. Paul and Duluth sent a letter to President Samuel Hill warning: "Your engines running over our tracks between Hinckley and Duluth are throwing a good deal of fire."[7] This had resulted in a fire south of Barnum, and Miller insisted that Eastern should relieve the St. Paul and Duluth of all damage claims which might arise. Samuel Hill immediately ordered that all nettings and ash pans be checked on their engines, and he so advised Miller.

Both railroads were relieved when the Kettle River bridge was completed and Eastern was again running on its own track. On September 18 Farrington wired both Hills the good news. To James J. in St. Paul he said, "First train crossed Kettle River Bridge 12:25 this morning."[8] To Samuel Hill, also in St. Paul, he wired, "Yes sir all trains Eastern Minn. running today over our line between Duluth and Hinckley."[9]

The Minneapolis Journal reported the estimated Eastern losses as $96,000[10] but James J. Hill assessed the loss to be $80,000 with insurance covering $60,000.[11] The Sixth Annual Report of the Great Northern Company for the fiscal year ending June 30, 1895, did not itemize any specific financial loss from the fire.

Although telephone service was available in the larger cities, cross-country communication was possible only by telegraph. Each railroad hired telegraph operators to relay messages from one station to another. Railroad crews relied implicitly upon their telegraphed messages along the road. Since the trains ran on single tracks and the fear of collision was great, any departure from the schedule had to be cleared by the officials and changes telegraphed to the stations on the road. During the fire when the wires were down, some trains were forced to run without orders, and nervous engineers and crewmen expected at any moment to collide head-on or run into the rear of another train stalled on the track.

Two companies, Western Union and the North American Telegraph Company, maintained telegraph service for the general public and for news correspondents. Just after the fire the bulk of news to other parts of the country was wired out of Pine City, the town closest to the fire zone. News reporters and telegraphers flocked to the burned area, set up emergency equipment and strung temporary lines to send out the initial first-hand reports. In Hinckley two days after the fire the Associated Press dispatcher sat on an empty beer keg tapping out his message on a dry-goods box. His copy, blurred by rain, was nailed to the "desk" with a railroad spike. Temporary wires had been strung between the black stumps which had once been the telegraph poles.

In Duluth when communication to the south was interrupted Saturday

*Remains of a
Hinckley building with
school in background.*

afternoon, that city was virtually isolated except for lines to the north. By
noon Sunday Western Union had one wire out of Duluth, and on this all
press news and commercial business had to be sent. Long press dispatches
piled up, including one to Chicago of 10,000 words. Thirty Western Union
linemen were sent out on handcars to replace every third pole and to string
miles of line. By Tuesday Duluth had a direct line through the burned area,
and in the three succeeding days more than 120,000 words were dispatched.
In addition to the news reports and personal communications, countless business messages were sent by the Relief Commission free of charge.

Immediately following the fire news correspondents from papers
throughout the country arrived at the burned district to send out on-the-
spot reports. The *New York World* sent young, crusading Nellie Bly to cover
the story. Four years earlier Miss Bly, born Elizabeth Cochrane, at age
twenty-two had broken the record of Jules Verne's fictional hero, Phileas
Fogg, in *Around the World in Eighty Days,* by circumnavigating the globe in
just a few hours over seventy-two days. When Miss Bly arrived from New
York on Thursday, September 6, she interviewed fire sufferers sheltered in
Pine City and then went on to Mission Creek, Hinckley and Skunk Lake
where she walked a total of fifteen to twenty miles with an escort. By 3:00
o'clock Friday morning she had written a 5,000 word report which she tele-
graphed to New York. On Friday she visited Duluth and returned to New
York one day later. Her three and one-half column article appeared in the
New York World on September 9.

EXCURSIONISTS

As soon as railroads resumed their regular schedules, Hinckley and other burned villages were overrun with people searching for living or dead relatives. The burned area also became a popular attraction for photographers, news reporters and sightseers. Visitors began collecting "souvenirs" from the ruins. In Hinckley local vigilantes were organized to patrol the town, and it was said that "any stranger wishing to secure relics of any description must be very slick indeed if he thinks to escape the eyes of all the numerous deputy village marshalls."[12] The deputies banished a number of suspicious-looking characters from the town.

But the curious came in droves. On Wednesday, September 5, hundreds of sightseers took the trains to Hinckley, stared at decomposed bodies and rambled over the ashes. *The Duluth News Tribune* described the event:

> When the north bound limited reached Hinckley yesterday, there was a mad rush by passengers from the cars to see the nine bodies which lay close to the tracks. Prominent among the ones who were most persistent in the attempt to gain a view of the blackened and distorted trunks and limbs were several mere girls. They got a close view and one of them turned deathly sick and would have fallen but for some helping hands that escorted her back to the chair car. The sight was too horrid for her as it was for many of the men and it is safe to say she will not manifest such undue haste to look at a lot of charred and naked human bodies again.[13]

To make matters worse the railroads began to run special Sunday "excursions" to the burned towns. Ironically the first trip on Sunday, September 16, was promoted by the St. Cloud relief committee to raise money for the fire sufferers. The Great Northern Railway Company provided the train free of charge, and sightseers paid $2.00 for an all-day trip with noon lunch served in the baggage car. The tour was advertised as one "no one should miss."

A train of eight coaches and a baggage car left St. Cloud at 9:00 Sunday morning and stopped at all stations to take on more passengers until about 300 were aboard. They stopped first at Brook Park, then went on to Hinckley where they stayed for three hours while "excursionists tramped over the ashes of the place." The local marshalls were not able to contain the swarm of sightseers. *The St. Cloud Daily Times* reported:

> A party of the St. Cloud excursionists found a hand in one of the heaps of ashes that indicated where a house had stood. The crowds visited the gravel pit, the mill site and all the places [of] interest. All returned to the train loaded down with relics. There was enough old truck carried away to start a junk shop. Ald. Kraemer was the most fortunate of the relic hunters. He brought back five silver dollars melted together. A. A. Wright had a grip with a piano inside, Ald. Alstrom had an ash kettle full of sundries and a pair of pinchers, Deputy Auditor Atkins had two flower vases, but they were stolen from him before he got home. Editor Eastman's most valuable souvenir was a 50 cent revenue stamp taken from the bottom of a beer keg. The cask had been burnt in two but the stamp escaped unscorched.[14]

The sightseers, loaded down with their loot, returned to St. Cloud at 6:00 p.m. The relief treasury was advanced by $475.00.

The following week Minneapolis and St. Paul newspapers ran notices promoting another Sunday excursion from the Twin Cities:

> Special to view Hinckley and area on St. Paul and Duluth railroad. Long stops made at Mission Creek, Hinckley and Skunk Lake. Round trip of 175 miles — $1.50. Leave Minneapolis on Sunday, September 23, at 9:00 a.m., back at 7:30. Lunch served on train. [15]

A train of twenty-one coaches pulled by two engines carried about 1,800 Twin Cities people to Hinckley and surrounding areas. A *Minneapolis Journal* reporter accompanied the expedition and described the ghoulish tour:

> The traveler on yesterday's excursion would have seen 1,800 connoisseurs in relics, and each one pursuing a specialty...frantic efforts of every man, woman and child to get something. Anything would do, from a cumbersome kitchen utensil to a bit of charred wood. One man was seen carrying to the train a large iron soup kettle containing an ax head and other iron truck, weighing fully 25 pounds, to judge from the way he staggered under the load. Another man had a coffee boiler, one of the monsters used in lumber camps. In this he had a section of chain, some horse shoes, files and a choice lot of hardware, dug out from the ruins of the blacksmith shop at Mission Creek. An elderly lady had a big basin containing a variety of blackened iron ware.... Among the 'truck' carried off by some people were the following: Two big ax heads, three circular saws...a gun barrel, a pick ax, a mass of fused glass and rubbish as big as a peck measure, large pieces of burnt wood, blacksmith tongs, etc. [16]

Some Hinckley sufferers, struggling to rebuild, cursed the invaders while others shook their heads in dismay. They all agreed that the "excursionists" should more appropriately be called "thieves."

REBUILDING HINCKLEY

One look at the fire-ravaged land prompted even the most confirmed optimist to predict that the future looked gloomy for the fire sufferers who planned to return and rebuild. Dire forecasts were made that once the lumber industries had no more forests to cut, towns and villages could not survive. *The Minneapolis Tribune* wrote, "[there is] little probability that Hinckley will rebuild to its former prosperous proportions. The Brennan Lumber Company is not expected to rebuild its plant. Without an enterprise of this kind, there is no future for Hinckley except as a junction point." [17]

Futility and despair must have seized many an otherwise buoyant citizen confronted with the task of beginning anew. A Duluth paper observed, "Hinckley is literally a place where 'joy has departed from its gates'." [18]

On Friday, September 7, Governor Knute Nelson visited Hinckley and was appalled at the sights. He said, "The state will assume charge here at once. We will erect a large warehouse, and with the assistance of the Hinckley relief corps will attend to the wants of all. This shows the most complete destruction by the elements that I ever have seen. Minnesota will never see her children suffer."[19]

But Angus Hay, who himself had lost everything but his files and *The Hinckley Enterprise* subscription book, announced reassuringly in Duluth papers just five days after the fire, "Hinckley will blossom like a rose in one month more. Buoyant...energetic and enterprising it will again extend its hand of prosperity, push and vim to the people of the world."[20] Hay's prediction appeared to be at least partially correct.

The local lumber companies did not rebuild to their previous size, but the Brennan Company and others did set up temporary operations to take care of the timber that could be salvaged from the burned area. Loggers were advised to lose no time in saving partly-burned trees before insects, worms and rot attacked them. When the lumber hit the markets, consumers were assured that lumber milled from the scorched trees in the burned area was in no way inferior to green lumber. In June, 1895, the Brennan Company had finished its operations in Hinckley, having moved the rest of its logs to Stillwater.

In the year of 1895 lumber production in the St. Croix valley hit its peak of 373 million feet.[21] Some of this was due to the large harvest of dead and dying trees from the fire region. The peak year of lumber output in the state was reached ten years later, but the fire hastened the end of the white pine industry in Pine County.

After the initial shock and hysteria of the fire, residents and observers began to view the effects of the fire objectively. Some people went so far as to claim the fire put Pine County way "ahead" of the other wooded areas of the state. This was "progress." *The St. Paul Pioneer Press* editorialized:

> The forest fires have brought with them benefits...which far more than compensate for the loss of property inflicted.... These tremendous tornadoes of fire have swept tens of thousands of acres completely clean of all underbrush, chips, leaves and all timber except charred remains of trees. They have accomplished in a few short hours what the labor of thousands of men could not have accomplished as completely in many years. They have made an immense clearing of all the ground, swept over, and covered with fertilizing ashes the grave of the great forest.... The ground is almost ready for the plow after removing the stumps.[22]

On Monday, September 10, the Hinckley city council assembled at the ruins of the burned city hall for its first meeting. All council members were among the fortunate ones who had survived the fire, but Mayor Lee Webster had hardly recovered from his desperate and futile search for his missing wife and from burying his parents who perished at Sandstone. In the ashes of the village hall lay the large bell that had tolled the approach of the fire. Treasurer S. W. Anderson was pleased to report that the village had $1,100 in the municipal treasury. The first action of the council dealt with protection of returning citizens by providing for a temporary "lock-up with iron cells" for law violators.[23]. Then discussion turned to rebuilding. The Hinckley Building Association was formed to work with officials of the State Commission and to see that building would progress in a systematic manner. Daniel McLaren was elected president of the group.

One of the first duties of the newly-appointed Building Association was to try to get the Great Northern and the Eastern Minnesota companies to commit themselves to rebuilding their depot on the former site so other businesses could establish locations accordingly. On September 10 Robert Saunders, secretary of the Association, wrote a letter to the railroad officials to that effect.[24] But the Hinckley Building Association did not know at that time that Samuel and James J. Hill were considering not only moving the depot to a different location in Hinckley but were contemplating shifting their terminal facilities from Hinckley to Sandstone, a move which would greatly diminish Hinckley as a railroad center.

On September 18 Samuel Hill sent an answer to Robert Saunders and the other Hinckley business men saying, "Station will be built near present round house,"[25] which meant it would not be located at its former site.

Angus Hay,
Editor of The
Hinckley Enterprise

Ten days later James J. Hill was vexed to read in *The Minneapolis Journal* that their intentions to move the facilities to Sandstone had leaked out. The article stated that Hinckley, having lost the lumber industry, looked to the railroads as a source of future employment and reconstruction, and the action about to be taken by the Eastern Railway of Minnesota would drastically affect its future. The paper indicated that the work about to begin in Sandstone was designed to make that location "one of the most extensive freight and storage yards of the Northwest."[26]

James J. Hill's dismay did not arise from the premature announcement of phasing out Hinckley's facilities and the effects on the town. He had little concern about that. What really annoyed him was that the news would reach the party that held property in Sandstone* which he hoped to acquire, and it would be a setback for the Eastern Minnesota and the Great Northern.[27]

At Hinckley citizens soon suspected that their town was not included in Hill's future plans. But Angus Hay expressed some of the local feelings regarding the Eastern Minnesota:

> The division of the Eastern is a nonentity as far as benefit to the village is concerned. If the Eastern moves its 'division' nobody will ever be any wiser — unless *The Enterprise* tells them it has gone.[28]

There are differing opinions as to the final location of the rebuilt Eastern Minnesota depot. Some local citizens of Hinckley claim is was built at the former site across from the gravel pit. But the correspondence in the

---

*W. H. Grant and the Minneapolis Trust Company each owned large portions of land in Sandstone.

Samuel Hill papers of the Eastern Minnesota Company on file at the Minnesota Historical Society Archives indicates that in May, 1895, the local business men and shippers of Hinckley made another attempt to have the station returned to its former location since the relocated station was inconvenient for the public and for shipping. Two signed petitions were sent to railroad officials to that effect.[29] Upon receipt of the petitions President Samuel Hill sought the counsel of General Manager Farrington, who advised against it, since moving the station back to its former location, he said, would increase operating expenses because trains would again have to make two stops, one at the depot and another at the water tank and junction. The station should not be moved back, Farrington said, unless Hinckley would agree to send *all* their business over the Eastern road, an impossible proposal which would be safe for the company to make.[30] Samuel Hill's reply to Mayor Joseph Tew on May 24, 1895, was short and to the point. It said, "Volume of business at that point is not sufficient to justify expense."[31]

The lumber was gone, the railroads were in a state of flux — only the charred land remained.

Looking toward the St. Paul and Duluth Railroad in Hinckley. Tents and temporary buildings in background.

145

Soon after the fire a tent city emerged among the ruins as men returned to bury the dead and begin rebuilding. One of the first structures to go up in Hinckley was a small cook shanty where three cooks, trained in lumber camps, and their assistants, worked long hours turning out a hearty workmen's menu of potatoes and beans (cooked in wash boilers), salt pork and beef, rye and white bread and hundreds of gallons of coffee and tea. In front of the shack was a long grub table where men ate their meals. Temporary railroad and telegraph facilities were set up in boxcars until better accommodations were available. The State Commission erected a shed to serve as relief headquarters, post office and storage depot for supplies.

Stray cows, horses and oxen were corralled. Two men milked the cows and drove them daily to a pasture which had not burned. Later hay and feed were shipped in by the Commission. As owners returned and were able to care for their animals, they claimed them. But an over-supply of homeless dogs plagued the town. It was noted that just following the fire, Hinckley had no children, but an abundance of dogs.

As soon as lumber arrived, merchants and business men started to build. Activity was a tonic for crushed spirits, and sounds of construction were therapeutic. Business establishments raced to see which would be the first to open, the leading contenders being the barber and the saloon-keeper. The barbershop won, and the saloon came in a close second. Newspapers reported that "a good many people directly interested in Hinckley do not relish the idea of a saloon being started as almost the initial industry of the new Hinckley",[32] but there was no way to avoid it since the village council had granted six saloon licenses during the summer before the fire.

On September 11 J. G. Howard, Superintendent of Construction, arrived in Hinckley with a crew of carpenters to begin work on homes for those who could not build their own. Secretary Hart arrived the following day, moving the relief headquarters from Pine City to Hinckley. Immediately the Hinckley Building Association and the council expressed to both men their concern about delays in the building of homes.

Shortly, construction began on a few houses, but the progress was not swift enough to satisfy Hinckley citizens. In the meantime the Hinckley people became disheartened, and some thought of leaving.

In early October David Allen Freeman wrote to his brother about the trials of rebuilding and the problems created by the hoards of "relic hunters" who pillaged the town:

> I got some lumber today to build a shack with. I gave my note for it. My insurance knocked me out of getting a house from the commission. And the Lord only knows when I will get my insurance. As you say it is awful discouraging to start in here again. Sometimes I have a notion to start down the track and never look at the place again. . . .
>
> Hinckley will never be to me what it was before though it is growing quite fast now and begins to look like a town. It has 4 saloons running now, one store, one barbershop and one blacksmith shop. . . . They [relatives] all want relics,

something Kate* had.... I might have saved lots of them. It had all been picked over by strangers so now...I do not think I could find much.[33]

*Kate perished in the fire.

Relief tents at Hinckley just after the fire.

But despite the delays in building and the onslaught of sightseers and souvenir collectors, Hinckley in one month had taken on the appearance of a "thriving mining camp arising from the wilderness."[34] The State Commission had built a combined supply depot and eating house which replaced the cook shanty. A hotel and several other business establishments were open, and several saloons were thriving. Some men erected temporary shanties in which they lived while they built their permanent houses, but most of them stayed in the State Militia tents pitched in the streets. Local Indians set up camp at the "Wigwam" near the Grindstone River west of the St. Paul and Duluth tracks where they waited for their clothing, food and supplies. Their provisions were issued from a place known as the "McDonald Shack."[35]

By October 5 it was reported that 150 homes were going up, and almost 100 more were about to be started. As homes were completed, women and children were allowed to return, and the town took on a more normal character.

Another sign of return to normalcy was the indication that some citizens thought of things other than the fire. It was the year of state elections, and Angus Hay and Dr. E. L. Stephan became worried that the fire may have played havoc with their political party in Pine County. When the two men visited the Republican state headquarters, Hay reported, "Republicans suffered more than the Democrats in the fire...especially in Hinckley where

Bell lies in ruins
of the Hinckley
Town Hall.

Temporary school built after fire. Dr. E. L. Stephan and children.

there were three Republican voters burned to death to every one Democrat."[36] Although it was true that Pine County had usually voted Republican, the statistics for the 1892 gubernatorial election indicated that Pine County men (women could not vote) cast 465 votes for Republican Knute Nelson and 495 for Democrat Daniel Lawler. In Hinckley 211 votes went to Nelson and 209 to Lawler. Hay and Stephan returned to Hinckley ready to restore party spirit along with houses and buildings.

As soon as enough children had returned, a temporary school was opened in one of the relief buildings. By December over sixty children had been enrolled, and more were expected as people returned. Classes were held in two sessions, with Miss Craig teaching the primary students from 9:00 a.m. to 12:30, and Prof. M. S. Collins instructing the older students from 12:45 p.m. to 5:15. During the bitter days of winter the box stove could not adequately heat the drafty classroom, so occasionally school had to be dismissed. But at Christmas warmth radiated as the children opened gifts sent to them by people near and far. The children of Rush City, suspecting that Hinckley children would celebrate a giftless Christmas, sent money to buy presents.

In June when the school year ended, the parents and community thought the pupils had made proper advancement in their studies under Prof. Collins and Miss Craig despite the unusual conditions that prevailed.

December 19, 1894, in the reborn town was a notable day. *The Hinckley Enterprise*, edited by the redoubtable Angus Hay, was back in print with a paper double the size of the former one. Not only did he publish local and area news, outspoken editorials and gleanings from the nation and the world as before, but he had added features for entertainment and enlightenment. There were adult serials, children's stories, science features, biographies of celebrities and a farm forum.

In bold print on the front page of the first post-fire issue appeared the following:

> 15 YEARS WORK IN 15 MINUTES!! The fire...did in 15 minutes what it would have taken the husbandman 15 years to accomplish. All nature is with us; it seemingly knew our needs, and came to clear the land. Come and see; no word can tell the opportunity afforded the farmer here since the fire.... Hinckley with her enterprise and energy will welcome the industrious home-seeker, but spurns the approach of a drone; industry only may enter here.[37]

The paper listed the businesses that were staying in Hinckley and noted that the St. Paul and Duluth railroad was building a large depot, one of the largest on their lines. And after three and one-half months of silence and restraint, Editor Hay could not resist lashing out at the local relief agents.

> Ever since the fire they have been hanging on like a lot of leeches, sucking the sustenance donated to a suffering people by a generous public. At the same time fire sufferers...who were competent to fill the positions applied for work. The running expenses have been too enormous. The public demands a statement and it should be given them at once. [38]

Succeeding issues of *The Enterprise* chronicled the rebuilding process with a weekly list of businesses opened, buildings completed and activities resumed. Many a waning spirit was buoyed by Hay's contagious optimism.

For those who managed to resettle before winter, life was anything but luxurious. The relief homes, though adequate, were small and drafty, and each family had been given only a minimum amount of furniture, utensils and supplies to tide them over until they could purchase more themselves. Groceries, consisting of basic staples, were given out for three months at a time, and winter clothing was issued to those who had none. Christmas was a lean time for families, and many considered that just being alive was all the gift they could afford.

But a few activities resumed. There was skating on the Grindstone if one had skates. The saloons were ever anxious for business, and the lumberjacks, although fewer in numbers, still provided free street-corner fistic entertainment. The school children were back at their lessons, and the Odd Fellows were erecting a hall at the Brennan Lumber Company site which they said would be one of the best in the state. Church members were planning to rebuild their churches as soon as they could pay for the materials. Inevitably the winter passed.

In March the village elections found Joseph Tew winning the mayor's seat over Dr. Stephan, with Lee Webster becoming treasurer and Andrew Stone, recorder. Through the spring and summer the council ordered the building of sidewalks and the erecting of chimneys to replace temporary stove pipes in relief homes. They proposed a 9:00 p.m. curfew for eighteen and nineteen-year-olds and passed ordinances that made it unlawful to disturb the peace by "shouting, yelling, singing, screaming, or by the use of loud, obscene, profane or vulgar language." They also voted to penalize fighting, quarreling, discharging firearms, drunkenness or intoxication in public places and made it unlawful to appear publicly in indecent or lewd dress. [39]

In April dignitaries including the Governor, members of the State Commission, railroad officials and mayors of towns and cities received the following hand-written invitation:

Market day scene in Hinckley, 1898

At eight o'clock on the evening of May First, Eighteen Hundred, Ninety Five, the new Town Hall, erected since the great holocaust of September last, will be dedicated to the Public by the Council and residents of the Village of Hinckley. You are cordially invited to be present as a guest of the village.
[Signed] Citizens' Committee[40]

The new town hall erected at the former site had been financed entirely with money from fire insurance and the city treasury, and the village fathers were justifiably proud of their accomplishment. The council chambers were on the second floor of the town hall, while the fire department occupied the ground floor. The Waterous engine, which had fought and lost the battle of September 1, had been rebuilt and stood ready to engage lesser fires.

The dedication of the town hall attracted a "prestigious assembly of dignitaries who felt that Hinckley was 'an adopted child'."[41] During the ceremony many speakers expounded on the courage of the present and the faith in the future of Hinckley. Angus Hay summed up the local feeling:

We look with pride upon our village hall — emblem of protection and justice. With justifiable pride we gaze upon it, for, has it not arisen to assert once more man's superiority to circumstances? To show that come what will, man, if he cannot face the storm, can at least hide till it is over and then appear on the scene, determined to do his part....

Our town will stand though a thousand destructions come upon us, and in its midst our temple which we dedicate tonight to the cause of justice.... God made the world, but we built Hinckley.[42]

REBUILDING

151

By the end of May the agents for the State Commission had concluded their work in Hinckley, and five local men were appointed to administer the state appropriations for rebuilding roads and bridges. Roads had suffered badly and had been almost impassable since the fire, with burned-out wooden bridges and corduroy roadbeds. New roads had to be constructed to farms and homesteads where former loggers and lumberjacks were settling on free farm land. New territory opened up as settlers moved to land bought at from $3.00 to $10.00 an acre. In mid-summer *The Enterprise* reported that farming had doubled in the past year, land sales were booming, and the building of roads was finally beginning.

With the advent of warm weather the tempo of activity increased. The state legislature approved money for the purchase of seeds, and farmers were busy grubbing out burned stumps, clearing the land and planting fields. There were free seed-potatoes and vegetable and flower seeds for anyone who wished to plant a garden. Citizens were urged to beautify the town, to plant trees and grass, paint their homes and build fences to keep cattle either in or out of their yards. The new St. Paul and Duluth depot got a coat of green paint, and badly-needed wooden sidewalks began to appear. The young lads lost no time in getting to their favorite swimming holes and just as they had done the summer before, were shocking boaters by swimming in the flesh. Dr. Stephan, the village health officer, called for the immediate disposal of decaying animal and vegetable matter remaining from the fire to allay the outbreak of disease. At the cemetery citizens had mounded and sodded the four trenches, planted trees and hedges and erected a fence to keep the cows out.

The crops that came from the scorched earth that first summer were bountiful beyond belief. It seemed that nature compensated for the death of the forests by producing a lavish harvest. Farmers reaped grain and root crops in such abundance there was no space to store them. There were record crops of corn, oats, berries and vegetables. Potatoes, free of potato bugs, had seldom grown so large. One farmer raised five potatoes which weighted twelve and one-half pounds.

Building continued through the summer. In August the Swedish Lutheran Church was dedicated, and 100 loyal members rejoiced that the edifice costing $2,000 was completely debt-free. The Presbyterians had also built a church, and the ladies of that congregation had sponsored one of the first social activities of the season — a bonnet social. The Catholics were anticipating starting their building soon.

One year after the fire the town gathered at the city hall for a solemn memorial service to pay tribute to those who died in the fire. Crowds filled the hall and overflowed outside where they listened in subdued silence to addresses and songs. The Hinckley Fire Memorial Association was then organized with Dr. Stephan as its first president. When the program was over everyone went in procession to the cemetery to lay flowers on graves, meditate, pray and sing.

The Hinckley citizens were proud of their town's recovery. In one year's time not only had buildings and homes been restored, but the people's faith and confidence had been revitalized. Through the experience they had discovered great inner strength. Angus Hay wrote fervently of his reborn village:

Hinckley is a queen. Without any pomp or parade, she is steadily growing more majestic. . . . She has passed through the fever of fire. Her future is as bright as the jewels in her crown. No tarnish on the band of gold — no wrinkle on her brow. Her subjects are as true, as brave and as loving as ever wore a subject's charm. Supreme, grand, but modest, she is still a queen upon her throne. [43]

Hinckley rebuilt.

REBUILDING BROOK PARK

At Brook Park the Rev. William Wilkinson was appointed relief agent by the State Commission. With the help of his son, Norman, he set up a supply shed where food, clothing and supplies were stored and dispensed as requisitioned by fire sufferers. As was the case in other burned villages, the sufferers were registered, and their needs were determined before permanent relief was authorized.

St. Cloud had voted to "adopt" Brook Park and give donated goods and money directly to that town instead of going through the State Commission. This triggered the confrontation between Alvah Eastman, editor of *The St. Cloud Journal Press,* and Agent Wilkinson. After being aired in the newspapers, the disagreement was mediated by the State Commission which took charge of rebuilding at Brook Park.

Before building could begin, the State Commission secured from the Kelsey and Markham Company an agreement giving each settler free title to two acres of land on which to erect a relief home and an extension of time on existing contracts. Not all former residents wanted to resettle in Brook Park. The Russian Jews had returned to Chicago, and a few other families had become discouraged at the thought of starting over and had decided to leave. But those who did return were determined to once more rebuild their ideal, though treeless, community.

St. Cloud and Stillwater gave generous amounts of money and supplies, and building progressed rapidly through the year following the fire. A singleness of purpose unified the town. Homes were erected, another school was constructed with assistance from the State Commission, and businesses were opened. No churches were built immediately, but everyone joined to support one Sunday School for children of all denominations. The Sunday School met in the school building, and the ladies of the town established a fund for the purchase of an organ.

In the spring more land was cleared for farming, and crops were planted. Some farmers turned to dairying since the fire had opened up pasture land. As in Hinckley, the harvest that year was bountiful. In May Angus Hay reported in *The Hinckley Enterprise* that a visit to Brook Park would surprise readers. He said the citizens of the town were a "strikingly intelligent class of people" who had made "wonderful improvements." He wrote, "New farms are constantly being taken and the people are happy."[44]

REBUILDING SANDSTONE

The rebuilding of Sandstone was affected by the same delays experienced in Hinckley. A camp of tents and an eating house appeared immediately to shelter and feed the workers who waited impatiently to rebuild. Temporary structures were quickly erected by businessmen, the railroad officials and the

State Commission. N. J. Miller of Duluth was appointed the relief agent and put in charge of building relief homes.

But unusual complications arose in Sandstone. James J. Hill was making plans (which he did not intend to make public until the propitious moment) to move the main terminal facility of the Eastern Minnesota from Hinckley to Sandstone. Hill wanted more land in the heart of Sandstone for railroad expansion, and he saw the advantage to his company of relocating the town site adjacent to his railroad. It seemed an attractive and profitable opportunity.

On September 8 his son-in-law, Samuel Hill, President of the Eastern lines, wrote James J. saying that the Relief Commission had offered to rebuild homes in Sandstone, "but as Grant holds town site bonds in excess of expenditures made I have asked that no building be erected owing to attitude of one creditor." Furthermore, he said, their quarries were unable to open yet and tents had been set up for refugees with buildings to be considered later. [45]

Somehow *The Minneapolis Journal* secured and leaked out information concerning Hill's plans. In an article published September 28 the paper said that work was about to begin on the new Sandstone railroad yards which would be "one of the most extensive freight and storage yards in the Northwest." The paper enumerated Hill's undisclosed plans in detail:

> These yards will be located on the south bank of the Kettle river, close to the bridge and half a mile from the old village. They will consist of about 30 tracks, with between 25 and 28 miles of total trackage and room for 2,800 cars. In connection will be a stone roundhouse of 25 stalls and other yard buildings on quite a large scale.... But little has been done at Sandstone in the way of rebuilding and it is likely that when work does go on it will be on the south side of the river, at the site of the new yards. [46]

The Rev. Wm. Wilkinson, Rector of St. Andrews Episcopal Church in Minneapolis. Relief agent at Brook Park.

REBUILDING

The day after the article appeared Hill sent a wire to General Manager Farrington saying he was chagrined at the item, and as a result of the article the hearing on the lease of the Kettle River Quarry was postponed. He wrote, "It is a serious loss and damage to 'us'. I do not know that we shall be able to at this time secure the property, owing to this premature publication."[47]

On October 2 Samuel Hill wrote to Farrington, "All matters affecting Sandstone have been definitely and finally abandoned."[48] But James J. Hill was not about to discard a lucrative idea. What transpired during October is uncertain, but the plans fell into place for the Hills. After three weeks of negotiating, James J. Hill made a godlike pronouncement: "This place shall flourish and prosper accordingly as I shall command." The *Duluth Herald* spelled out the details:

> [The] new plat is made by the Northern Land Company which means James J. Hill as much as anything else, with northern on it, and the town is expected to contain 2000 people within one year. The yards are enlarged and six new tracks will be laid.[49]

On December 27, 1894, the *Pine County Courier* revealed more of Hill's plans for Sandstone when it announced: "The Minnesota Sandstone company having capital stock of $250,000 has filed papers of incorporation with Samuel Hill" and four other stockholders for the purpose of running the quarry.[50] Subsequent papers indicated that the Minnesota Sandstone Company had platted and had begun to sell newly-acquired lots west of the tracks. In February the railroad was able to take over another thirty acres through condemnation proceedings.[51] Within months after the fire the quarries were working at full capacity and employing many men, and by March, 1895, the town had reached a population of over 700. Things were going well for the Hills and for Sandstone.

"There are no kickers in Sandstone," said Relief Agent Miller. "People are in better shape than before the fire."[52] The promoters of Sandstone felt that it would soon become the metropolis of Pine County.

CHAPTER **8**

Assessing the Fire

"I S THE END of the world!" "Doomsday has come!" Terrified people screamed the words as they fled in panic before the firebrands that hurled through the air igniting everything about them. As they prayed to God to save their souls, some thought they were living through the last dread days on earth, that the fire and brimstone of old Sodom and Gomorrah had descended upon them. Others believed a cyclone of fire had been driven in by the wind.

There were various theories as to its cause. Some said it must have been a streak of summer lightning that ignited the woods, or spontaneous combustion of charcoal dust and carbon in parched resin-filled air. Ignatius Donnelly, the Populist leader, theorized that it had been a meteorite or a comet with a tail of fire. People in neighboring communities thought the blackened afternoon sky was due to an eclipse of the sun.

After the disaster those of a more pragmatic nature speculated that it may have been caused by the sparks from a lumberjack's bonfire or a carelessly-lit pipe. Or it may have been from a farmer burning his land to clear it, a widely-used and accepted practice. Those who lived near the railroad tracks were certain it was started by sparks spewed by the train engines, which at that time had no spark arresters, or cinders from those with faulty nettings or overflowing ash pans. Insurance companies, flooded with fire claims, charged publicly in the "Report of the Pine Land Investigating Committee" that the fire had been set by timber thieves to cover up their illegal practice of cutting trees from lands to which they had no rightful claim. Any one of these or a combination of several could have started the *Great Hinckley Fire* in a tinder-dry forest ready to ignite.

It is common knowledge that the summer of 1894 had been one of the driest and hottest in Minnesota history. Newspapers reported the severe

ASSESSING THE FIRE

157

Burned district surrounding Hinckley.

drought conditions, the unbearable heat and the local fires that burned through July and August.

To arrive at the most accurate picture of what happened and why, one can draw on the conclusions of qualified forestry specialists and fire control scientists who have analyzed the forest and weather conditions that existed at that time. In addition meteorologists and climatologists have interpreted weather and climatic factors from existing records and data.

Forestry specialists agree that the timber companies in the past left the forests in the worst possible condition, setting the stage for uncontrollable fires. The pine slashings left by the loggers throughout the woods grew drier as time progressed and created the most dangerous of all fuel supplies. Conifers are especially susceptible to fire, with their high resin, or pitch, content. Openings and clearings within the heavily forested areas increased the fire hazards as light and air were admitted to speed up the drying process.

Forest litter and undergrowth caused the surface fires to ravage the forest floor swiftly. The fire spread to the crowns of the trees, was carried to other tree tops by sparks and fireballs blown ahead by strong winds. In places, ground fires continued to burn fallen timber, stumps and roots, and bore into the humus of the forest floor. The fires that smoldered and tunneled into the ground were especially damaging since they destroyed roots and seedlings and changed the chemical composition of the soil.

A United States Department of Agriculture Forest Service Study, *Climatic Conditions Preceding Historically Great Fires in the North Central Region,* made in 1969 by Donald A. Haines, Meteorologist, and Rodney W. Sando, Associate Fire Control Scientist of the North Central Forest Experiment Station, has a detailed analysis of the weather conditions that preceded seven well-known Midwest fires from 1870 to 1920 in Illinois, Michigan, Minnesota and Wisconsin. The Hinckley fire is included in this report along with the Fire of 1871 in Peshtigo, Wisconsin; the Baudette, Minnesota, Fire of 1910, and the Cloquet, Minnesota, Fire of 1918.

Haines and Sando have cited the difficulties in making the study since records of pre-fire conditions of earliest fires were not complete. Terms such as "drought" are vague and open to many interpretations. However, by 1894 there were several efficiently run weather stations in eastern Minnesota collecting data. Information from four stations, St. Paul, Cambridge, Collegeville, and Sandy Lake, was used to determine the pre-fire conditions at Hinckley. Their conclusions are as follows.

1. All seven fires studied occurred during September or early October.
2. The Hinckley Fire destroyed the smallest forested area although in any fire it is difficult to determine the exact area burned.
3. The pre-fire conditions in 1894 were more serious than in any of the other fires. At Hinckley the period before the fire showed much less precipitation than in the other fires. Sixty days before the fire there had been only 12% of the normal amount of rainfall, thirty days before the fire there had been 20% and fifteen days prior to the fire only 2% of the normal amount. In St. Paul the precipitation total for June, July and August of 1894 was the lowest in 128 years of keeping records. Figures show the average precipitation for those months to be 10.85 inches. In 1894 it was 2.00 inches. Sandy Lake, the station nearest Hinckley, recorded the severest precipitation deficiency of all four stations.
4. When it did rain in Hinckley prior to the fire, rainfall was much less frequent.
5. The temperature records showed the summer of 1894 to be an abnormally hot season. In the Hinckley area there were four to five times the number of hot days than normal. Collegeville reported there were sixteen days in July over 90° (the normal is three days). The temperature in the ten days before the fire averaged 10° above normal.
6. In 1894 an additional report from Duluth showed the relative humidity averaged almost 9% below normal for June, July and August.
7. On the day of the fire, Collegeville reported the maximum temperature to be 95% F., the wind blowing at 20 miles per hour and the relative humidity at 28%.

Earl L. Kuehnast, the State Climatologist with the Department of Natural Resources, states it another way in a preliminary study of the relationship of major forest fires to July-August precipitation. He says that in the immediate area around Hinckley, rainfall measured only one-half to one and one-half inches for the two-month period prior to the 1894 fire. July and August of 1894 were the driest in Minnesota since the National Weather

Service began keeping records in 1890. He also indicates that strong, hot, dry southerly winds blowing in advance of low pressure systems greatly increase the fire danger, especially if fires are already burning. In the Hinckley Fire the maximum temperature was about 20° F. above normal maximum temperature, the winds were from the southwest and fires were burning in areas to the south and southwest. [1]

Rodney Sando, University of Minnesota, College of Forestry, has come to the conclusion that the fire over Hinckley was the converging of two fire systems, one that started south of Brook Park near Henriette and what was then the Quamba station, the other beginning near Beroun directly south of Mission Creek. When the two fire systems came together at Hinckley, they created their own whirlwind with a cyclonic rotation of air. Those who witnessed the fire aptly called it a "tornado" or "cyclone of fire." The fire also created its own explosive gases that rolled into gigantic fireballs that were hurled long distances through the air. Sando has concluded that most of the people apparently died of asphyxiation, rather than burns, as the oxygen became depleted and a high concentration of carbon monoxide formed in the overheated air. The fact that some bodies showed few signs of burns bears this out, and others, which were badly charred, were in many cases burned after the victims had suffocated. [2]

The summer of 1894 was the driest in Minnesota weather records, but the summer of 1976 threatened to be as dangerous. The stage was set for a replay, and on a smaller scale it occurred again on September 7, 1976, at the Huntersville State Forest near Park Rapids, Minnesota.

Analysts of forest fires say that fires, like storms, develop distinct temperaments and personalities. The Hinckley Fire showed itself to be one of great eccentricity. It was ill-tempered and malicious, vindictive and spiteful, and entirely unpredictable as to what it sought to burn and what it chose to spare.

This was no passive fire. It did not crawl or creep but burst and exploded. It roared, seethed and boiled. On the ground it swept forward in walls and cylinders of flame, in the air it soared in massive balls of fire and gas. Its heat was intense and searing and it devoured kingly pines in minutes, yet spared fragile saplings close by.

As people returned to the burned area, they witnessed the erratic behavior of the fire and stood in awe of its power. It had levelled the town of Hinckley so that scarcely a chimney or gutted wall remained upright. Sidewalks and street corners were obliterated. Yet the Eastern Minnesota railroad water tank and roundhouse stood without even showing blisters on the painted surfaces. In the woods near Mission Creek the fire burned a stand of green timber yet capriciously skipped over a flimsy tarpaper shack. In a garden at Hinckley carrots, onions and potatoes were cooked in the ground and surrounding trees were completely destroyed, but a fragile picket fence stood unharmed. Near Hell's Gate quarry a wagon remained intact with

*Coins melted by fire.
On exhibit at Hinckley
Fire Museum.*

*Tin plates burned
in the fire.
On exhibit at
Hinckley Fire Museum.*

spokes of just one wheel burned. Telegraph poles were burned off in the middle leaving stumps on the ground and tops dangling from wires. At the Sandstone railroad yards from a long string of boxcars, the fire chose to burn only three in different places.

The blast-furnace heat of the fire melted and fused glass to wire screen, transformed crockery and tinware into shapeless masses and liquified metal coins into lumps. In a hardware store a keg of nails became a solid chunk of metal, and barrels of water were reduced to metal bands.

ASSESSING THE FIRE

161

Melted printers' type on exhibit at Hinckley Fire Museum.

Burial crews uncovered other oddities. Three melted silver dollars were found on one badly-burned body while only two feet away lay undischarged gunpowder in a partly-melted flask. In a swamp near Hinckley searchers found the remains of a woman and a little girl. Under the woman were the charred leaves of a Swedish Bible, while on the streets of Duluth seventy-five miles away, were found what appeared to be pages from the same Bible. In a root cellar near Skunk Lake several people were found horribly burned, but the wooden door and log walls of the cellar weren't even discolored by smoke.

The fire played bizarre games with domestic and wild animals. Frightened wolves, bear, deer and small animals were said to have sought refuge in creeks and ponds alongside humans with no apparent fear of people or each other. Twenty-five snakes and dozens of field mice were found alive together in an old well at Sandstone. Two horses were badly burned, but the wagon load of hay they were pulling was unharmed. Another team had turned into charred corpses, but the harnesses they wore were still intact. At the depot the body of a faithful Newfoundland dog was found still guarding the burned trunk of its owner. When a young boy opened the door of the oven of a cookstove in a demolished house, out jumped a lively, healthy chicken. Elsewhere a little kitten emerged from an outhouse, burned but alive. Hundreds of dead chickens littered the streets of Hinckley, yet two days after the fire one proud rooster and twelve hens appeared at the cooks' shanty to peck at the crumbs from the table.

As the initial shock and trauma of the fire passed, survivors began to relate the many extraordinary experiences to each other and to their offspring. In time the story of *The Great Fire* became more than a tragic episode and an historical event. It became a legend.

People have asked, "How did the fire end?" To this question there was no definite answer. There was no miraculous windshift or downpour of rain, and certainly no man-made efforts were able to halt its progress.

Although fires were reported "raging," a term used liberally and loosely by newspapers of the day, in many areas of northern Minnesota, Wisconsin and Michigan before and after September 1, the major fire zone referred to as the Hinckley Fire took on the shape of a huge oval. It reached from what is now Beroun, Henriette and Quamba on the south, to Askov (then called Partridge) and Finlayson to the north. It covered generally an area sixteen miles wide and thirty miles long, totalling 480 square miles, or 307,200 acres. Some authorities say there were 160,000 acres of forest land burned;[3] others put the figure at 350,000 acres.[4] When the fire reached the northern boundaries Saturday evening, it had expended much of its fury, and the wind had abated. It might be said the fire "blew itself out," another loosely defined expression. But fires continued along railroad tracks and threatened villages through most of September.

On September 3 the papers told of burial parties working in Hinckley in the rain, a light drizzle, that hastened the decomposing of unburied victims. But the precipitation was negligible and localized.

Reports from Chicago on September 4 indicated that smoke from forest fires continued to endanger navigation on the Great Lakes from Duluth to Buffalo. On the south shore of Lake Superior visibility was down to one-hundred yards, and many boats were being delayed at Sault Ste. Marie with resultant shipping losses.

On the same day rains were reported falling in Wisconsin, checking temporarily the fires that had destroyed farms, villages and untold acres of forest land there. But on succeeding days fires had flared up again until a drenching rain on September 7 extinguished most of them. But those rains did not reach Minnesota. *The Duluth News Tribune* repeated a familiar warning:

The whole country is a gathering of small fires which a little wind will develop into a dangerous conflagration. The immense deposits of peat are burning fiercely several feet below the surface of the ground and it will need a steady and heavy rain for some days to put them out.[5]

ASSESSING THE FIRE

Although a major conflagration did not occur again, fires did continue to cause grave concern and near-panic. In Pine City the memorial service scheduled for the afternoon of Sunday, September 19, was postponed when the sky turned bloody red and smoke rolled over the town. The citizens and refugees crowded aboard trains that had been held there until the threat was over. In Mora, where the fire originated, citizens had turned their animals loose and had fled to an island in Lake Mora where they waited for two hours before they felt it safe to return to their homes. A shift in wind saved the town. At the same time more fires threatened towns to the north from Barnum to West Duluth, where an all-too-familiar sickly yellow sky worried residents.

Throughout all of September north-central Minnesota continued to be a veritable tinderbox ready to explode. Reports came in of threats of fire near Little Falls and Brainerd to the west and along the railroad tracks to Duluth where trains were still spreading sparks along the route. In late September and early October the much-needed rains came and caused one editor to comment, "Now we have an abundance of rain when we don't need it."[6]

Hinckley — where the depot stood.

CHAPTER **9**

People and the Fire

BOSTON CORBETT

T WAS BOSTON CORBETT who supposedly fired the fatal shot that killed John Wilkes Booth, President Lincoln's assassin. Historical accounts indicate that Corbett, whose given name was Thomas P. Corbett, achieved considerable fame after the shooting in 1865. Several years later he moved to Kansas where he enacted a melodramatic scene in the state legislature which resulted in his commitment to the Topeka Asylum for the Insane in Kansas. On May 26, 1888, he escaped. The remainder of Corbett's life is summed up with the statement, "He disappeared forever."

On the list of those that died in the Hinckley Fire, compiled and certified by Dr. D. W. Cowan, Coroner of Pine County, on November 24, 1894, appeared the following:

Corbett, Thos. — Age 57; residence, Hinckley; not identified; supposed to have perished in swamp one-half mile north of Hinckley. [1]

On September 5, 1894, *The St. Paul Pioneer Press* reported:

Three lumbermen from one of O'Neill's camps east of Sand Creek...left the camp Saturday afternoon with a team and five in the party. They were forced to abandon the team and in the mad rush for safety two fell behind. One of them was a man upwards of sixty years old named Corbett. After the fire was over the three who escaped vainly endeavored to find their companions. [2]

Two days later another notation appeared in *The Duluth News Tribune:*

Noble Wilson's searchers went after the body of old Tom Corbett who was watching a lumber camp east of the village. They found no trace of the man and are certain he is among the dead. [3]

Boston Corbett

In a collection at the Hinckley Fire Museum are two first-hand accounts written by fire survivor Frank Haney, a lumberman, who in 1894 worked at Gus Sexton's logging camp near the Kettle River four miles east of Hinckley. One report is dated August 18, 1954, and is signed by Haney; the other is not dated or signed, but the information indicates that Haney wrote both reports possibly for the Hinckley Fire Pageant of 1954. Haney would then have been 82 years of age.

On the day of the fire Tom Corbett, Chris Sexton, Frank Haney and his friend, Noble Wilson from the O'Brien camp nearby, were at the Sexton camp. Corbett had been hired by the Sextons for four seasons to provide deer and game for the camp, and during the long winter nights he had related his past experiences to the lumberjacks. As far as anyone at camp knew, he had no friends or relatives. He wrote no letters, received no mail and did not claim his pension. When he died there was no one to inform of his death. Corbett (spelled "Corbet" in the report) was described as a small, elderly man, weighing about 140 pounds. Although he had adopted the name "Boston Corbett" upon his conversion at a Boston revival meeting, when he came to Hinckley he was known as Tom Corbett from Boston.

Following is a summary of Tom Corbett's story as told by Frank Haney:

Thomas P. Corbett was born in England in 1832 and emigrated to the United States at the age of seven. His youth was wild until he "saw the light" at a revival meeting in Boston, and following the example of Christ's disciples, changed his name to "Boston Corbett." He read the Bible faithfully and preached whenever and wherever people would listen. During this period he was employed as a hat-maker in Danbury, Connecticut.

At the outbreak of the Civil War Corbett was one of the first to volunteer. During the war he was captured and sent to the Andersonville Prison in Georgia, where he formed a Bible class and preached to prisoners. After his parole he was confined to a hospital for several months suffering from ill health. When he recovered he joined another New York company and served to the end of the war.

After President Lincoln was shot by John Wilkes Booth in April of 1865, Corbett was among the first to volunteer to go on the manhunt for Booth. The orders for the troops were "capture but not kill." When Booth was shot, Corbett admitted that it was he who had fired the fatal bullet. He was arrested, but since his act had made him somewhat of a hero, he was merely reprimanded for his actions and released. Later he received $1,650 in reward money.

After his mustering-out on August 17, 1865, Corbett returned to his former occupation of hat-making in Camden, New Jersey. He continued to preach and was given a full-time job as pastor of a Methodist Church. Soon, however, his reputation led the parishioners to feel he was not suitable to be a minister of the Gospel.

Corbett then moved westward to Kansas where he homesteaded seven miles from the town of Concordia. Here he adopted a hermit's life in a small two-room cabin, subsisting for several years on his pension and what little he could make from farming and cattle grazing. He became sullen and moody and met visitors at the door with a rifle.

When farming failed, Corbett was given a token job as assistant door-keeper at the Kansas State Capitol. This job appealed to him, and he proudly appeared for duty with his army cap and his .38 "hot leg" strapped to his Civil War belt. He relished the attention this brought him, and when asked, gladly led in prayer at the beginning of legislative sessions. But on February 15, 1887, when the raucous legislators were embroiled in an especially boisterous session and one legislator shouted mockingly to Corbett to lead them in prayer, Corbett was so incensed by the blasphemy he drew his gun and shouted, "Legislature is adjourned." He was promptly arrested, tried, pronounced insane and sent to an asylum in Topeka. In 1888 he escaped and fled to the remote lumbertown of Hinckley, Minnesota.

In 1890 Corbett was settled in a small cabin east of Hinckley where he earned a living supplying deer, game and fish to customers. There were no game laws or restrictions, and wildlife was abundant. That fall he was asked to provide venison for the logging camp run by the four Sexton brothers one-half mile east of the Kettle River. Corbett found camp life to his liking and agreed to join the Sextons the succeeding winters.

In August, 1894, four Sexton brothers and a hired man went out to the camp to prepare for the coming logging season. There was marsh hay to be put up for the horses and supplies to be brought in. At the end of August the smoke that had persisted in the woods all summer seemed particularly heavy, and the threat of fire worried the men. As a precaution they cleared the campyard of burnables and loaded an empty box built of planks on a wagon for valuables in the event they should have to make a hasty get-away.

On September 1 conditions seemed threatening. The wagon was stationed at the office door, and a harnessed team stood ready in the barn. Chris Sexton, the teamster, was assigned the job of loading the most important records and supplies in the wagon, hitching up the horses and fleeing to safety if necessary. The other brothers had gone to another camp for supplies.

Frank Haney and his friend, Noble Wilson, were on their way to pick cranberries and had stopped in at the Sexton office for directions to the patch. Suddenly the sky grew dark, and flames shot through the woods less than sixty rods from the camp. They heard Corbett yell a warning from outside. He had walked to the Sexton camp from his cabin four miles away. In a matter of minutes the fire was upon them. Chris Sexton quickly hitched up the team, the men piled into the wagon and with the horses at full gallop they tried to outrun the fire. As the road narrowed and entered a thick stand of pine, fallen trees soon blocked the road. They unhitched the horses to fend for themselves and continued to race on foot towards the river as fire blazed in the tops of the pines above them. Haney clutched his gun which he was prepared to use if he should be trapped by the fire. Corbett, being older and slower, followed behind the other men. A flaming tree crashed just in front of him as he ran, and he didn't have a chance.

After a torturous dash through the woods, the other men managed to reach a log-landing in Sand Creek where they found an embankment for protection. They lay in the water, covering their heads and faces with wet clothing. Here they stayed while the inferno roared over them, and trees blazed on all sides. Deer dashed in panic through the flames, and fish died in the heated water. A dog joined them in the river and buried his nose in the wet mud.

In minutes the fire raced on and a deathly stillness ensued. The three survivors lay on the warm sand with covered heads until 9:00 o'clock Sunday morning. But old Tom Corbett had perished somewhere back in the woods.

As indicated by the newspapers Nobel Wilson and others searched for Corbett's body, but no remains were identified as his. Those who knew him never saw him again, and they were certain he was a victim of the fire. Coroner Cowan added Corbett's name to the death list and guessed his age mistakenly to be fifty-seven. Corbett would have been sixty-two.

The names of Frank Haney and the four Sexton brothers are on file in the State Commission relief ledgers at the Archives of the Minnesota Historical Society. All of the men indicated that the Gus Sexton camp was their place of residence, and all entered claims for relief at Pine City. Frank Haney's registration stated that after the fire the only property he had left was his shotgun (which he carried with him through the fire) valued at $14.00 and the clothes he wore. He was given an outfit of clothing and $5.00 in cash. The Sexton brothers received only clothing. 4

The information given by Frank Haney correlates remarkably with historical records. An inquiry to the Kansas State Historical Society in November, 1976, verified that although several people had been known to impersonate Corbett, to the best of the Society's knowledge, Corbett was never seen again after his escape from the Topeka asylum. 5

Historians and scholars will continue to disagree on the circumstances surrounding Booth's death, but are in agreement that Boston Corbett, the man alleged to have killed him, dropped out of sight after his escape from Topeka. It appears that Frank Haney, lumberman at Hinckley, wrote the final chapter of Corbett's story. If Corbett had wanted to disappear forever, what better place than in a remote spot deep in the forests of Minnesota?

Engineer James Root

One of the most applauded, but not necessarily the most deserving, railroad hero of the day was fifty-one year old Jim Root. Following the fire his fame reached both coasts of the United States and spread abroad. Awards, medals, tributes and money contributions were showered upon him with glowing testimonials to his courage and heroism. Poems were composed in his honor.

Root was described as a modest, amiable man of medium height with an open, honest face and an unassuming manner. He was known as a person of great will and determination. There were hints that he was plagued by ill health.

James M. Root was born in Greenbush, New York, in 1843 (or 1844). His long and varied railroading career started early. In 1857 at age fourteen he began working with the Hudson River road. After three years he railroaded for a short time in Indiana, and in 1861 enlisted as a minute-man to fight against the Morgan raiders. After he was mustered out he returned to railroading as engineer and conductor of a work train on the Louisville and Nashville line. During the war he was sent to the front at Knoxville, Tennessee, and began the march with Sherman. He soon returned to Atlanta where he engineered Sherman's advance train. Until the close of the war in 1865 Root ran a hospital train and a prisoner train at Andersonville and Chattanooga.

Following the war Root left the south and came to Hastings, Minnesota, to visit an uncle. He worked at a lumber mill and logging camp near Stillwater and in 1869 married Mrs. E. M. Fox of that town. In 1870 he took a job with the St. Paul and Duluth Railroad Company as engine dispatcher at Duluth and in 1871 became an engineer, a job which he held until the time of the fire. [6]

In the 1890's railroads across the country were striving to set new speed records. In 1891 the Empire State Express had attained a speed of 50.7 miles per hour. Root was hoping some day to beat that record with his Limited, but Saturday, September 1, 1894, was not the day to try. Root never did set a new speed record but created a different record of sorts. It was figured that from Hinckley to Skunk Lake "crawling backward at an estimated 18 miles per hour, he had saved 50 lives a mile." [7]

Root's five-mile run back to Skunk Lake captured the attention of the press and the public. Root himself told and retold his story for publication, including minute details of the explosion in the cab, the injury and loss of blood, fainting at the throttle, returning to consciousness to find the steam pressure down, fainting again, being revived by McGowan and collapsing on the cab floor from exhaustion. Some of the press reports and accounts in books differ to some degree, either from reporter's interpretations or from Root's telling, but they all indicated without a doubt that Root had played the role of hero that day.

After Root was rescued at Skunk Lake early Sunday morning, he was brought to Pine City, where his wife met him and accompanied him home to White Bear Lake. He arrived there about noon on Sunday. Two doctors checked him over early in the afternoon and reported that his condition was not serious, though he suffered from minor cuts, burns and mental strain. By Monday morning his eyes and hands were almost normal.

At 6:00 o'clock Sunday evening reporters gained entry to Root's darkened bedroom for an interview and heard him recount haltingly the adventures of the prior day. Through the following week correspondents flocked to Root's home to draw out more details from the hero. Flowers and congratulatory messages poured in, and curious people gathered outside his house to catch a glimpse of him.

The accolades were endless. Newspapers large and small featured articles about Engineer Root. *The New York Times, Chicago Tribune, Chicago Post, Syracuse Post* and other nationally known papers applauded his bravery. *The Chicago Inter Ocean* gushed, "His soul is the stuff of which heroes are made in this world — archangels in the world beyond."[8] *The London Daily News* said that Root's action was that of "purest heroism" and called on Englishmen to do something to recognize the astonishing deed.[9] On September 5, 1894, Root's hometown paper, *The White Bear Lake Breeze,* proudly ran his complete story. Duluth, Minneapolis and St. Paul papers featured long articles on him and collected funds for medals.

On September 3 the Minneapolis relief committee issued a tribute to Root saying, "An emergency which tried the mettle of manhood confronted J. M. Root on this occasion and he proved himself its master....On Saturday morning he was a locomotive engineer; today he is a hero."[10]

Prominent Minneapolis citizens presented Root with an inscribed citation for bravery on September 18, and four days later Congressman Dave Mercer of Omaha, Nebraska, promised to get congressional recognition for Root in the following session. Mercer stated:

> I propose to introduce a bill at the next session of congress to give James Root a medal for his bravery during the Hinckley forest fires....I have determined that railroad heroes shall be honored, and while I am at it, I'll see that the fireman and the entire crew are officially recognized by congress for their brave and efficient service on that ill starred occasion.[11]

But not everyone joined in applauding Jim Root. Among the passengers who had boarded the Limited at Duluth were those who criticized the engineer for not stopping the train at Carlton when the unusual conditions first became evident. Root in his own defense claimed there was nothing alarming other than the thick smoke which was a frequent occurrence that summer.

FROM THE ASHES

170

He had assumed that as soon as they neared Hinckley everything would be fine.

There were complaints that the rest of the railroad men were being overlooked while Root basked in the spotlight. People indicated that Porter Blair and Fireman McGowan had performed just as admirably as Root during the crisis at Skunk Lake. And it was pointed out by some critics that Root really risked nothing, since when he could go no farther he was forced to back up to Skunk Lake or perish. Whereas Engineer Best and Conductor Powers of the Eastern Minnesota were faced with the difficult decision of how long it was safe to hold the train at Hinckley and took a great risk when they delayed departure to take on as many refugees as possible.

After the fire Jim Root did not return immediately to his job with the railroad. Instead he was on a "lay-off" during the first days of October and travelled to New York to enroll his twenty-year-old son in college. In New York he was contacted by a theatrical agent who wanted him to appear as a locomotive engineer in the play, *The Ride for Life,* scheduled to run in the Grand Opera House in New York City. Root explained later to reporters that he had at first resisted the idea since he didn't want to "parade himself," but the agent persisted and asked, "What'll it take for two weeks?" Root facetiously replied, "$500 a week." "Done," said the agent and drew out a contract. [12]

The play opened in the Grand Opera House on Monday evening, October 8, and ran for *one* week. It was advertised in *The New York Times* as follows:

ENGINEER JIM ROOT — THE HERO OF HINCKLEY, WHO SAVED 300 LIVES and drove his engine through a hell of flame will run the locomotive in A RIDE FOR LIFE. [13]

The play was described as a "comedy-drama" with tropical scenes of New Orleans and the Mexican border and unusual effects of a "steam locomotive which plays a prominent part in the action." [14] After the opening *The White Bear Lake Breeze* ran a special report from New York saying:

Mr. Root did not have much to say, but he carried the hero away from death on his flying train and gained the plaudits of a packed house. "The Ride for Life" is an excellent play of the sensational type, its lover is the tenderest, its hero the most heroic and its villain of the deepest dye. Every foot of space was filled tonight, and the short season allotted to this new attraction is certain to be a profitable one. [15]

The New York Times was not as kind in the review that followed opening night. The paper said the locomotive was a "cross between a '1492' street car and a teakettle" and described Root's performance:

He is not. . . a particularly impressive spectacle, being exactly such a looking man as locomotive engineers always are, grimly pallid of face, heavy of build, and inexpressive of feature, but no doubt he is a hero — or was. Of course, there is no legal, or even logical, objection to driving an engine through a blazing forest and saving a lot of lives one day, and then earning money by posing as a freak the next. It's all right, only one can't help wishing that Mr. Root had gone into burglary or almost any of the lesser crimes instead of trading on his glory and making himself, and heroism cheap, cheap, cheap. [16]

In Minnesota most of the city and small town papers made little reference to Root's short theatrical experience. *The Prison Mirror* of Stillwater did criticize him for allowing himself to be used by a shrewd manager to swell his bank account, but the hometown *Lake Breeze* defended Root saying he had never claimed to be an actor and would have been foolish not to earn in two weeks what normally it would take six months to earn as a railroad engineer.

When he returned to Minnesota, Root said when interviewed that he was tired of the acting business and added:

> It may be all right for a young fellow...but I'm getting too old to be an actor. It keeps a man up too late at night, and I never did like a night run. The only thing that caught me was the salary, and of course I couldn't refuse that. Furthermore, the canvas engine made me more nervous than a forest fire and a property man makes a very unsatisfactory general superintendent. [17]

After his short-lived acting career Root returned to the St. Paul and Duluth Railroad and engine 69 which had been overhauled. He continued to work for the company until he retired in New York on a railroad pension.

On December 14, 1911, *The New York Times* listed the following entry with the death notices: "ROOT-James, 992 Washington Av., Bronx, Dec. 12. Funeral today."[18] A longer article appeared in *The Times* on December 15 telling of Root's heroism during the fire. In the article it indicated that Root had "died at his home, 217 E. 77th St. at the age of 67 years." It further stated that Root had retired three years before on a pension. [19]

It is uncertain where Jim Root is buried. One source of information stated that he was brought to Stillwater, Minnesota, the home of his wife. [20] However there is no record of his burial at either of the two Stillwater cemeteries nor does Washington County, where Stillwater is located, show any entry of Root's burial in the county. [21]

Fireman John McGowan

The heroic deeds of John McGowan, the plucky fireman aboard Root's train, were submerged in the crush of attention heaped upon Engineer Root. McGowan's acts did not have sufficient drama and flair to capture public attention, nor did McGowan ever write his own story for publication. Root made the headlines; the other railroad men were mentioned in the by-lines.

Occasionally some newspaper reporter would tell of the heroism of McGowan as they wrote the Skunk Lake story, and a few letters to editors protested that Root got all the glory while other equally deserving heroes were ignored. The editor of *The Duluth News Tribune* was of that opinion when he wrote:

> Much has been said of brave, faithful Jim Root and he deserves every good word that has been spoken and written about him. He does not deserve all the fame, all the glory won in that grand ride with death coming on. Fireman McGowan's noble act has been lost sight of to some extent in the admiration that has existed over Jim Root's heroism. It should be told again and again that no less a hero than Root is McGowan. [22]

At the time of the fire John McGowan lived in St. Paul and had been employed by the St. Paul and Duluth Railroad for seven years. As fireman he was responsible for stoking the coal fire to keep the steam engine going — a hot, dirty job, especially on a sultry day such as September 1.

As the train backed up to Skunk Lake, it was McGowan who discovered and revived the unconscious Root at the throttle. Had he not rescued Root, the train would have stopped, all its passengers undoubtedly would have burned, and the Skunk Lake drama would have had a disastrous ending.

When they came to Skunk Lake, McGowan was at the door helping people off the platform. It was he who returned to the engine with another man during the height of the fire and carried Root to safety in the water, saving the engineer's life a second time. Later McGowan disconnected the engine from the still-burning coal car so the ailing Root could spend the night safely in the shelter of the cab.

Yet nowhere in the interviews granted and the accounts written by Engineer Root was there gratitude expressed to McGowan for saving his life and selflessly attending to the welfare of the passengers. Nor did Root ever hint that McGowan was indirectly responsible for rescuing the trainload of people.

Little is known of McGowan's life before or after the fire, except that he was said to have been "killed by the overturning of his engine at Mahtomedi, some twelve years after the death of Jim Root." [23] Since the source of this information had stated mistakenly that Jim Root died in 1907, it is not certain when McGowan's death occurred.

Porter John Blair

John Blair was the good-natured porter who tended to passengers on board the Limited as it ran between St. Paul and Duluth. Regular patrons said his face was a "friendly beacon to travelers."[24]

On the day of the fire Blair performed his usual duties on chair car No. 56. As conditions became worse, his calm disposition was tested to the limit. After the train came to a halt near Hinckley and began the famous reverse ride back to Skunk Lake, Blair was said to be the steadiest man on board. He moved through the burning coach reassuring frightened passengers and calming terrified children. He passed out water to drink, moistened towels to cover faces and quieted the religious fanatic who alarmed the rest with screams of doom. As people crowded from the train at Skunk Lake, Blair assisted them and made repeated trips back to the coaches to rescue children. He was one of the last to leave the doomed train when he was certain all passengers were off.

While the waves of fire blew over the terror-stricken people in Skunk Lake, Blair used the fire extinguisher he had taken from the train to put out sparks that ignited clothes and hair. Through the long night he moved from group to group finding extra clothing for women and children and reassuring distraught survivors that they were safe and would be rescued.

When asked how he managed to keep his composure, Blair replied, "I thought of my wife and babies and said to myself, 'John, if there ever was a time you need to be cool and clear-headed it is right now' and I just resolved I would not lose my head, and if I had to die, I would do so without making a fool of myself."[25]

Although Blair's honors did not begin to compare with those showered on Jim Root, he was recognized at a gathering in his home town of St. Paul on September 13. It was announced that:

> ...a public meeting will be held at Market hall...by the Afro-Americans of St. Paul and all others interested as a testimonial to John W. Blair, colored porter of the St. Paul and Duluth limited train burned at Skunk Lake, who was one of the heroes of the awful holocaust.[26]

Many people attended the meeting and listened to stories of Blair's heroism aboard Root's train. The Rev. R. C. Quarles, pastor of the Pilgrim Baptist Church, made the following observation:

> We have seen in blazing headlines the praises of brave Engineer Root and the other members of the train crew, but I have looked in vain for the name of John W. Blair as a great hero of the terrible occasion. I am glad, John W. Blair, that among those who had the coolness and manhood to make a record on that terrible night, that there was a black face with a white heart.[27]

The Hon. C. C. O'Brien, who was a passenger aboard the train, was the principal speaker and noted:

There are many witnesses to his heroism who are ready and willing to give such testimony and who say that he is at least entitled to an equal share of honors with the engineer of the ill-fated train. Mr. Blair was constantly on the lookout for those who wandered into danger and brought them back. Many can testify to the fact that they owe their lives to his efforts. He could have deserted the train and sought his personal safety, but he chose to remain and do his whole duty as a man toward those under his charge. He is a credit, not only to his race, but to mankind and his deeds of bravery shall not go unsung. [28]

Blair was presented with a gold medal in the shape of the Legion of Honor cross suspended from a bar in the facsimile of Blair's chair car No. 56. The inscription on the medal read:

Presented by the St. Paul & Duluth R.R. Co. to JOHN WESLEY BLAIR for gallant and faithful discharge of duty on Limited train, No. 4, in Forest Fires, Sept. 1, 1894. [29]

Blair's modest response to the award was, "All I can say is that on that awful night I did what I thought to be my duty. The memories of this night and the kindness you have shown me shall always be cherished by me as long as I live." [30]

Conductor Thomas Sullivan

When thirty-four year old Conductor Thomas Sullivan called "All aboard" at the Duluth depot to load up the 1:55 p.m. Limited for its routine trip to St. Paul on September 1, it was fortunate he did not know what the next twenty-four hours held for him.

As the train went south, Sullivan noticed the darkening sky but thought nothing of it since it had been that way for two months. He assured nervous passengers that everything was all right. But when the train stopped one mile north of Hinckley, Sullivan saw the fire approaching like a cyclone and said to Root, "Jim, we cannot stay here long; we will have to go back to a place of safety." [31] Then the Hinckley refugees came running to the train. Sullivan estimated that between 150 and 160 people climbed on, which together with the passengers already aboard brought the total to about 300.

As the train went in reverse to Skunk Lake, the explosion which shattered Root's cab window also broke all the windows on the west side of the coaches. Sullivan described the ensuing panic in the crowded first class car as one of the worst sights he had ever witnessed. People screamed in terror, and Sullivan shouted for them to be quiet and remain calm. This restored some degree of order.

Sullivan noted in his published report that Porter John Blair was "as brave a man as I ever saw."[32] He told of the courage of the lady who handed him wet towels to keep the last car from burning, and he admired Mrs. Saunders, who calmly administered to the seven children in her care. Sullivan commended the entire crew for the way they performed under duress.

During the time the Limited was backing and when it had come to a stop at Skunk Lake, Sullivan was worried that freight No. 12, which was supposed to have been following them, would either be burned or would crash into them. This prompted him to head north on foot as soon as all the passengers were off the train at Skunk Lake. He felt it his duty to intercept the freight, get word of the disaster to his superiors and order relief for the people at Skunk Lake. Brakeman Monahan and others from the train also headed up the tracks in scattered groups.

The flight to the next station was torturous. Guided only by the tracks, Sullivan was forced at times to lie on the ground to get a breath of air. All the while he suffered intense pain in his burning eyes. At about 6:00 p.m. he arrived at the Miller station which had up to that time escaped the fire. A. L. Thompson, telegraph operator, informed Sullivan that the freight he had worried about, under Engineer Kelly and Conductor Roper, had been held at Willow River but was ready to proceed south as far as was possible. Sullivan gave Thompson a message to be sent to Duluth telling of the burned Limited and requesting a relief train for the people at Skunk Lake. The message was scarcely tapped out when fire hit the Miller station and forced everyone to flee farther north.

Up the tracks they met the freight heading south. Sullivan told Kelly and Roper they wouldn't be able to reach Skunk Lake since bridges and culverts were burned, but the two trainmen wanted to see how far they could go. They promised to pick up Sullivan and the others when they returned. There were then 21 in the group.

When the people reached Finlayson station, they found milk to drink and water for washing. Sullivan bathed his burning eyes. But the fire relentlessly pursued them again and drove them out to a gravel pit near the tracks two miles farther north. By that time Sullivan and others from Skunk Lake had run ten hellish miles barely keeping ahead of the flames. After an hour of waiting they heard the welcome sound of the returning freight on its way back to Willow River.

The freight stopped, and Kelly and Roper helped everyone to board it. At Rutledge, the next station, Sullivan learned that a relief train from Duluth was on its way to try to reach the survivors at Skunk Lake. With this knowledge Sullivan collapsed from exhaustion and lay in the caboose until he was helped out at Willow River. Many of the others had to be led off the train since they, too, were nearly blind from the fire and smoke. The citizens of Willow River administered to the sorry band until the relief train arrived about 11:00 p.m. to take them to Duluth.

Sullivan was brought to St. Mary's Hospital where he was treated for burns and exhaustion. Reports circulated to the effect that he had lost his senses and was delirious. He kept asking about the child he thought he had thrown to safety out of the window of the Limited, but a passenger on the train stated positively that Sullivan had thrown no child out the window, and that he may have been anxious over the welfare of a little girl who had been put in his custody on the train at Duluth. The little girl was saved with the others at Skunk Lake.

On Monday Sullivan's wife came to be with him, and on Tuesday he had recovered sufficiently to return to his home in St. Paul where he continued to recuperate for some time.

Sullivan's actions were given occasional commendation, but he was definitely in the shadow of the engineer of his train. The editor of *The Duluth News Tribune* in giving recognition to the other railroad heroes wrote of Sullivan:

> Conductor Sullivan, too, did his duty, encouraging and helping the passengers and working with might and main to save life. The fact that he went through such awful scenes in his work of saving, that after the cars had been cleared and the train burned, his mind temporarily gave way shows what he did and how his thoughts were with his passengers. Even in his temporary derangement, his thoughts were upon one little girl who had been placed in his charge before the train left Duluth. [33]

A report of Thomas Sullivan's death appeared in *The St. Paul Pioneer Press,* May 13, 1927. The brief notice stated that Sullivan had been born in Ireland in 1860 and had come to the United States at age twelve. When he was twenty he was hired by the St. Paul and Duluth Railroad Company and had spent 47 years in its service. He died of apoplexy in 1927 at the age of

67, leaving his wife and daughter, Grayce. His funeral was held at the St. Mark's Church in St. Paul, and he was buried in the Oakland cemetery. Thirty-three years after the fire Thomas Sullivan was credited in the newspaper with "one of the greatest acts of heroism of the Hinckley holocaust."[34]

HEROES OF THE EASTERN RAILWAY OF MINNESOTA

Engineer William Best

On the day of the fire William Best, engineer of passenger train No. 4 of the Eastern Railway Company of Minnesota, had an opportunity to redeem his recently tarnished reputation. Although Best was reported to be one of the most able engineers in the northwest, he had been criticized during the Great Northern strike earlier that year for walking off the job and deserting a trainload of passengers on an open track where they were in danger.[35] But Best proved himself a hero on September 1.

Just after the fire, at the request of the railroad officials, Engineers Best and Barry and Conductor Powers each filed an official accident report with the Great Northern Company. The information given in all reports is essentially the same, but Best's account tells of the contention that arose between the two engineers as the combined trains began to take on refugees at Hinckley. In bold handwriting Best wrote:*

> I went to meet Cond. Powers. Before I got to him our train started. I then run for the Engine & set the Air Brakes. Cond. Campbell [came] telling me that Engineer Barry was going to pull the pin if we did not go. I then released the air. He then . . . whistled to go. I again set the air Brakes & did not leave the Engine often while we was in Hinckley as every little while he would try & start. He sent Brakeman Beach back to till me to let the Brakes go or we would be all Burnt up but I would not let them off untill we had used all the time we could. It was the hardest Place I ever stood in. I was thinking what if I should Loose the train after all but their is one thing I should not have been here to write this but Providence Judged diferent.[36]

---

*Best's report appears as he wrote it. The spelling has not been altered, but punctuation has been added for clarity.

Best's and Powers' decision to hold the train a few more minutes might have been a tragic one. Best recounted the sights in the village and the imminent danger:

> The train Crews was doing noble work loading the People into the cars. It then become so hot it was imposible to stay anny longer & those that was left could not get to us. I never will forget the...Poor People running & falling in the street, & cattle with them, calling out for God sake hold the train but our time had come. Our train was doomed to stay anny longer...The Mills & Houses was in one great sheat of flame. They burnt so fast I could see all inside of the houses. Bed room sets and Just as the house would be inside. Then it would all fall to-gether....It was terrible but grand....We had done all...that mortals could do under the Circumstances. [37]

As the train went northward over the fiery route, Best applied the brakes at each bridge to slow the train so the two brakemen, who rode on the outside of Barry's engine, could signal Barry to cross. When they reached Sandstone, Best and Barry overruled the decision of the two conductors to remain there. As they left Sandstone and warily crossed the Kettle River bridge, they could hear the roar of the fire behind them. Best wrote of the remainder of the trip:

> We started again for home Leaving Deth & Distruction everywhere....We all felt relieved when the train was safe out of the fire....On arriving at West Superior we Cut our Engines off & a switch Engine took the train to Duluth as our Eyes was Burnt so bad we could not go much farther. With the help of an all Just Providence we arrived at nine p.m. all well. [38]

With their arrival at West Superior, Best's duties for the day were over and he went home to treat his impaired eyesight and rest from the nervous strain. Among the awards and honors bestowed upon the railroad crews, very little recognition was given to Best individually. A few newspapers set up "Heroes' Funds" for all railroad men. *The New York Evening Post* collected $16.00 for Best and Fireman Ford for heroism, an amount both men turned over to the relief fund for the fire sufferers.

William Best was one railroad hero whose judicious acts and coolheaded decisions were not adequately recognized at the time. It will never be known how many people were saved at Hinckley because Best held a firm grip on the air brakes for a few more crucial moments.

Engineer Edward Barry

If Engineer Edward Barry had uncoupled his freight engine from the front of the combined Eastern trains at Hinckley and left, as he threatened, some 500 passengers and Hinckley refugees would not have lived to relate the story. Had he pulled out with his engine and abandoned the rest of the train, Best's engine at the rear would have been helpless, the carloads of people would have been sacrificed and Barry would have received no medals for heroism.

Conductor Powers of the passenger train was officially in charge of the combined crews because of his seniority over the others. If Barry had disobeyed orders from his superior, he would have jeopardized his position with the railroad company. He no doubt would have been soundly reprimanded and penalized, and his reputation would have been irreparably damaged.

But Barry was anxious to leave the burning town and several times gave the two sharp whistles to signal the departure of the train. Fortunately for the people of Hinckley, he was restrained by Best who held the train back with the air brakes in the engine at the rear.*

As soon as Best released the brakes and the train was on the road out of the burning town, Barry's performance was above reproach. The trip north of Hinckley was especially arduous for Barry since he was in the front pulling the load with his engine in reverse, relying only on the two brakemen to flag him safely across the burning bridges. His eyes were badly affected by the smoke and fire, and by the end of the trip he was almost blind.

At Sandstone Barry and Best were in agreement that the train should continue northward instead of stopping as the conductors recommended. This proved to be a wise decision, since Sandstone was completely burned in less than an hour after the train left. Barry maintained his composure as the heavy train crossed the burning wood trestles of the precarious Kettle River high bridge, and he brought it safely across just minutes before the ends collapsed.

Barry wrote about the harrowing ride in the accident report submitted to the Great Northern Company:*

> The wood work on the Engine was on fire and I put it out with water from the Tank. I had to keep throwing water on my self as my clothes caught on fire. We arrived at Kettle River Bridge and the fire had just got too burn the lower timber. I new if we stoped we wer all lost so I puld the throttle wide open and got across all right. If I had stoped we would have bin all burnt so I doon the best I could too save my own life and the...passengers we had on [the] train....Could hear

---

*Barry did not mention this incident in his accident report, or in the account he wrote for publication.

---

*The report appears as Barry wrote it with unaltered spelling. Only punctuation has been added for clarity.

180

the cyclone coming so I run quite fast till I got too Mansfield. When I got too Kerrick I could hardly see and thought I couldent goo any farther but the folks said so mutch I puld out and arrived at West Sup. [39]

When the train arrived at Superior, Barry and Best were relieved of their duties, and another engine took the train to Duluth. Barry was disabled and suffering from impaired eyesight. He went to his home in Superior to rest and treat his burned eyes. In three days he was back at work.

Engineer Barry and Conductor Campbell, also of the freight train, each were awarded gold medals by the Hinckley fire sufferers in recognition of bravery and heroism. Barry was aware of the importance of his own act of courage. He wrote in his accident report: "If it hadn't bin for me they all would have bin lost", and at the bottom of the page he could not restrain himself from adding, "I think I am deserving of the credit instead of Best."[40]

When Barry retired he had been with the Great Northern for twenty years and was considered one of the company's best locomotive engineers. He died on July 26, 1904, at St. Joseph's Hospital in St. Paul after a year of suffering from heart disease. Barry was forty-six years of age and was survived by his wife. The funeral was held at the St. Mary's Catholic Church followed by interment at Calvary Cemetery. His death notice in the *St. Paul Dispatch* stated:

> Mr. Barry distinguished himself in the great Hinckley fire by running a train into the burning woods about Hinckley for the rescue of people there. For this brave act he was presented with a gold medal which he prized highly. [41]

Engineer Barry was given a distinction not accorded any of the other railroad heroes — Barry township in Pine County was named in his honor. [42]

Conductor Harry Powers

On Saturday, September 1, when Conductor Harry D. Powers of the Eastern Minnesota Railway loaded passenger train No. 4 at Duluth for its 1:00 p.m. departure for St. Paul, he had aboard some illustrious passengers. Three of them were judges, and they all praised Powers for his conduct through the crisis at Hinckley. Said one judge:

> He acted a noble part; never for an instant did he lose his self possession. He advised every one to keep perfectly cool; saw nothing but harm could come of excitement; helped the people onto the train; kindly but firmly refused to delay for a moment to take baggage on board; said to women who frantically demanded delay that they might secure some household goods, "Mrs. we cannot wait for that baggage. We will gladly take you, get on board. It is your only chance." Lifted the children on board with the deftness and tenderness equal to that of a mother's love. [43]

A Hinckley resident who boarded the train said, "Con. Powers of the Emergency Train was the coolest man I ever saw in my life. The way he kept his nerve was something wonderful."[44]

When the two trains were couple together at Hinckley, it was Powers' decision, in consultation with Engineer Best, to hold the train at Hinckley as long as possible to allow more people to get aboard before leaving town. If the train had burned with all its passengers, Powers would have been the individual held responsible. Powers and Best were both involved with thwarting Barry's attempts to leave Hinckley. Fortunately for everyone their decision turned out to be correct.

Powers was employed by the Great Northern Railroad for many years and gained respect in the company as a capable conductor. After the fire newspapers accorded him a considerable amount of public recognition. Samuel Hill of the Eastern Minnesota presented him with a gold watch inscribed: "Presented to H. D. Powers for his heroism on September first, 1894."[45]

THREE DOCTORS

Dr. D. W. Cowan

One of the first men to go to the rescue of Brook Park survivors was Dr. D. W. Cowan of Hinckley. He was with a crew that arrived at Brook Park from Mora on Sunday afternoon, bringing provisions and medical supplies to sufferers sheltered in the unburned boxcars and the wrecked St. Cloud and Hinckley train.

After the rescue work at Brook Park Dr. Cowan turned his attention to duties as coroner of Pine County. It was his responsibility to make the official report of the dead, a monumental task. The doctor mustered all his organizational skills and systematically went about the distasteful work. He instructed search and burial parties in the procedure, advising them to obtain as much information as possible about each victim, noting the name and address of the person, where the body was found, by whom, where it was buried, what valuables or marks of identificaiton were found, in whose custody valuables were left and the names of friends or relatives. A record was compiled for each victim. Coroner Cowan's task was compounded since many victims were burned beyond recognition and positive identification was impossible. But he worked indefatigably and efficiently, moving from one burned settlement to the next to inter and record the dead. *The St. Paul Pioneer Press* said of Cowan's work:

His personal loss has not prevented him from doing most efficient work at Hinckley. His labors have been almost beyond endurance, but he has responded to every demand upon him with an alacrity and an energy which has accomplished wonders. [46]

When Dr. Cowan filed the coroner's report November 24, 1894, he had certified the deaths of 413 people of Pine County. Of these 314 were listed by name, including those who were not positively identified but were assumed to be from a given family or residents of nearby homes. The remaining 99 were listed as "Unknown."

Dr. Cowan was Hinckley's first doctor, having come to town in 1891. He had established a drug store with J. M. Currie of Mora in charge. In 1893 Cowan was joined by Dr. Stephan, just out of medical school. Cowan had living quarters and an office in a convenient spot at the Currie home across from the St. Paul and Duluth depot.

After the fire Dr. Cowan was more fortunate than most of Hinckley's residents. Although his drug store was a total loss, it was insured for $500, and the doctor owned $600 in stock. The State Relief Commission records indicate that he was given $150 worth of lumber and labor to rebuild and later received an oilcan, oil, a stove and stove pipes totalling $4.30. He was also paid $100 a month for October and November for medical services to fire sufferers. [47]

After the fire Dr. Cowan remained in Hinckley for a few years before moving to Sandstone.

Dr. E. L. Stephan

On display at the Hinckley Fire Museum is a small well-worn black appointment book in which the last handwritten entry reads, "Great Fire." It belonged to Dr. Ernest L. Stephan who, when the fire struck, ran back to his burning office to pick up the book and a few other items before catching the Eastern Minnesota train for Duluth.

Although Dr. Stephan had been in Hinckley only a year and a half, he had established himself not only as a capable doctor and surgeon, but as an energetic citizen and advocate of the town. To help pay his expenses while at the University of Minnesota Medical School he had taken a variety of jobs, among them serving as a church musician and taking night calls for a Minneapolis doctor. After internship and graduation in 1893 he moved to Hinckley as an associate of Dr. Cowan. There he had an office at the Cowan drug store.

On the day of the fire Dr. Stephan was driven from his office by the oppressive heat. After sensing the danger he ran to the houses in the south end of town, telling anyone still remaining to flee to the Eastern depot and board the train. He then helped families reach the train and put some twenty children aboard before climbing on himself. On the way to Duluth Dr. Stephan went from car to car reuniting separated families.

When the train arrived in Duluth, the doctor took a short respite, then loaded his pockets with brandy and carron oil and caught the first train back to the burned area. The train, in charge of W. V. S Thorne, Superintendent of the Eastern Railway, left at 5:00 Sunday morning to investigate the damage to the railroad lines. On board with Dr. Stephan were Douglas Greeley, manager of the Morrison Hotel at Hinckley, and a few other Hinckley men.

The train's progress along the way was slowed by fallen trees and debris which had to be removed from the tracks. One mile north of Partridge the train stopped at a burned bridge, and as many men as could rode a handcar

Dr. E. L. Stephan leading a 4th of July parade in Hinckley in 1899.

while the rest walked to Sandstone and the burned Kettle River bridge. The men forded the river near the bridge and climbed up the bank to the annihilated village of Sandstone. Here they counted over forty-five dead bodies scattered about the streets. The men continued walking to Hinckley and arrived there at 5:00 p.m. Sunday evening. They were the first party to return of those who had left on the Eastern Minnesota train twenty-five hours before. At Hinckley they found that the relief trains and crews had arrived from Pine City and Rush City, and many survivors had been rescued. Dr. Stephan joined the others in searching for more survivors and helping the injured. Throughout the following days the doctor continued to administer aid where needed.

On the registration blank in the State Relief Commission files it was noted that the doctor lost all his belongings, his entire library of books and his surgical instruments. Dr. Stephan asked for no assistance other than payment for the medical services he rendered. He was given one mackinaw outfit and two suits of underwear totalling $6.00 and was paid $100 a month by the Commission for his services for September, October and November.[48]

From 1893 to 1896 Dr. Stephan served as Pine County Superintendent of Schools, presiding over twenty-four school districts. Each year he conducted public examinations for candidates who wanted teaching certificates in teachers' summer sessions held in Pine City. There were courses in physical culture, psychology, methods, civics and one in physiology which was taught by the doctor himself. During the session Editor Angus Hay made some droll observations about the dashing young doctor and his forty-three students, forty of whom were young women. He wrote:

> It is expected that the teachers will be amply able to take care of themselves after Dr. Stephan has finished his course in physiology. The doctor says he shall dwell on "the heart and its affections"....No one but a superintendent and a single one at that, knows how much mental strain is put upon a man who is obliged to look after forty young ladies. Our superintendent looks care worn already. We wonder why he does not appoint some assistants.[49]

Later Hay wrote, "Many young ladies seem to have lost their hearts in Dr. Stephan's class."[50] One year later in June, 1896, Dr. Stephan married Clara Hay, sister of Editor Angus Hay. Miss Hay had taught school at Lake Pokegama and Finlayson and was no doubt one of those who attended the young County Superintendent's physiology class.

The Stephans made their home in Hinckley where they raised two children, Helen Ruth and Angus, and a foster son, Raymond. The doctor performed miracles of surgery on kitchen tables, delivered nearly 5,000 babies, set countless broken bones and treated a profusion of illnesses and diseases. He made town and country calls until his death in 1950 and went to great lengths to reach his patients, even taking to handcars, manure spreaders and snowshoes when other transportation failed. Summer or winter he

Dr. E. L. Stephan at age 79.
1948 photo

never wore a hat, and in later years his snowy white mane flying in the wind was a familiar sight. He was appointed physician and surgeon for both railroads, served for a time as president of the local school board and was Selective Service examiner during World Wars I and II. During the flu epidemic of 1918 Dr. Stephan had fewer than the normal number of mortalities, and other doctors sought out his treatment — plenty of rest, oranges and sweating.

In 1947 Mrs. Stephan passed away, just ten months after they celebrated their fiftieth wedding anniversary. Dr. Stephan died November 13, 1950, following a brief illness, at the age of eighty-one. He had given fifty-seven years of dedicated service to Hinckley.

Dr. Inez Legg

At the time of the fire Hinckley's health was in capable hands with three well-qualified doctors in town. Dr. Inez Legg, a graduate of the Women's College of the New York Infirmary, ran a small hospital at her residence across from the bank. She made calls to neighboring communities where she stopped over with friends between trains.

Dr. Legg hired local girls to help care for the hospital patients, one of whom was Mary Anderson (Kofoed). Mary said of Dr. Legg, "She was a very fine lady. I worked for her for a year and a half and learned so much from her. But she was having a hard time making a living because people didn't pay their bills. She was terribly discouraged and was going to move to Duluth."[51]

The State Commission report indicates that Dr. Legg was in Hinckley the day of the fire, and on September 5 her name appeared on the list of refugees sheltered at Hotel Duluth. The doctor lost all her personal belongings, hospital equipment and furniture, medical supplies and library. She did save some of her surgical instruments. At Duluth she was given $15.00 in cash together with groceries, furniture, bedding, drugs and household items totalling $116.82. A notation on her relief application said, "This lady is by all means deserving. She practiced medicine in Hinckley and is estimable in every way — all you can give would be well placed. M. S. Collins."*[52]

After the fire Dr. Legg went to West Duluth, then in May, 1895, set up practice at Carlton, Minnesota. The fire had made Dr. Legg's move from Hinckley decisive.

TWO CLERGYMEN

Father E. J. Lawler

"For heaven's sake, leave all you have! Get to the gravel pit, run to the river. Hinckley will be destroyed."[53] That was the urgent message carried through the streets by sentinel Father Lawler. When the fire alarm had sounded early Saturday afternoon, he had rushed to the fire station with the firemen and had witnessed in the next two hours the helplessness of the fire department in containing the spreading flames. The priest knew then that a catastrophe was upon them.

Father E. J. Lawler, age thirty-five, was a revered and respected man in the town. He worked tirelessly for the betterment of the communities he served — Hinckley, Mission Creek and Sandstone. At the time of the fire he had just recovered from typhoid fever.

After alerting the townspeople the Father tended to his own safety. He fled with his housekeeper through the blazing streets to the Grindstone River where he joined the Tew family and others. It was then about 4:00 p.m. As

---

*Mr. Collins was the head of the Hinckley school and was employed as a clerk by the State Commission, first at Duluth, then at Hinckley.

the searing flames roared overhead, Father Lawler pulled off his surplice, wet it and covered the crippled Grandma Tew, who sat on a rock on a tiny strip of land in the Grindstone. He also tore his coat into segments to cover others. When his housekeeper fainted and fell in the water, he kept her from drowning until she revived. One man begged the priest to hear his final confession, but the Father thought it his sacred duty to pronounce absolution on all the souls gathered there. But the exertion took its toll on the brave priest, and soon he fell faint from exhaustion. Fortunately a young lad saved him by holding his head above water until he gained consciousness.

Some of the people who had sought shelter in the Grindstone died, most of them being victims of the river, not the fire, but Father Lawler survived. The priest, however, suffered from shock, and his eyes were so affected by the smoke and flames that he was almost totally blind.

After the fire had passed, he was led to the gravel pit where he lay, blinded and partly unconscious, until after 1:00 o'clock Sunday morning when he was rescued by a crew from Pine City. He was carried to a relief train and taken to Pine City where he was treated for a few days before being transferred to St. Mary's Hospital in Duluth. Here he had a prolonged recovery.

Although the Father had lost all his personal belongings in his parish quarters in Hinckley, his requests for relief were modest. He was given $25.00 in cash and $25.00 worth of clothing.[54] As he was recovering from his injuries, the Catholic Society of Pine City and Hinckley built a parsonage for him at Pine City,[55] a home he probably never occupied.

No one knew how many lives the good priest saved that day.

The Reverend Peter Knudsen

Father Lawler said of the Rev. Knudsen, pastor of the Hinckley Presbyterian Church, "[He] is a royal man. I firmly believe that he would lay down his life to serve another without a thought that such a deed deserved any special credit."[56] That statement from a Roman Catholic priest at a time when ecumenism was not widely practiced was a distinct compliment.

Pastor Knudsen had arrived in Hinckley only four months before the fire, having come from Brainerd, Minnesota. Although he resided at Hinckley, he also conducted church services at Sandstone and Pine City.

When the fire struck, the Pastor and his wife went to the Eastern Minnesota depot to help others aboard, but when the train left they refused to leave, saying, "Others are left in the village, we must go back if possible and help them to the gravel pit."[57] So the train left without them, and they

The Rev. Peter Knudsen
Pastor of Hinckley
Presbyterian Church

Mrs. Peter Knudsen, wife
of the pastor of Hinckley
Presbyterian Church

headed back toward the burning town. They went only a few steps when flames enveloped them. Twice Mrs. Knudsen fell and was ready to die, but as the smoke lifted for an instant, they saw an empty wagon under which they crawled until it, too, began to burn. Fortunately the gravel pit was nearby, and they managed to reach its shallow waters with about 100 other people. Animals, too, sought the pit, their usual watering hole. Every person was saved there except one man who was trampled by a cow and drowned.

When the fire had passed, the survivors climbed up the banks and surveyed the ruined town. But Mrs. Knudsen, being of a practical nature, took a tin pail that had been found at the Eastern water tank, squatted down and milked a cow. The pastor found some watermelons in a nearby garden and brought them to the gravel pit. Using the scooped-out rinds for cups, they gave the fresh milk to the children to drink.

After the fire the pastor was immediately involved with rescue and burial work in Hinckley. On Monday, September 3, he participated in a burial ceremony at the Hinckley cemetery, and on Sunday, September 9, he was one of the speakers at the memorial service held at Pine City.

The Knudsens, as others, lost everything, but he prudently carried $300 insurance. The Relief Commission gave him $100 in cash, a few household items, six chairs, garden seeds and enough groceries for *five* people.[58] Since the couple was childless, it can be assumed that they "adopted" three survivors after the fire.

The church lost 25 members in the fire, but the pastor soon revived the waning spirits of the remaining parishioners, and by mid-October he had them erecting a new edifice. The Knudsens continued to serve Hinckley until June, 1895, when he was formally installed as the minister of the Presbyterian Church in Pine City. A local paper called the courageous clergyman "the sort of person who cannot be appalled by difficulty and [one who] is working unceasingly for the upbuilding of Hinckley."[59]

Mrs. Joseph Tew's jewel case containing money, jewelry, glasses and family Bible which she carried on relief train to Duluth. On exhibit at Hinckley Fire Museum.

FOUR FAMILIES

The Tew Family

On Saturday afternoon when Joseph Tew, the local drayman who had been out fighting fires, could see that Hinckley was doomed, he raced home, loaded his large family on his dray and headed for the Eastern Minnesota train. There were nine of them — his wife, June, their seven children and Grandma Tew, who was crippled from sciatica rheumatism.

When they got to the depot, the train was already jammed with people, but June and six of the children managed to squeeze into a car. Joseph, the eldest daughter, Lizzie, and Grandma could not get aboard so they climbed back on the wagon and headed north to the Grindstone River. When the fire bore down upon them, Joseph unhitched the horses and helped Grandma to a rock on a small island in the river. Father Lawler, his housekeeper and several others came to the same spot.

As the fire moved over them, Father Lawler removed his surplice, wet it and threw it over Grandma Tew. She survived unharmed as did Joseph and Lizzie, but the bodies of the horses were found burned near the bridge. When it was possible to leave the shelter of the river, the Tews went to the Eastern Minnesota roundhouse, the only remaining building in the town, and were put aboard a train to Pine City.

June Tew and her children arrived safely in Duluth on the crowded Eastern train. They first stayed at the Armory, then were assigned to quarters at the Congregational Church, later were moved to the Bethel. For several days after arriving in Duluth they didn't know if the other members of the family had survived.

Their house at Hinckley was completely destroyed, but it was said that a crucifix and a cross were found unharmed. Three weeks after the fire the family returned to Hinckley and lived in a small shack that Joseph had hurriedly constructed. Although the Tews carried $300 insurance, he was given a No. 2 relief home, the larger size, which cost $171.90. In addition the family received groceries, furniture, clothing, horse collars, hay, corn and seed potatoes. [60]

M. S. Collins, relief clerk, wrote on the application blank:

> Mr. Tew is a hardworking industrious man. He has a large family and is quite heavily in debt, but thinks he can get a little time. He has no present ready resources, is in great need of help and is certainly deserving. He can probably get as many references as any man in Hinckley. [61]

A few days after the family had returned to Hinckley, one of the sons died, and five months later their daughter Mary died, both supposedly from effects of the fire. [62]

On display at the Hinckley Fire Museum are some relics remaining from the Tew family. There are the pennies saved by Joe Jr. which had melted into one lump inside an old butter crock. There is also a china doll carried by daughter Mary to Duluth and a small chest which contained money, jewelry, glasses and a Bible that Mrs. Tew brought with her on the train.

China doll carried by Mary Tew
on the relief train to Duluth.
On exhibit at Hinckley Fire Museum.

FROM THE ASHES

The Greenfield Family

When the fire struck the Marvin Greenfield home, five miles north of Hinckley near Skunk Lake, Mr. Greenfield went to the cellar of their house with his wife, their six children, a hired man, a neighbor and his two sons. As fire consumed the house above them, the floor gave way, and the dining room table crashed through to the cellar. They all managed to get out except the hired man who was trapped below, and the eldest Greenfield daughter who, in confusion, ran back into the burning house. The others fled to a potato patch and lay down in the rows. Mr. Greenfield dashed from child to child to tear burning clothes from their bodies until the fire forced him to lie down and cover himself as best he could. He heard ten-year old Charlie scream that his mother's clothes were afire, but there was no way to reach her in the height of the blaze. When the flames subsided Charlie was still alive, having saved himself by rolling in the dirt, but Mrs. Greenfield was severely burned over two-thirds of her body. Mr. Greenfield suffered from badly-burned eyes. Later the bodies of four children were found in the potato patch, and the daughter's remains were recovered from the ashes of the home.

Mr. and Mrs. Greenfield and Charlie were brought first to Pine City, then moved to the Homeopathic Hospital in Minneapolis where Marvin received treatment for his eyes and later for pneumonia. Charlie received only slight injuries, but Mrs. Greenfield was so severely burned she was given little chance for recovery. However, after intensive hospital care for months, she returned to Hinckley in March, 1895.

When he had recovered, a disheartened Mr. Greenfield returned to Hinckley to rebuild. He was given $100 cash and $30 worth of lumber for a home. The Relief Commission also supplied them with food, clothing, household items, furniture, farm implements, hay and seeds. Not including a charge of $33.59 for Mrs. Greenfield's lengthy hospitalization, the family was rehabilitated for a total cost of $468.24. [63]

The Hinckley Enterprise wrote of this family, "Sadly, but bravely, they accept their loss." [64]

The McNamara Family

When he knew that Hinckley would not escape the fire, John McNamara, section foreman of the St. Paul and Duluth railroad, hurried his wife, Annie, and their five sons to the depot to catch the 4:00 o'clock Limited to Pine City. As they left their house, Annie grabbed her black leather purse. No sooner had they arrived at the crowded depot than the roof caught fire, and

Mrs. John McNamara's purse containing $3,500 was found under body of one of her sons. On exhibit at Hinckley Fire Museum.

everyone had to evacuate the building. The McNamaras, along with others, ran north on the St. Paul and Duluth tracks and caught Root's train to Skunk Lake. They did not stop at the lake but continued running north on the tracks and in the confusion became separated. Thirteen-year old Peter and ten-year old Jim got to Rutledge where they caught the same relief train that took Conductor Sullivan to Duluth. At Duluth both boys were suffering from smoke and damaged eyes but when interviewed were confident their mother and brothers were safe.

In the pre-dawn hours Sunday morning Mr. McNamara was found near Skunk Lake by a rescue team that came from Hinckley. He was dazed and did not know the whereabouts of his family. For a time he and a rescuer searched along the tracks but found no trace of the missing McNamaras. John then went on his way north to Rutledge.

Late Saturday night when Dave Williams' rescue crew from Duluth had been working its way to Root's train, they found several victims of the fire along the tracks a few miles north of Skunk Lake. One was a woman, and close by were some children. Under one child was found a black leather purse. In the dark the men tried to pry it open, but the clasp held fast, so they threw it on the handcar. When morning came they forced open the purse and found cash and certificates of deposit totalling $3,500. The purse belonged to Mrs. McNamara. In Duluth Mr. McNamara was notified of the purse and the probable death of his wife and two sons. He was surprised when told of the contents of the purse as he had no idea that his wife had saved that much money. He hoped it was a case of mistaken identity.

McNamara boarded a relief train to Skunk Lake to identify the bodies. When he saw them, he at first could not be sure they were his family, but later positively identified his wife and assumed that two bodies nearby were those of his sons, fifteen-year-old John and nine-year old Michael. The purse was returned to McNamara. It was said that his wife had saved the money for many years for the education of her sons. The day after the fire John Jr.

was to have left for school at St. Thomas in St. Paul. Mrs. McNamara and the two sons were buried in Rush City.

The Relief Commission records indicate that the McNamaras had lived in a railroad company house which burned along with the family belongings. The only property remaining was a cow and some land which Mr. McNamara owned in Hinckley. No mention was made of the $3,500 found in his wife's purse. After the fire John rented a house in Rutledge where he hired a housekeeper to stay with his three remaining sons. He was given furniture, household utensils, groceries and building materials amounting to $146.64. [65]

In the spring of 1895 *The Hinckley Enterprise* noted that when John McNamara moved to Rutledge, Hinckley had lost a good citizen.

The Fraser Family

When it appeared that Hinckley was doomed, Al Fraser tried to get his young wife and three small children, ages four, two, and seven months, aboard the Barry-Best train, but it was so jammed that only one child was taken aboard. The Frasers raced back toward town, jumped on an empty wagon pulled by a team of horses and just ahead of the fire galloped north up the road across the Grindstone bridge. On the other side of the bridge the wagon caught fire. Fraser quickly unhitched the team and turned them loose while the wagon burned. Just then another riderless team and wagon came toward him. Fraser caught the horses and found some barrels of water and a trunk of clothes on the wagon. He hastily immersed his two children in a barrel and wrapped wet clothing from the trunk about his wife. Two men came dashing down the road and jumped in the other barrels. In fifteen minutes the fire had swept over them. They all survived. But from the nearby swamp where 127 Hinckley people had taken shelter, they heard one piercing cry as the fire struck, then ominous silence. All had perished in the marsh, presumably from suffocation before their bodies burned.

The Relief Commission ledgers indicate that Mrs. Fraser needed medical care for fire injuries through September. The family had lost everything and was given $175 in cash, groceries and clothing to begin another life. [66] It is not known what happened to the child that was put aboard the train to Duluth, but the Fraser escape became an oft-repeated Hinckley legend.

Mary Anderson Kofoed of Hinckley at age 100.

CENTENARIAN

Mary Anderson Kofoed

"Television! Who would have thought I'd be talking about the Hinckley Fire on television," said Mary Anderson Kofoed on her 100th birthday.

On October 7, 1976, Hinckley's oldest survivor of the fire faced the cameras and recalled the day that she said "froze in my memory." She was seventeen at the time, just five weeks away from her eighteenth birthday.

On the day Mrs. Kofoed turned 100, Hinckley citizens dropped in at the small white frame house where she lived with her daughter, Mabel Anderson, to leave cards, flowers and gifts. A television crew from the Twin Cities squeezed into the tiny living room with its paraphernalia to grind out footage for the evening telecast. When the day ended, Mrs. Kofoed admitted it was exciting but she was a bit weary.

Prominently displayed in the living room was a "Citation of Honor" signed by Governor Wendell R. Anderson which acclaimed her an "outstanding centenarian, one of Minnesota's foremost pioneers, who has contributed significantly to more than one half of the Nation's birthdays."

Mrs. Kofoed was born in Sweden in 1876 and came to Hinckley with her pioneer parents, Nels and Tilda Anderson, at the age of three. She was the eldest of the six children and on her 100th birthday was the only one of her family still living. The Andersons' first home was in Hinckley's earliest depot which her father bought for $20.00. Two years later they moved to a new home one block south of the St. Paul and Duluth depot where they lived until the fire destroyed it. Mr. Anderson sold the lot in town and moved to his acreage one-half mile south of Hinckley where he farmed for many years.

After the fire Mary returned to Hinckley for a time, then attended the Agriculture School at St. Paul for one year. She taught school for three years at Worthington, Minnesota, where she met John Kofoed, whom she married in 1904. They lived at Worthington two years, then moved to the family farm at Hinckley where they lived for forty years before moving into town.

John Kofoed passed away in 1975 at the age of 99 after seventy years of marriage. Mrs. Kofoed died on November 10, 1977, at the age of 101. Among their living descendants are two children, four grandchildren, sixteen great-grandchildren and four great-great-grandchildren.

It cannot be estimated how many times Mrs. Kofoed related the story of the *Great Fire*. She might have wanted to put the tragic episode out of her mind years ago but for inquisitive people who urged, "Tell us about the fire, Mary."

Here is Mary's story as told to one inquisitive person:

The Hinckley Fire story is like the Bible to me — it never grows old. That day we were busy as usual, the men had gone to work in the morning with their dinner pails never dreaming that before the day was over some of them would lose their loved ones and their homes. The summer had been so hot and dry the grass was all brown, and everything was scorched. There was smoke in the air all the time from fires burning around town.

That Saturday I had gone across the tracks to take care of Grandma Dunn, a little blind woman. Her son, Tommy, the telegraph operator at the St. Paul and Duluth station, came home at noon for dinner. He was worried. "Dress up mother, Mary," he said, "I'll get you tickets on the Limited for Pine City. It looks bad and I'm afraid the town will go." He went back to the depot.

I fixed up Grandma Dunn and covered the haystack — everyone had a cow in those days — all of Pine County was one big pasture — and we went to the depot. Grandma's daughter and four children had just walked in from the country and they came, too. I thought we'd be the only ones there, but in fifteen minutes about 200 people had rushed in. Then someone opened the sliding doors to the freight room and shouted, "Get out of the depot — the roof is on fire! Run for your lives!"

Nels Anderson family
taken two weeks
before the fire.
Top: Jennie, Anna
Middle: Nels Anderson, Charlie,
Mrs. Anderson, Mary
Front: Albert, Jarda

FROM THE ASHES

Mary Anderson [Kofoed]
at age 20 [Year 1896]

Everyone ran out to the street. The wind was blowing so hard you could hardly stand. It was thick with smoke and red hot cinders were falling. I told Grandma's daughter to lead her while I ran to the lumber company store and tried to get in. To my good fortune, the door was locked. I looked back, like Lot's wife, and saw the fire boiling out the depot windows. Right then I prayed to the Lord to save my soul because I knew my body would perish. The whole town seemed to be on fire in an instant.

But just then a man came clipping along the wooden sidewalk pulling two children. I can still hear his deep voice saying, "Oh my God, we'll die." I grabbed his coat-tails, and we ran for another block. Then I saw Mrs. Kronenberg come running with her six children. "Hurry up, Mary," she shouted, "We can get on the train."

"But I haven't any money," I said.

"Oh to dickens with the money," she yelled, "Today we're running for our lives."

Then I got courage — there was hope we could get out of town. We were among the last to get on. They had put two trains together with two engines and every boxcar they could find. They put me in the caboose, and Mrs. Kronenberg and her children went to the baggage car. The train was packed full.

Oh what a sight it was when the train left, one to sicken the strongest of men. That picture just froze in my mind — to see people running after the train, screaming for it to stop — and of course we couldn't stop because the fire was so close, and if the bridge had burned we would have been trapped. I looked back and saw them drop in the streets.

On the train there was such sorrow and uncontrollable grief; mothers didn't know if their husbands or children were on the train or left back in the fire. Children were crying for their parents. I didn't know what happened to my own family until Dr. Stephan found me and led me to the baggage car. There I saw my whole family sitting on the floor, all alive, and were we glad to be together again!

PEOPLE AND FIRE

That Saturday morning my father had been out at the farm fencing and had come back to town for dinner. When it got bad, he unharnessed the horses and let them shift for themselves. He told my mother to take a sheet and collect the most precious things — but there was no time for that. They had to leave everything. They each took a child by the hand and ran to the depot where they were put in the baggage car. My sister had been taking care of a sick woman that day, and she made it to the train, too. Grandma Dunn was also on the train, but her son Tommy died as he ran toward the river. I lost my aunt, uncle and two cousins.

When we got to Sandstone the trainmen had an argument about crossing the high bridge which was burning, but we made it across just a few minutes before it collapsed.

We got to Duluth about 9:00 o'clock that night. They gave us hot tea and bread and butter. Oh it tasted good! The people of Duluth were so good to us. We stayed at the Armory Saturday and Sunday nights, then on Monday morning we went to stay with my uncle who lived in Duluth.

My father headed right back to Hinckley Monday morning. He bought a tent, some quilts and pillows and with Charlie, my brother, who was ten, took a train back there. We had lost everything of course, except the money he carried — about $40.00. The horses were burned, too. They dug potatoes at the farm — we had a good potato crop even though it was dry, and he cleared up the land. As soon as the Relief Commission got lumber, he built us a 24 x 16 foot house, with two good rooms, out in the country. For $40.00 he got it plastered, and it was so nice and warm. Then he found a box stove out in the woodshed that hadn't burned, and he put that in the house.

We made out all right. My father sold two lots in town; we got $200 for those. And we had $550 of insurance money. I peddled some of our potatoes in Duluth for $40 more.

My mother, the younger children and I went back to Hinckley on October 7, my eighteenth birthday. We got in on the noon train. I had bought some nice rolls at a Duluth bakery, and we cooked some coffee in a syrup pail and had a birthday party in our new house.

At Hinckley we got a few groceries and other things from the Relief Commission, but since my father had insurance we weren't entitled to very much. There were others who had nothing. But I bought second-hand furniture in Duluth — just what we had to have. For $40.00 I got a stove, two beds, some chairs and a table. We still have the table, and it's still as good as ever. I paid only a dollar for it.

At Christmas time our minister came to town, and he had no place to stay so I invited him to our house. We had no eggs or milk in the house, but a nice lady who had a cow gave us a pail of fresh milk, and my mother cooked some mush. The minister said it tasted so good. And we didn't have sheets for the bed, so I quickly basted together two strips of muslin and made sheets for the hay mattress and a pillow case. He said he never slept better. That evening we all went to church and had our Christmas program. There were presents for everyone — blankets, sheets, pillow cases — things we could use.

My father cleared more land, bought a team of horses, a cow and a heifer, a wagon and a sled. In the spring we planted a garden — my how things grew! We had wonderful crops that year after the fire.

We were all so glad to be alive. We had a home and plenty to eat and my father said, "We can all put our feet under our own table again. Thank the Lord."[67]

FROM THE ASHES

IN MEMORIAM OF
MRS. MARY KOFOED

BORN
October 7, 1876

PASSED AWAY
November 10, 1977

Oldest known survivor of the
Great Hinckley Fire of 1894

A year ago, at the age of 100, Mary was presented a Citation of Honor
by the Governor of Minnesota.

Fire Museum Committee

TWO UNUSUAL CHARACTERS

Alfred G. Highton

On Wednesday morning, September 19, 1894, the steamer *India* docked at the Duluth harbor after a trip up the Great Lakes from Buffalo, New York. An elderly, bearded gentleman with flowing gray locks stepped ashore with the other passengers. He was followed by his valet who carried his bags. They went to the Spalding Hotel where the old gentleman, who had been observed to have an "excitable manner," requested quarters for himself and his man. Hotel Manager Frisbee assigned them a room and the visitor signed the register with a flourish — "A. G. Highton and servant, Portland, Ore." He announced that he was the owner of a mining company in Portland, had the backing of Boston bankers and was on his way west to tend to his many investments.

Later that morning Highton talked loudly and freely about his mines and numerous business ventures. Then he was off for a day of sightseeing along the boulevard and a cruise in the bay. Following that, he visited the Great Northern ticket office and talked to City Ticket Agent Walter Whitten about ordering a special train to the west coast. Agent Whitten was delighted with the prospect of making such an advantageous sale. But first, Highton said, he wanted to secure a private Pullman to take him to St. Paul that evening. Whitten arranged for a sleeper car on the Omaha line costing $109 for which Highton wrote a check on the Bank of Commerce of Buffalo, New York. Whitten endorsed the check, and the Omaha agent accepted it.

That evening Highton invited Agent Whitten and some acquaintances from the *India* to be his guests for a planked whitefish dinner at the Spalding Hotel. After the feast Highton expressed his sorrow at leaving Duluth, but explained he had to catch his train for St. Paul. He paid his hotel bill with a $100 check endorsed by his newly-acquired friend, Whitten. With his valet and bags he boarded his private Pullman and was off to St. Paul.

At 7:15 Thursday morning the train pulled in at the St. Paul station. Highton and his servant immediately checked in at the Merchants Hotel. After breakfast he strutted about boasting that he was buying the Spalding Hotel in Duluth and was negotiating with Pillsbury to buy half a dozen flour mills. At noon Highton appeared impeccably dressed and after lunch sat with Hotel Manager Carson on the veranda where they smoked expensive cigars ordered by Highton and charged to his hotel bill. Highton talked of his mines in the west and almost persuaded the hotel manager to invest in his mining stock. Then the conversation turned to the recent Hinckley Fire, and Highton's eyes filled with tears as Carson told him of the suffering of the survivors. Highton said, "By Jove, that's too bad. I'm going to do something for those people."

With a flourish he wrote out a check for the relief fund on the Bank of Commerce for $1,000 and handed it to Carson, who was astounded and impressed by the size of the check. But Highton brushed aside the generous gift with, "It's nothing at all, my dear sir." [68]

At 1:00 p.m. Highton appeared dressed in a neat gray travelling suit, and with his valet carrying his "traps" he boarded an electric streetcar for Minneapolis. He had heard from Carson the names of the men on the State Fire Relief Commission, so he ordered a carriage to drive him from the streetcar to the office of Charles A. Pillsbury, Chairman of the Commission. After conversing for some time with Pillsbury about business affairs, they talked of the Hinckley Fire. Highton once again pulled out his checkbook and casually wrote out a check to the relief fund and handed it to Pillsbury. The check was for $20,000. Highton left the surprised, and by then suspicious, Pillsbury holding the check.

Pillsbury immediately telephoned Kenneth Clark, Treasurer of the Commission, and asked him to come to his office. Clark appeared, bringing with him the $1,000 check Highton had written earlier. The two men had just decided to investigate the open-handed Highton when Detective Doyle of the Minneapolis Police Department walked in looking for Highton and announcing that he was wanted in Duluth for forgery. After a short search Highton was arrested and put in jail at the Central Police Station.

In the meantime worried parties in Duluth had been wiring east and west checking on Highton's credentials. Ticket Agent Whitten was informed that Highton had no account at the Bank of Commerce of Buffalo and had no Boston backers. Furthermore, the New York police had just run a bulletin on Highton (alias Deitsch, Miller, Murdock, Haviland, Hosard and Wheeler) saying he was a "jailbird who had served time for passing bogus checks." [69] He also had a record in Portland and was known on the west coast for his shady transactions. He reportedly had sold a salt mine fifty miles out in the Atlantic to Albert B. Fish of Jersey City for $90,000 and had sold pine timber land, to which he had no claim, to lumber companies. Highton had escaped prosecution because the victims usually chose not to expose the swindles and suffer public ridicule.

Agent Whitten and Chief of Police Armstrong went to Minneapolis to identify and return the prisoner to Duluth. When the train arrived at the Duluth station Friday night, a large crowd of spectators had gathered to see the "high-spender" they had read about in the papers. Highton complained about the people staring at him and continued to protest as he was locked in a cell by himself. He did admit to being thoroughly drunk for days, but blamed others for allowing him to throw away his money.

Highton's valet returned to Duluth with a pathetic tale of his employer's ill-kept promises. The young man, unemployed, had been hired at Buffalo and had been promised good pay, travel and adventure. He was not only deceived, but Highton had borrowed most of the lad's own money to pay for lavish living aboard the *India*. When last heard of, the unfortunate valet was wondering how to get back to Buffalo.

On Monday, September 25, Highton was arraigned before Judge Powell in Duluth and charged with grand larceny in the second degree based on the $109 check. A demure Highton, somewhat recovered from his indulgence, pleaded "Not guilty."

The official records at the Office of the Clerk of District Court at Duluth indicate that on February 25, 1895, a grand jury returned the verdict of "Guilty" for the crime of grand larceny in the second degree. On March 12, 1895, Alfred G. Highton was sentenced to hard labor at the State Prison at Stillwater, Minnesota, for six months.[70]

The case was closed, and the fire relief fund was without the $21,000.

Emma Hammond

The "respectable" people of Hinckley did not talk about these "ladies." The village council had not allowed them to set up their establishment inside the incorporated city limits, so they operated their business one mile east of town at the end of a well-trodden path. *The Hinckley Enterprise* hardly ever mentioned them unless they made news in unusual ways, such as the time in early 1894 when "Mabel Gonzale, an in-mate of the house of ill-fame near Hinckley, was examined by E. Veenhoven, judge of probate, and Drs. Cowan and Stephan . . . and pronounced insane and committed to the state asylum at St. Peter." The paper further stated that the prostitute had been a comely, well-educated lady of Spanish descent. Miss Gonzale died during her first night of confinement at the St. Peter State Hospital. Her mother came from Montana to claim her body.[71]

In Hinckley, as in most lumber towns where men collected, there was a "house of entertainment," or a "sporting house," as it was called locally, that flourished. The women were there during the fire, and as everyone else, they had to seek shelter.

Stewart Holbrook tells of a Mrs. Garrity who ran a house for the "entertainment of loggers and other lusty men" on a thoroughfare east of Hinckley. He says that at 4:00 p.m. Mrs. Garrity realized it was too late to reach the railway station so, after tucking bills into her black lace stockings, she and four of her girls ran to a pool in the Grindstone River where they had bathed in the summer. But Big Mary, who weighed 300 pounds, was caught in the fire and was badly burned before she reached the pool. According to Holbrook, Mary lived, but was under doctor's care for months. Mrs. Garrity was said to have returned to business in Hinckley shortly after the fire.[72]

No other reports were found to verify the existence of Mrs. Garrity, but the Duluth, Minneapolis and St. Paul papers just after the fire tell of a woman whose description is similar to that of Big Mary.

On September 5 *The Duluth News Tribune* noted, "Emma Hammond, who will die, is a large fleshy woman, who kept a house of ill fame at Hinckley. She is horribly burned all over her body."[73]

Dr. Albert Higbee reported to the Minneapolis Citizens' Relief Committee that Emma Hammond was among the ten seriously injured people who were moved from Pine City to Minneapolis on September 4. His report indicated the following:

> At St. Mary's Hospital Emma Hammond, age 48 years, burned on nearly every portion of her body; recovery very doubtful. Do not think this case demands the charity of the committee only so far as medical attendance is required. [74]

On September 9 *The Duluth News Tribune* again reported on Mrs. Hammond:

> Mme. Maggie, or Emma — for she has several names — who used to run a brothel at Hinckley, is dying at a Minneapolis hospital. Her burns are frightful and she suffers untold agonies, yet she exclaimed almost cheerfully when being removed from Pine City to Minneapolis: "I ain't got any kick coming; most of my girls are dead and I want to die to [sic]; I regard my present pains as punishment for my sins." [75]

In the meantime a *St. Paul Pioneer Press* correspondent at Hinckley wrote:

> Three bodies of inmates of a bawdy house a mile east of town were found...by Bull Hanly. These were three of the seven from the same house, who left the safe place in the Grindstone river to get valuables at the house. The fire cut off their return to the river, and they sought safety in an oat field near the house. The bodies were badly burned and could not be recognized. [76]

An interview in October, 1976, with Frank Patrick, a survivor of the fire, revealed that his father, John Patrick, had a homestead near the house of ill repute east of Hinckley. When the bodies of the three women were found after the fire, they had been buried in a field belonging to the Patricks. After a time four posts and a barbed wire fence had been erected to enclose the burial spot. Not liking the idea of this addition to his property, Mr. Patrick contacted the county commissioner to see if the bodies could be moved to the cemetery. The commissioner consented and hired Patrick to do the disagreeable job. The badly decomposed remains were disinterred and reburied in one of the four trenches in the cemetery. Whether these three were included in the number of 248 who died in Hinckley is not known. [77]

The relief registration blank in the State Commission files indicated that Mrs. Emma Hammond, a widow, was born in Ohio. Her occupation was listed as "Domestic — prostitute." She had lost all of her belongings in the fire and gave no address of friends to contact. A notation by the agent indicated that she was "Terribly burned, will probably die." [78]

A later entry in the State Commission ledger book showed that Mrs. Hammond was given transportation to Minneapolis (to the hospital) amounting to $1.90 in September and was paid $110 on February 26, 1895, an amount undoubtedly covering hospital expenses for her extensive care. [79]

(It had been recommended by the Commission that hospitals be paid $1.00 a day for care of fire victims.)

It is not certain when Mrs. Hammond left the hospital, but a report from the St. Mary's Hospital in Minneapolis dated April 26, 1895, indicated that besides being burned severely she had developed pneumonia and was just beginning to care for herself, but was not at that time able to go back to work.[80]

Registration Blank

Name *Hammond Mrs Emma* Birth place *H.A. Ohio 15*

Wifes Name *Widow*, Birth place

·Children, Birth place

Residence *Hinckley*, How long, How long in

Minnesota

Occupation *Domestic Procured*

Did he own his home. If mortgaged, for how much.

$. How much insurance $

What property left *None*,

Value $.

Address of friends *Has None*

Ability of

Needs *Terribly burned Will probably die*

Wants to go to *Mnpls*

CHAPTER **10**

In Remembrance

MONUMENTS AND SURVIVORS

FEW YEARS after the fire the citizens of Hinckley felt it would be appropriate to erect a monument to those who perished in the fire. After a few unsuccessful attempts to raise the necessary money locally, Mayor John Craig sought help from Representative T. H. McKusick of Pine City, a local legislator. Rep. McKusick agreed to introduce a bill requesting aid from the state for the erection of such a monument. After County Attorney R. C. Saunders had drafted the bill, McKusick presented it to the House. On March 14, 1899, McKusick sent an optimistic telegram to the local committee saying, "I have the monument bill by the tail in the House. Have moved it in there. Watch for results."[1] Three days later the results were forthcoming and McKusick wired, "Monument bill recommended to pass. Shake."[2] On April 7, despite some opposition, a bill passed appropriating $2,500 for the monument, to be erected under the supervision of the local committee.

After receiving several designs and bids from various companies, the monument committee, under the guidance of Chairman Saunders, and the city council decided to award the contract to the Arnold Granite Company of St. Cloud. The monument was to be a tapering square shaft of alternating blocks of polished and rough faced St. Cloud gray granite. It was twelve feet wide at the base, fifty-one feet nine inches tall, and weighed sixty tons. The cost was not to exceed $2,400.

Registration for relief by Emma Hammond of Hinckley

IN REMEMBRANCE

207

On August 11, 1900, the monument committee decided what lettering was to be inscribed on the four sides of the base. On the west side looking toward the town were to be the words:

DEDICATED SEPTEMBER 1st A.D. 1900 THIS MONUMENT IS DEDICATED TO THE PIONEERS OF CIVILIZATION IN THE FORESTS OF MINNESOTA.

On the north facing the trenches was to be the inscription:

IN MEMORIAM. IN THE FOUR TRENCHES NORTH OF THIS MONUMENT LIE THE REMAINS OF TWO HUNDRED AND FORTY EIGHT MEN, WOMEN AND CHILDREN, RESIDENTS OF HINCKLEY, WHO PERISHED IN THE FIRE WHICH THIS MONUMENT WAS ERECTED TO COMMEMORATE.

On the east side were to be the words:

SEPTEMBER 1st A.D. 1894. ON THE FIRST DAY OF SEPTEMBER A.D. 1894, BETWEEN THE HOURS OF THREE AND FIVE O'CLOCK IN THE AFTERNOON A FOREST FIRE SWEPT OVER CENTRAL PINE COUNTY DEVASTATING FOUR HUNDRED SQUARE MILES OF COUNTRY, CONSUMING THE VILLAGES OF HINCKLEY, SANDSTONE, MISSION CREEK AND BROOK PARK, AND DESTROYING MORE THAN FOUR HUNDRED AND EIGHTEEN HUMAN LIVES.

The south side facing the road would bear the words:

THE GREAT HINCKLEY FIRE. THIS MONUMENT IS ERECTED BY THE STATE OF MINNESOTA UNDER AN ACT OF THE LEGISLATURE APPROVED APRIL 7th A.D. 1899, TO THE MEMORY OF FOUR HUNDRED AND EIGHTEEN MEN, WOMEN AND CHILDREN WHO PERISHED IN THE GREAT HINCKLEY FOREST FIRE OF SEPTEMBER FIRST A.D. 1894.

At a service held exactly six years after the fire on September 1, 1900, the monument was dedicated. A long line formed and processed to the Rosehill cemetery where floral tributes were placed on the trenches. The Hon. T. H. McKusick gave the dedication address. In the audience was Edward Barry, engineer of the Eastern Minnesota freight, who had returned for the occasion. When the ceremony was over the survivors who lingered to look at the tall slender shaft had a sense of well-being in knowing "This we have done for our dead."

The monument has remained a source of local inspiration and pride through the years. Many visitors have come to read the inscriptions, gaze on

*Monument in the Rosehill Cemetery
in Hinckley. 1976 photograph.*

209

*Inscription at base of
Hinckley monument.*

Inscription on monument

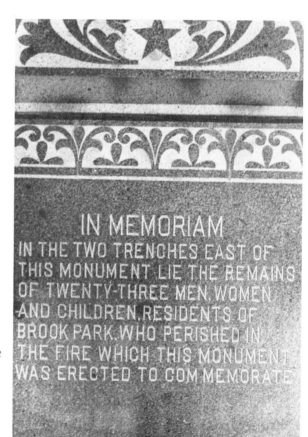

FROM THE ASHES

the four trenches, look to the east across the fields where once lifted a majestic forest and to the west toward the refashioned village, while reflecting on the pioneer spirit that shaped the transformation.

In the Brook Park cemetery, one mile southwest of that town, another monument honors those who lost their lives there. The monument, erected by the State of Minnesota and dedicated on October 1, 1915, is an unpolished gray granite shaft rising from a tiered stone base. The inscriptions on the polished granite panels at the base indicate that 23 of the 26 who perished in the fire lie buried in two trenches to the east of the monument.

Each September through the years after the fire the Hinckley survivors gathered to pay tribute to their deceased companions. The organization became known officially as "The Hinckley Fire Survivors' Association." This group continued to meet yearly, and those survivors who had moved away often journeyed back for the annual reunion.

In 1944, on the 50th anniversary of the fire, the town prepared a special celebration for the survivors — a banquet, program and a memorial service. At that time the name of the organization was changed to "The Hinckley Pioneers' Association" to include those who settled in town just after the fire. The group continued to meet until 1964, but the numbers had dwindled to a handful, and the remaining members agreed to dissolve the organization. They turned over the remaining funds to the Minnesota Historical Society to be used to "publicize the Hinckley Fire Area with suitable markers."[3]

In 1954 the town commemorated the 60th anniversary by re-enacting on two evenings the events of the fire in the Hinckley Fire Pageant which attracted considerable attention. The 75th anniversary was marked in 1969 by another memorial service with nineteen survivors in attendance.

Four trenches in Rosehill Cemetery in Hinckley. Photo 1976

Hinckley Fire Museum, 1976.

HINCKLEY FIRE MUSEUM

A few months after the fire when the St. Paul and Duluth Railroad Company rebuilt its depot at Hinckley, Angus Hay called it a "magnificently large depot...the largest on their lines."[4] It stood at its former site, commanding a view toward the redeveloping business district. In the spring when it was beautified with a coat of "bottle green paint" and the grounds were graded and shade trees planted, it was clearly the most handsome structure in the new town.[5] The inside of the building was no less impressive, with its separate men's and women's sides and its horseshoe eating counter, "The Beanery," where hungry passengers fortified themselves with a sandwich and a piece of pie served at a polished cherry wood counter.

After years of railroad service, followed by use as a warehouse, the depot had lapsed into a state of disrepair and abandonment. In 1970 it was bought by the citizens of Hinckley from the Burlington Northern Railroad Company for $1.00, and in 1971 the restoration process began. Funds came from the state legislature, the Bicentennial Commission, the Minnesota Historical Society, the Pine County Historical Society and local donations. It was a people's project completed largely by the labor of local citizens who were concerned with preserving the town's unique heritage. Residents bought bundles of shingles, and the Duluth National Guard donated their weekends to re-roof the building. Much of the foundation was replaced, the outside paint stripped and repainted, and the original floors refinished. The Hinckley Fire Museum was dedicated on Sunday, September 5, 1976, with twelve survivors of the fire as honored guests.

Inside the museum one enters the world of logging and lumbering as it was in its prime in the 1890's. Lumberjack tools, fire fighting equipment and items that went through the fire are on display. A mural depicting the exodus from Root's train at Skunk Lake dominates an entire wall. The telegraph office of heroic Tom Dunn, who lingered too long at his key, has been reconstructed, and a diarama of pre-fire Hinckley fills an entire room. In the beamed freight room there is a display of railroad equipment and a stage for lectures and small productions. Upstairs the quarters of the depot agent have been restored with 1890 furniture and pieces that have come from relief homes in the area.

On May 7, 1973, the museum was added to the National Register of Historic Places under its official name, the "Hinckley Depot." The museum is a favorite spot for classes of students, tour groups and hundreds of travellers who stray off the nearby freeway. One is bound to come away with a kindled awareness of life as it was in the forests of Pine County and a sense of drama of the *Great Fire* that swept the town from existence.

*The gravel pit has become
Memorial Park in Hinckley.
Photographed 1976.*

IN REMEMBRANCE

213

Monument at Brook Park

CHAPTER 11

Other Aspects

CONSERVATION

AMERICANS have been notorious for squandering the country's natural resources in the name of "progress." The abundant forests which once extended over a large portion of the land were regarded as limitless, adequate for everyone's needs forever. So with the blessing and encouragement of the government, lumber companies were able to lease or buy enormous tracts of woodlands at low cost. The best trees were ruthlessly harvested, the inferior ones either left standing or scrapped, piles of slashings and brush were strewn on the forest floor to dry and ignite at the first touch of flame. Lumber became an everyday commodity and was sold for tremendous profit. Huge timber dynasties emerged, fat, prosperous and wielding great influence.

A few farsighted people raised their voices in protest over the rape of the land. One such voice was that of General Christopher Columbus Andrews, U.S. Minister to Sweden and Norway from 1869 to 1877 during the Grant administration. Andrews was a Minnesotan and a conservationist. While in Sweden he had seen a superior system of forest supervision and management at work, and he advocated a similar plan for the United States. Ironically, in August, 1894, just nine days before the Hinckley Fire, C. C. Andrews had presented a paper, entitled "The Prevention of Forest Fires", at a meeting of the American Forestry Association in Brooklyn, New York.[1] At the time of the fire Andrews noted that Minnesota had a law making it a misdemeanor to start a forest or prairie fire that endangered lives or property, but there was no implementation for its enforcement.

A few attempts had been made earlier in Minnesota to call attention to the importance of forest management and conservation. In 1876 the Minnesota State Forestry Association was organized, the first of its kind in the nation. In 1889 Professor Green was teaching a course in forestry at the University of Minnesota, and by 1892 the Populists, Minnesota's third party under the leadership of Ignatius Donnelly, had adopted a platform calling for conservation of water resources, management of forests, fire prevention and curbs on private ownership of timberland. But citizens and government officials remained apathetic and unconcerned until the shock of September 1, 1894.

Following the fire newspaper editors began to clamor for government supervision of forest lands, fire patrols and a state fire warden system, interstate fire controls and regulations to force lumber companies to clean up their litter. The editor of *The St. Paul Pioneer Press* advocated the creation of a state forestry commission and reprimanded an apathetic public:

> For many a weary year *The Pioneer Press* has urged the cause of forestry before an indifferent public. We have done a little tree planting, even that gradually dying out through indifference; but as to taking care of the magnificent forest... there was no thought of that. At least we are happy to see there is public opinion beginning to form on the subject. [2]

On October 3, 1894, a Forest Fire Prevention Convention met in St. Paul and adopted resolutions calling for legislation to be passed at the next session of the legislature. Recommendations were made favoring the appointment of a state fire commissioner, erecting fire towers and forming fire patrols, requiring lumbermen to burn their rubbish, making railroad companies responsible for fires caused by them and obliging farmers to secure permits to burn.

In December, 1894, after a two-year study, an exhaustive report of the Pine Land Investigation Committee was filed with Governor Nelson on sixteen topics relating to lumber, forests and stumpage. In the report charges were made that "stumpage thieves" bribed appraisers to get false estimates of timber lands, purchased land at one-quarter to one-half of its value by fraudulent methods and cut timber from public lands to which they had no claim. Furthermore, the report charged that the Hinckley Fire was set by the thieves to "cover up their stealing of timber on state lands." [3] The report called for legislation to curb the exploitation of timber lands and measures to protect forests.

The fire of September 1 and the subsequent investigation reports shook legislators into limited action. In 1895 laws were passed to implement methods to preserve state forests and prevent fires. They were similar to laws passed ten years earlier in New York state. C. C. Andrews was appointed the first Chief Fire Warden of the state at a salary of $1,200 a year. He was given authority to prevent and extinguish fires, but was given a budget of only $6,000 a year, plus an additional $5,000 for fire emergencies. The appropriation was totally inadequate to patrol twenty million acres of forest land. In 1897 efforts were made in the legislature to repeal the new forestry law. The attempts failed, but the forestry budget was cut from $6,000 to $5,000 where it remained until 1909 when $21,000 was allowed. Despite the lack of money C. C. Andrews continued to expend every effort to promote and enforce forest conservation and management. In 1898 he was finally granted the aid of a stenographer.[4] In 1899 the legislature appointed a State Forestry Board to manage state timber land.

After the laws of 1895 had been in effect for five years, J. J. Folsom, who replaced Angus Hay as editor of *The Hinckley Enterprise*, assessed their local impact. He said:

> A few persons have been convicted and punished the past year for carelessly causing fires. Fire wardens, however, are reluctant to institute criminal proceedings; and [are] unwilling to make criminal complaint against a man, who perhaps will be their neighbor or townsman through life.[5]

But legislation was at least one step forward for a wasteful nation.

REPEAT PERFORMANCE

Will it happen again? Yes, emphatically. Fires have taken and will continue to take their toll as long as there are forests to burn, contributing weather conditions and natural or human igniters.

In the 24 years following the Hinckley Fire there were three major fires in Minnesota. It is difficult to determine accurate figures on the number of acres burned and lives lost since authorities differ as shown in the table below:

Name of Fire	Date	Reference	Acres burned	Lives lost
Hinckley Fire	Sept. 1, 1894	Elmer	160,000	413
		Larson	350,000	— —
		Mitchell	350,000	418
		Plummer	160,000	418
Chisholm Fire	Sept. 11, 1908	Elmer	20,000	0
		Larson	400,000	— —
		Mitchell	150,000	0
Baudette Fire (and Ontario, Canada)	Oct. 7, 1910	Elmer	300,000	42
		Larson	360,000	— —
		Mitchell	360,000	29
		Plummer	300,000	42
Cloquet Fire	Oct. 12, 1918	Elmer	770,000	538
		Larson	200,000	— —
		Mitchell	200,000	432
		Holbrook	250,000	538

Eighty-two years after the Hinckley disaster another lesser fire of similar character and origin struck again. On September 7, 1976, a spark from a farmer's hay-making machine ignited dry grasses and started a fire that raced into three counties and three state forests in north-central Minnesota. The fire took its name from the Huntersville area where it originated. Before it was contained it had spread over 23,000 acres in Wadena, Hubbard and Cass counties, and had burned into the state forests of Huntersville, Foothills and Badoura. The fire zone was located 25 miles southeast of Park Rapids and 200 miles northwest of the Twin Cities.

The preface had a familiar ring — severely dry and hot weather during the preceding summer with record high temperatures of 95° F. in Duluth and 98° F. in the Twin Cities the day of the fire, lakes and rivers reduced to alarmingly low levels, incendiary conditions in forests and marshes, peat bogs smoldering through the summer, gusting southwest winds up to 45 miles per hour, and sparks from motor vehicles or farm equipment.

Even the fire behaved as it had 82 years earlier. It leaped, burst and exploded, it shifted in erratic patterns and licked over tree tops at unusual speed. It came with searing flames that lifted into fifty-foot walls of fire. Masses of flame and gas were hurled through the sky in room-size fireballs. It roared, skipped, jumped and expended most of its fury in one terrifying day.

"You're witnessing something that is quite rare," said veteran forester Clifford Carlson to a news reporter after spending 26 unbroken hours of fire fighting. "It might compare with the Hinckley Fire of 1894."[6]

The Sunday before the Huntersville Fire, foresters in the area were gravely concerned when the 110-foot watch-tower at Sebeka was toppled by vandals. With forests in dangerous fire conditions the U.S. Forest Service needed every advantage of spotting potential fires early. On Monday helicopters hovered over the area with intra-red sensors trying to locate "hot spots" in peat bogs.

On Tuesday at 11:28 a.m. a lookout on duty at the Nimrod tower reported seeing a curl of suspicious smoke three miles southeast of the small settlement of Huntersville. A forester immediately jumped on his caterpillar with attached fire-plow and started to the fire. A crew of twenty fire fighters was soon on its way, and an aerial water-drop was ordered. A farmer was the first one at the scene and tried in vain to plow a fire-break in front of the blaze. When the fire fighters arrived, they worked at the rear and flank of the fire. In an hour the first bomber swooped over with fire retardant. But the flames were not to be stopped or deterred.

By 1:00 p.m. the fire had burned a strip one mile long and one-quarter mile wide and was heading toward a stand of dry jack pine. Two local fire trucks arrived to protect the homes in the path of the fire, and more men and equipment arrived to dig fire-breaks. But efforts proved useless. By 4:00 p.m. the fire, fanned by a brisk southwest wind, had gained in velocity and strength and had spread to a length of five miles.

The people, who lived on farms scattered throughout the area, saw the red-orange glow and watched the billows of smoke roll high overhead. Some of them packed their belongings into pick-up trucks and campers and headed away. But ever-curious sightseers jammed roads and obstructed evacuation and fire fighting attempts. Overhead helicopters and bombers circled and dropped thousands of gallons of water and fire retardant, but the fury and tempo of the fire increased. By 4:30 a front one mile wide and eight and one-half miles long was headed directly toward the $350 million Badoura Tree Nursery.

About 5:00 p.m. as the fire came within one-half mile of the nursery, almost imperceptibly the wind began to shift, first to the west, then to the northwest. The fire turned on itself, and what had been its length became a nine-mile front travelling southeast toward the settled part of the area. People who had watched the fire to the west found themselves directly in its path. One group of fifteen, who became trapped, could not be rescued by helicopter but were saved in the middle of a recently harvested oat field.

Fire fighters continued to battle along the flank of the newly-shaped fire, and water-drops from the air continued. The blaze still moved in its erratic pattern, hurling ahead in immense columns, exploding on the ground like incendiary bombs, or rolling through the air in immense fireballs. But fortunately there was less fuel to feed on in the fields and pastures.

At 9:00 p.m. a weather miracle occurred. The wind subsided, the temperature dropped, and a gentle rain began to fall. It wasn't much of a rain, but it subdued the monster. Crews lost no time in plowing fire-breaks around the periphery to keep it contained.

Through succeeding days the flames smoldered and rekindled, but the fire fighters were on immediate alert to extinguish them. The surface blazes were not safely contained until the end of September. Fires had tunneled deep underground into peat bogs where they continued to burn through the fall and winter. The hunting season was closed while the threat of fires existed.

Fortunately the Huntersville Fire was not similar to the Hinckley Fire in terms of area covered or lives and homes lost. No one died at Huntersville, and property loss was minimal compared to other fires. Six homes, one combination store and gas station, out-buildings, several unoccupied dwellings and farmers' hay stacks were lost. Several fire fighters and residents experienced near-tragedies and suffered from shock, burns and fatigue.

Although most of the newspapers reported that the Huntersville Fire was started by a hay-making machine, there were witnesses who claimed it was begun by a motor bike, a careless smoker or an electric fence. Whatever the cause, the effect was just as disastrous. The fire burned 23,000 acres of land, 5,000 of which was pine up to fifty years of age. The Department of Natural Resources estimated the timber loss at $1,500,000 and the cost of fighting the fire to be about $1,000,000.

Not reckoned in dollars and cents was the loss of wildlife. Some fleet animals outran the fire, others such as rabbits seemed to have a premonition OTHER ASPECTS of disaster early enough to escape, but hundreds of deer, game birds and small animals were trapped and perished. Those who viewed the area following the fire said death appeared to be prolonged and without mercy. Slow-moving animals such as porcupines and raccoons didn't have a chance. The fire also destroyed ground cover and browse and tunneled deep into the humus where it continued to cause trouble for months afterward. [7]

Both the Hinckley Fire and the Huntersville Fire were disastrous in their own ways, but the Hinckley Fire was clearly one of greater dimension. Yet it appears that in 1976 the Sikorsky, Bell and Hiller helicopters, the B-26, B-17 and C-119 planes, the caterpillars and fire-plows, scores of National Guardsmen, foresters and volunteer fire fighters, "hotshot" crews from Idaho, Montana and Florida, sophisticated ground-to-air communications and infra-red sensors were almost as ineffective as the nineteen-man fire department of Hinckley with the Waterous steam engine.

Historical Notes

PLACES

Brook Park. The village of Brook Park was developed in 1893 by the Kelsey and Markham Land Company. The original railroad station was called Pokegama, as was the township, a name adopted from the Ojibwa Indians meaning "water which juts off from another water." The Great Northern Railway Co. later changed the station name to Brook Park to correspond to the post office name. This town, eight miles southwest of Hinckley, was the first village to be totally destroyed by fire.

Finlayson. The village of Finlayson was named in honor of David Finlayson, the owner of one of the first sawmills in the area. The post office was established in 1887.[1] Although this small settlement on the St. Paul and Duluth Railroad at the northern edge of the fire zone was not totally destroyed, the fire did cause extensive damage to homes and property.

Hell's Gate. Between two and three miles north of Sandstone the Kettle River narrows into a channel of swift water and rapids appropriately named Hell's Gate. During the spring drives massive log jams would occur. In 1894 the Hell's Gate quarries were in operation and provided temporary shelter for some of the Sandstone refugees. The area is now contained within the Banning State Park.

Hinckley. In 1868 logging officially began on what was to become the site of the village of Hinckley when two men, Mulvey and Carmichael, set up their operation near the Grindstone River. In 1869 Captain W. H. Grant of St. Paul brought a portable sawmill over the Government Road, and a year later a dam was constructed on the Grindstone. The McCain brothers built a larger mill near the dam which was later sold to the Brennan Lumber Company, a branch of the Rust Owen Lumber Company of Eau Claire, Wisconsin.[2]

The village and township of Hinckley were named in honor of Isaac Hinckley, a civil engineer who was president of the Philadelphia, Wilmington and Baltimore Railroad and a stockholder in the St. Paul and Duluth Railway Company.[3] He had the village platted by the Western Land Association in 1870, but the plan with a central diagonal intersection was not adopted.[4] In 1872 the township was formed, and in 1885 the village was incorporated.[5]

Before railroads were built, Hinckley was connected to the outside by the Government Road constructed for military purposes by the United States government between 1850 and 1860.[6] Supplies, mail and passengers were brought in by wagon and stage coach over the rough corduroy road which ran two and one-half miles east of town. In the spring of 1894 a citizens' petition led eventually to the construction of a road parallel to the Northern Pacific tracks from Hinckley to Pine City. This became Highway No. 1 and later No. 61.

Miller. In 1894 Miller was a small railroad settlement on the St. Paul and Duluth Railroad at the junction of a spur track which went eastward to the Hell's Gate quarries. Miller was one of the six communities reported to have been totally destroyed by the fire, along with Brook Park, Mission Creek, Hinckley, Sandstone and Partridge. It was later named Groningen.

Mission Creek. The original village of Mission Creek had been named for the nearby creek which flowed south to join the Snake River west of Pine City. The creek had been named earlier for the Ojibwa mission built on Lake Pokegama in 1836.[7] Mission Creek, three miles south of Hinckley, was the second town to be totally destroyed by fire.

Partridge (Askov). In 1894 Partridge, a small settlement on the Eastern Minnesota Railroad northeast of Sandstone, was one of the last villages to be completely burned. The township of Partridge had been named for one of its first settlers. Twelve years after the fire the Danish People's Society negotiated the purchase of 20,000 acres of cut over and burned land in the area to be sold to Danish settlers. In time this community became known throughout the United States for its preservation of Danish heritage and its many cooperative ventures. In 1908 it was named Askov in honor of the distinguished Askov School in Denmark.

Pine City. When Pine County was first organized, Chengwatana (Ojibwa for "town of pines") was its county seat. In the early 1870's the court house was moved to Pine City, a village which was platted in 1869 and incorporated in 1881.[8] Pine City, fourteen miles south of Hinckley, was the town nearest the fire zone which was not burned, and its 1,000 citizens provided valuable assistance to fire refugees.

Pine County. Pine County, in the upper St. Croix Valley in east central Minnesota, was named for the pineries of white and red pine that once grew extensively in the region. The county was established in 1856 but not organized until 1872.[9] At the time of the fire over 4,000 people lived in the county.

Pokegama (See **Brook Park**)

Sandstone. Before Sandstone was established, the town of Fortuna existed, though mainly on the map as a point where the Government Road crossed the Kettle River.[10] Fortuna had been designated as the county seat of Buchanan County in 1857, but in 1860 the legislature approved the annexing of Buchanan to Pine County, effective in 1862. Fortuna never achieved identity as a town. Instead the settlement of Sandstone emerged when W. H. Grant of St. Paul opened the quarries along the Kettle River in 1885. Sandstone was platted and incorporated in 1887.[11] In 1894, when fire destroyed the town, the main industry was sandstone quarrying, with lumbering as its second most important business.

RAILROADS

The Eastern Railway of Minnesota. In 1894 the Eastern Railway of Minnesota, a branch of the Great Northern, was officially a seventy mile portion of the route extending from Hinckley to West Superior, Wisconsin. In 1882 the Minneapolis and St. Cloud Railroad Company had built a line connecting Hinckley to St. Cloud. One year later it was acquired by James J. Hill's St. Paul, Minneapolis and Manitoba Railway Company.[12] In 1887 Hill organized the Eastern Railway of Minnesota to link the Hinckley-St. Cloud line with Duluth and West Superior, where he owned Great Lakes docks, grain elevators and a fleet of lake ships. The connection between Hinckley and Superior was completed in 1889. That same year Hill organized the Great Northern Railway Company and brought together the lines under that name. However, the section between Hinckley and Superior continued to operate under the Eastern Railway Company of Minnesota with James J. Hill's son-in-law, Samuel Hill, as its president (Samuel Hill was no relation to James J. Hill). The Eastern had a ninety-year contract with its parent company to use the Great Northern tracks from Hinckley to the Twin Cities and the terminal facilities at Minneapolis and St. Paul.

The St. Paul and Duluth Railroad. In 1868 the Lake Superior and Mississippi Railroad Company built a line connecting St. Paul to Wyoming, Minnesota. One year later it extended the line three miles north of Hinckley, and in 1870 it reached Duluth. The railroad became the property of the St. Paul and Duluth Company in 1877 and was acquired by the Northern Pacific in 1900.[13]

Chapter References

Chapter 1. THE TIMES — 1894

Hinckley

1. Fred G. Plummer, *Forest Fires: Their Causes, Extent and Effects* (U.S.D.A., Forest Service, 1912), p. 30.
2. *The Hinckley Enterprise,* Aug. 8, 1894, p. 6.
3. Ibid., May 3, 1894, p. 1. (Also other issues through summer, 1894).
4. Ibid., July 25, 1894, p. 4.
5. *The Duluth News Tribune,* Sept. 5, 1894, p. 1.
6. Albro Martin, *James J. Hill and the Opening of the Northwest* (New York: Oxford U. Press, 1976).
7. *The Minneapolis Journal,* Sept. 4, 1894, p. 1.
8. Elton T. Brown, *A History of the Great Minnesota Forest Fires* (St. Paul: Brown, 1894), pp. 177-8.

Pine County

9. Theodore C. Blegen, *Building Minnesota* (Boston: D. C. Heath, 1938), p. 256.
10. *The Hinckley Enterprise,* vol. 1, no. 1 (Memorial Edition Commemorated to the Survivors of the Great Hinckley Fire of Sept. 1, 1894), p. 3; Agnes M. Larson, *History of the White Pine Industry in Minnesota* (New York: Arno, 1972), p. 364.
11. Manuel Conrad Elmer, *Timber, America's Magic* (No. Quincy, Mass.: Christopher, 1961), p. 36.
12. *The Hinckley Enterprise,* Dec. 19, 1894, p. 1.

The State of Minnesota

13. Joseph A. A. Burnquist, ed., *Minnesota and Its People,* vol. 1 (Chicago: S. J. Clarke, 1924), p. 326. (From Gov. Nelson's Inaugural Address).
14. Ibid., p. 227.
15. Blegen, *Building Minnesota,* p. 256.
16. Martin, *James J. Hill,* pp. 411, 415, 416.
17. *The St. Paul Pioneer Press,* Sept 4, 1894, pp. 1, 5.

Chapter 2. THE FIRE

1. *The St. Cloud Daily Times,* Aug. 31, 1894, p. 3.
2. Ibid., Sept. 1, 1894, p. 2.

Brook Park

3. William Wilkinson, *Memorials of the Minnesota Forest Fires* (Minneapolis: Wilkinson, 1895), p. 25.
4. *The Hinckley Enterprise,* June 26, 1895, p. 8.
5. Frank R. Holmes, *Minnesota in Three Centuries,* vol. 4 (Minneapolis: Publishing Society of Minn., 1908), p. 227; *The Duluth Herald,* Sept. 7, 1894, p. 1.

Mission Creek

6. *The St. Paul Pioneer Press,* Oct. 6, 1894, p. 6; *The Duluth News Tribune,* Oct. 6, 1894, pp. 1, 6.

Hinckley
7. Wilkinson, p. 52.
8. Antone A. Anderson and Clara Anderson McDermott, *The Hinckley Fire* (New York: Comet, 1954), p. 44.
9. Wilkinson, p. 169.
10. Stewart H. Holbrook, *Burning an Empire* (New York: Macmillan, 1943), p. 18.

Sandstone
11. *The St. Paul Pioneer Press,* Sept. 5, 1894, p. 1.
12. *The Duluth News Tribune,* Sept. 10, 1894, p. 1.
13. *The Rush City Post,* Sept. 7, 1894, p. 1.

Partridge
14. *The Duluth News Tribune,* Sept. 6, 1894, p. 4.
15. *Report of the Minn. State Commission for the Relief of Fire Sufferers to the Gov., St. Paul,* 1895, p. 19.

Finlayson
16. Ibid., pp. 19, 38.

Chapter 3. TRAINS TO THE RESCUE

The Eastern Railway of Minnesota
1. *Great Northern Railway Co., Time Table,* Sept. 20, 1894.
2. *Great Northern Railway Co., Eastern Railway Co. of Minn., Samuel Hill Subject Files,* file 94, Minn. Historical Society, Archives and Manuscripts Division, St. Paul (Accident report of William Best).
3. Wilkinson, p. 170.

The St. Paul and Duluth Railroad
4. Wilkinson, p. 129.
5. Ibid.
6. *The Minneapolis Tribune,* Sept. 3, 1894, p. 1.
7. Wilkinson, p. 139.
8. Ibid., p. 131.
9. Ibid., pp. 146-7.
10. Brown, *A History of the Great Minnesota Forest Fires,* pp. 97-9.
11. *New York World,* Sept. 9, 1894, p. 5.

The St. Cloud and Hinckley Train
12. *The St. Cloud Daily Times,* Sept. 3, 1894, p. 3.

Chapter 4. AID FOR SURVIVORS

Duluth
1. *The Duluth News Tribune,* Sept. 2, 1894, p. 1.
2. *The Hinckley Enterprise* (Memorial edition), p. 1.
3. Wilkinson, p. 236.
4. Ibid., p. 239.
5. *The Duluth News Tribune,* Sept. 3, 1894, p. 2.

Pine City
6. Wilkinson, pp. 191-2.
7. Ibid., p. 192.

Rush City
8. Ibid., p. 211.

226

St. Cloud

9. *Report of the Minn. State Commission,* p. 17.

Help for Brook Park

10. Wilkinson, p. 212.

Aid for Sandstone

11. *The St. Paul Pioneer Press,* Sept. 4, 1894, p. 2.
12. *Great Northern Railway Co., Eastern Railway Co. of Minn., Samuel Hill Subject Files,* file 94, (telegram from Farrington to Samuel Hill, Sept. 3, 1894).

Chapter 5. THE DEAD AND THE MISSING

Burial around Hinckley

1. Holbrook, *Burning an Empire,* p. 26.
2. Wilkinson, pp. 121-4.
3. *The St. Paul Pioneer Press,* Sept. 4, 1894, p. 2.
4. *The Hinckley Enterprise* (Memorial edition), p. 1.
5. *The St. Cloud Daily Times,* Sept. 5, 1894, p. 1.
6. Wilkinson, pp. 105, 118.
7. *The Duluth News Tribune,* Sept. 6, 1894, p. 1.

Burial around Sandstone

8. Wilkinson, p. 310.

Missing Persons

9. *The Duluth News Tribune,* Sept. 7, 1894, p. 1.
10. Ibid., Sept. 3, 1894, p. 4.
11. Ibid.
12. Wilkinson, p. 112.
13. *The Duluth News Tribune,* Sept. 9, 1894, p. 10.
14. *The Hinckley Enterprise,* June 26, 1895, p. 18.
15. Mary Anderson Kofoed, interview, Hinckley, Minnesota, Oct. 8. 1976.

Chapter 6. RELIEF

Pine City

1. *The Duluth News Tribune,* Sept. 5, 1894, p. 1.
2. *Report of the Minn. State Commission,* p. 4.

Duluth

3. *The Duluth News Tribune,* Sept. 4, 1894, p. 1.
4. Ibid., Sept. 8, 1894, p. 1.
5. *Duluth Herald,* Sept. 7, 1894, p. 5.
6. *The Duluth News Tribune,* Sept. 10, 1894, p. 2.
7. Ibid., Sept. 6., 1894, p. 1.
8. Ibid., p. 2.
9. Ibid., Sept. 8, 1894, p. 5.
10. Ibid.

Donations

11. *The Minneapolis Journal,* Sept. 3, 1894, p. 2.
12. *The Duluth News Tribune,* Sept. 2, 1894, p. 4.
13. Ibid., Sept. 3, 1894, p. 1.
14. *The Minneapolis Tribune,* Sept. 6, 1894, p. 1.
15. *Duluth Herald,* Sept. 7, 1894, p. 5.
16. Ibid.

17. *The Minneapolis Tribune,* Sept. 12, 1894, p. 10.
18. *Report of the Minn. State Commission,* p. 25.
19. Ibid., p. 10.

The State Fire Relief Commission

20. *Report of the Minn. State Commission,* pp. 6-7.
21. Ibid., pp. 11-13.
22. *The Duluth News Tribune,* Sept. 19, 1894, p. 4.
23. *The Minneapolis Journal,* Sept. 20, 1894, p. 4.
24. *The Rush City Post,* Sept. 21, 1894, p. 1.
25. Ibid., Oct. 19, 1894, p. 1.
26. Ibid., Dec. 21, 1894, p. 1.
27. Ibid.
28. Ibid., Jan. 4, 1895, p. 1.
29. *The Hinckley Enterprise,* Jan. 2, 1895, p. 1.
30. Ibid.
31. *The Rush City Post,* Jan. 11, 1895, p. 1.
32. *The St. Cloud Journal Press,* Sept. 20, 1894, p. 5.
33. *The Minneapolis Journal,* Sept. 21, 1894, p. 2.
34. *The Minneapolis Tribune,* Sept. 21, 1894, p. 5.
35. *The St. Cloud Journal Press,* Sept. 27, 1894, p. 2.
36. *Governor's Files, Minn. Commission for Relief of Sufferers, 1894-95,* boxes 2, 3, Minn. Historical Society, Archives and Manuscripts.
37. *Report of the Minn. State Commission,* p. 12.
38. Wilkinson, p. 398.
39. *Great Northern Railway Co., President's Subject Files,* file 2679, Minn. Historical Society, Archives and Manuscripts.
40. *Report of the Minn. State Commission,* pp. 10, 19.

Chapter 7. REPAIRING AND REBUILDING

1. "Bob Murphy's Reporting at Large," *The Minneapolis Sunday Tribune,* Aug. 30, 1964, p. 1-B.
2. *Great Northern Railway Co., President's Subject Files,* file 2679, (telegram from J. J. Hill to J. S. Kennedy in N.Y., Sept. 13, 1894).
3. *Great Northern Railway Co., President's Subject Files,* file 2679.
4. Ibid.
5. Ibid.
6. Ibid.
7. *Great Northern Railway Co., Eastern Railway Co. of Minn., Samuel Hill Subject Files,* file 94, (telegram from Miller to Samuel Hill, Sept. 13, 1894).
8. *Great Northern Railway Co., President's Subject Files,* file 2679.
9. *Great Northern Railway Co., Eastern Railway Co. of Minn., Samuel Hill Subject Files,* file 94.
10. *The Minneapolis Journal,* Sept. 6, 1894, p. 6.
11. *Great Northern Railway Co., President's Subject Files,* file 2679, (telegram from J. J. Hill to J. S. Kennedy in N.Y., Sept. 13, 1894).

Excursionists

12. *The Duluth News Tribune,* Sept. 6, 1894, p. 1.
13. Ibid.
14. *The St. Cloud Daily Times,* Sept. 17, 1894, p. 3.
15. *The St. Paul Pioneer Press,* Sept. 20, 1894, p. 5.
16. *The Minneapolis Journal,* Sept. 25, 1894, p. 6.

Rebuilding Hinckley

17. *The Minneapolis Tribune,* Sept. 3, 1894, p. 3.
18. *The Duluth News Tribune,* Sept. 6, 1894, p. 1.
19. Ibid., Sept. 8, 1894, p. 1.
20. Ibid., Sept. 6, 1894, p. 1.
21. Theodore C. Blegen, *Minnesota, a History of the State* (Minneapolis: U. of Minn. Press, 1963), p. 325.
22. *The St. Paul Pioneer Press,* Sept. 10, 1894, p. 4.
23. Ibid., Sept. 12, 1894, p. 1.
24. *Great Northern Railway Co., Eastern Railway Co. of Minn., Samuel Hill Subject Files,* file 108-115.
25. Ibid.
26. *The Minneapolis Journal,* Sept. 28, 1894, p. 8.
27. *Great Northern Railway Co., Eastern Railway Co. of Minn., Samuel Hill Subject Files,* file 108-115, (telegram from James J. Hill to Farrington, Sept. 29, 1894).
28. *The Hinckley Enterprise,* Jan. 30, 1895, p. 8.
29. *Great Northern Railway Co., Eastern Railway Co. of Minn., Samuel Hill Subject Files,* file 366.
30. Ibid.
31. Ibid.
32. *The St. Paul Pioneer Press,* Sept. 12, 1894, p. 1.
33. David Allen Freeman, excerpts from letter to his brother, Oct. 8, 1894, Hinckley Fire Museum.
34. *The Minneapolis Journal,* Sept. 21, 1894, p. 2.
35. Anderson, *The Hinckley Fire,* p. 67.
36. *The Minneapolis Journal,* Sept. 26, 1894, p. 2.
37. *The Hinckley Enterprise,* Dec. 19, 1894, p. 1.
38. Ibid.
39. Ibid., May 15, 1895, p. 1.
40. Great Northern Railway Co., *Eastern Railway Co. of Minn., Samuel Hill Subject Files,* file 94.
41. *The Hinckley Enterprise,* May 8, 1895, pp. 1, 8.
42. Ibid., p. 8.
43. Ibid., Oct. 16., 1895, p. 8.

Rebuilding Brook Park

44. *The Hinckley Enterprise,* May 29, 1895, p. 8.

Rebuilding Sandstone

45. *Great Northern Railway Co., Eastern Railway Co. of Minn., Samuel Hill Subject Files,* file 108-115.
46. *The Minneapolis Journal,* Sept. 28, 1894, p. 8.
47. *Great Northern Railway Co., Eastern Railway Co. of Minn., Samuel Hill Subject Files,* file 108-115.
48. Ibid.
49. *Duluth Herald,* Oct. 24, 1894, p. 8.
50. *Pine County Courier,* Dec. 27, 1894, p. 5.
51. Ibid., Feb. 7, 1895, p. 1.
52. *The Duluth News Tribune,* Dec. 14, 1894, p. 8.

Chapter 8. ASSESSING THE FIRE

1. Earl L. Kuehnast, *Preliminary Study — The Relationship of Major Forest Fires to Previous July-August Precipitation,* Sept. 17, 1976; Earl L. Kuehnast, interview, University of Minnesota, St. Paul, Oct. 15, 1976.

2. Rodney Sando, interview, University of Minnesota, St. Paul, Oct. 15, 1976.
3. Elmer, *Timber, America's Magic,* p. 84; Plummer, *Forest Fires,* p. 30.
4. Larson, *History of the White Pine Industry in Minnesota,* p. 345; Mitchell, *Forest Fires in Minnesota,* p. 69.
5. *The Duluth News Tribune,* Sept. 6, 1894, p. 4.
6. *The Pine County Pioneer,* Oct. 5, 1894, p. 8.

Chapter 9. PEOPLE AND THE FIRE

Boston Corbett

1. Wilkinson, p. 106.
2. *The St. Paul Pioneer Press,* Sept. 5, 1894, p. 2.
3. *The Duluth News Tribune,* Sept. 7, 1894, p. 1.
4. *Governor's Files, Minn. Commission for Relief of Sufferers, 1894-95,* box 4.
5. Mrs. V. P. Allbert, Librarian, Kansas State Historical Society Reference Report, Nov. 19, 1976.

Heroes of the St. Paul and Duluth Railroad

6. Brown, *A History of the Great Minnesota Forest Fires,* pp. 147-9.
7. *The St. Paul Pioneer Press Sunday Pictorial Magazine,* Sept. 3, 1967, pp. 14-15.
8. *The Duluth News Tribune,* Sept. 9, 1894, p. 10.
9. *The Lake Breeze,* Sept. 5, 1894, p. 4.
10. *The Minneapolis Journal,* Sept. 4, 1894, p. 2.
11. *Duluth Herald,* Sept. 22, 1894, p. 3.
12. *The Duluth News Tribune,* Oct. 4, 1894, p. 5.
13. *The New York Times,* Oct. 7, 1894, p. 10.
14. Ibid.
15. *The Lake Breeze,* Oct. 10, 1894, p. 4.
16. *The New York Times,* Oct. 9, 1894, p. 4.
17. *The Lake Breeze,* Nov. 21, 1894, p. 1.
18. *The New York Times,* Dec. 14, 1911, p. 13
19. Ibid. Dec. 15, 1911, p. 13.
20. Anderson, *The Hinckley Fire,* pp. 98-9.
21. Information from the Washington County Historical Society, Stillwater, Minn., Jan. 21, 1977.
22. *The Duluth News Tribune,* Sept. 8, 1894, p. 4.
23. Anderson, op. cit. p. 99.
24. *Duluth Herald,* Sept. 7, 1894, p. 1.
25. Ibid., Sept. 7, 1894, p. 1.
26. Ibid., Sept. 13, 1894, p. 1.
27. Wilkinson, p. 163.
28. *The St. Paul Pioneer Press,* Sept. 13, 1894, p. 10.
29. Wilkinson, p. 163.
30. Ibid.
31. Ibid., p. 147.
32. Ibid., p. 149.
33. *The Duluth News Tribune,* Sept. 8, 1894, p. 4.
34. *The St. Paul Pioneer Press,* May 13, 1927, p. 1.

Heroes of the Eastern Railway of Minnesota

35. *The Minneapolis Journal,* Sept. 4, 1894, p. 1.
36. *Great Northern Railway Co., Eastern Railway Co. of Minnesota, Samuel Hill Subject Files,* file 94.
37. Ibid.
38. Ibid.

39. Ibid.
40. Ibid.
41. *St. Paul Dispatch,* July 27, 1904, p. 7.
42. Warren Upham, *Minnesota Geographic Names* (St. Paul: Minn. Historical Society, 1969), pp. 410-11.
43. Wilkinson, p. 56.
44. Brown, *A History of the Great Minnesota Forest Fires,* p. 173.
45. Wilkinson, p. 56.

Three Doctors

46. *The St. Paul Pioneer Press,* Sept. 7, 1894, p. 1.
47. *Governor's Files, Minn. Commission for Relief of Sufferers,* 1894-95, box 3 (registration card), box 4 (ledger book).
48. Ibid.
49. *The Hinckley Enterprise,* July 10, 1895, p. 1.
50. Ibid., July 24, 1895, p. 1.
51. Mary Anderson Kofoed, interview, Hinckley, Minnesota, Oct. 8. 1976.
52. *Governor's Files,* op. cit.

Two Clergymen

53. Wilkinson, p. 52.
54. *Governor's Files,* op. cit., box 4 (ledger book).
55. *The Pine County Pioneer,* Oct. 5, 1894, p. 8.
56. Wilkinson, p. 57.
57. Ibid.
58. *Governor's Files,* op. cit. box 3 (registration card), box 4 (ledger book).
59. *The Rush City Post,* Oct. 12, 1894, p. 8.

Four Families

60. *Governor's Files,* op. cit. box 4 (ledger book).
61. Ibid., box 3 (registration card).
62. Mrs. Lydia Clark Stanchfield, personal account of the Hinckley Fire, Hinckley Fire Museum. (Mrs. Stanchfield is a daughter of Joseph Tew.)
63. *Governor's Files,* op. cit., box 4 (ledger book).
64. *The Hinckley Enterprise,* Mar. 13, 1895, p. 8.
65. *Governor's Files,* op. cit. box 3 (registration card), box 4 (ledger book).
66. *Governor's Files,* op. cit. box 4 (ledger book).

Centenarian

67. Mary Anderson Kofoed, interviews, Hinckley, Minnesota, Aug. 14, 1974, Oct. 8. 1976.

Two Unusual Characters

68. *The St. Paul Pioneer Press,* Sept. 21, 1894, p. 1.
69. Ibid.
70. Office of Clerk of District Court, St. Louis County, Duluth, Minn., Nov. 9, 1976 (answer to inquiry).
71. *The Hinckley Enterprise,* Jan. 4, 1894, p. 4.
72. Holbrook, *Burning an Empire,* p. 19.
73. *The Duluth News Tribune,* Sept. 5, 1894, p. 1.
74. Wilkinson, p. 343.
75. *The Duluth News Tribune,* Sept. 9, 1894, p. 9.
76. *The St. Paul Pioneer Press,* Sept. 8, 1894, p. 2.
77. Frank Patrick, interview, Hinckley, Minnesota, Oct. 8, 1976.
78. *Governor's Files,* op. cit. box 3 (registration card).
79. Ibid., box 4 (ledger book).
80. Wilkinson, pp. 353-4.

Chapter 10. IN REMEMBRANCE

Monuments and Survivors

1. *The Hinckley Enterprise* (Memorial edition), p. 4.
2. Ibid.
3. Irene Patrick Nelson, letter to Mrs. Newman, Feb. 14, 1966, Hinckley Fire Museum.

Hinckley Fire Museum

4. *The Hinckley Enterprise,* Dec. 19, 1894, p. 8.
5. Ibid., June 26, 1895, p. 8.

Chapter 11. OTHER ASPECTS

Conservation

1. Alice E. Andrews, *Christopher C. Andrews...Recollections: 1829-1922* (Cleveland: Clark, 1928), p. 285.
2. *The St. Paul Pioneer Press,* Oct. 7, 1894, p. 4.
3. Ibid., Dec. 22, 1894, pp. 1-2.
4. Andrews, op. cit. p. 286-9.
5. *The Hinckley Enterprise,* Sept. 8, 1900, p. 3.

Repeat Performance

6. *The St. Paul Pioneer Press,* Sept. 9, 1976, p. 1.
7. Other sources for the Huntersville Fire story: Allen Wickman, "A History of the Great Fire," *Park Rapids Enterprise,* Sept. 25, 1976, pp. 10-11; *The Minneapolis Star,* Sept. 8, 9, 1976; *St. Paul Dispatch,* Sept. 8, 1976; *The St. Paul Pioneer Press,* Sept. 9, 1976; Joe Gummerson, interview, St. Paul, Minnesota, Oct. 28, 1976.

HISTORICAL NOTES

1. Upham, *Minnesota Geographic Names,* p. 412.
2. *The Hinckley Enterprise* (Memorial edition), p. 1.
3. Upham, op. cit.
4. Map surveyed and platted by Joseph Turner, surveyor for Western Land Association, Dec. 10, 1870. Hinckley Fire Museum.
5. Upham. op. cit.
6. Grover Singley, *Tracing Minnesota's Old Government Roads* (St. Paul: Minn. Historical Society, 1974), p. 20.
7. Upham. op. cit. p. 413.
8. Ibid.
9. Ibid., p. 410.
10. Singley, op. cit. p. 21.
11. *Minnesota Legislative Manual 1975-1976* (St. Paul: State of Minn.), p. 505.
12. Richard S. Prosser, *Rails to the North Star* (Minneapolis: Dillon, 1966), p. 142.
13. Ibid., pp. 138, 155.

Bibliography

PUBLISHED SOURCES

Akermark, Gudmund Emanuel. *Eld-cyklonen or Hinckley Fire,* trans. William Johnson. Askov, Minn.: American Publishing Co., 1976. Originally published in Swedish under title *Eld-cyklonen eller Hinckley-branden,* Minneapolis: Companion Publishing Co., 1894. Republished by the Pine County Historical Society.

Anderson, Antone A., and Clara Anderson McDermott. *The Hinckley Fire,* New York: Comet Press, 1954.

Andrews, Alice E., ed. *Christopher C. Andrews...Recollections: 1829-1922,* Cleveland: Arthur H. Clark Co., 1928.

Bettmann, Otto L. *The Good Old Days — They Were Terrible!* New York: Random House, 1974.

Blegen, Theodore C. *Building Minnesota,* Boston: D. C. Heath, 1938.

Blegen, Theodore C. *Minnesota, a History of the State,* Minneapolis: University of Minnesota Press, 1963.

Blegen, Theodore C., and Philip D. Jordan. *With Various Voices,* St. Paul: Itasca Press, 1949.

Brown, Elton T. *A History of the Great Minnesota Forest Fires,* St. Paul: Brown Bros., 1894.

Burnquist, Joseph A. A., ed. *Minnesota and Its People,* vols. I and II, Chicago: S. J. Clarke Publishing Co., 1924.

Carter, Samuel. *The Riddle of Dr. Mudd,* New York: G. P. Putnam's Sons, 1974.

Daly, George Anne and John J. Robrecht. *Illustrated Handbook of Fire Apparatus,* Philadelphia: INA Corp., Archives Dept., 1972.

Easton, Augustus B., ed. *History of the Saint Croix Valley,* vol. II, Chicago: H. C. Cooper, 1909.

Eisenschiml, Otto. *In the Shadow of Lincoln's Death,* New York: Wilfred Funk, 1940.

Elmer, Manuel Conrad. *Timber, America's Magic,* North Quincy, Mass.: Christopher Publishing House, 1961.

Fiftieth Anniversary of the Great Hinckley Fire of September 1, 1894, Hinckley, Minn., 1944.

Folwell, William Watts. *A History of Minnesota,* vols. III and IV, St. Paul: Minnesota Historical Society, 1969.

Forestry in Minnesota. State of Minnesota, Department of Natural Resources, St. Paul, 1971.

Forrester, Izola. *This One Mad Act,* Boston: Hale, Cushman and Flint, 1937.

Grant, William H. *Sandstone's Gift Souvenir,* 1899.

Great Northern Railway Co. *A Condensed History of the Great Northern Railway,* St. Paul: Great Northern Railway Co., 1952.

Great Northern Railway Co. *Sixth Annual Report of the Great Northern Railway Co.,* 1895.

Great Northern Railway Co. *Time Table,* September 20, 1894.

Guthrie, John D., *Great Forest Fires of America,* U.S. Department of Agriculture, Forest Service, 1936(?).

Haines, Donald A., and Rodney W. Sando. *Climatic Conditions Preceding Historically Great Fires in the North Central Region.* North Central Forest Experiment Station, U.S.D.A. Forest Service Research Paper NC-34, St. Paul, Minn. 1969.

Haines, Donald A., and Earl L. Kuehnast. "When the Midwest Burned," *Weatherwise*, vol. 23, no. 3, American Meteorological Society, June, 1970.

Harrison, Frederick G. *Cinders and Timbers*, Cloquet, Minn.: Frederick G. Harrison, 1967.

Holbrook, Stewart H. *Burning an Empire*, New York: Macmillan, 1943.

Holbrook, Stewart H. *Holy Old Mackinaw*, New York: Macmillan, 1938.

Holbrook, Stewart H. *James J. Hill*, New York: Alfred A. Knopf, 1955.

Holmes, Frank R. *Minnesota in Three Centuries*, vol. 4, Minneapolis: Publishing Society of Minnesota, 1908.

Johnson, Byron Berkeley. *Abraham Lincoln and Boston Corbett*, Waltham, Mass.: Byron Johnson, 1914.

Kelsey, Lucy N. *September Holocaust*, Minneapolis: A. Roper, 1894.

Larson, Agnes M. *History of the White Pine Industry in Minnesota*. New York: Arno Press, 1972.

Larson, Agnes M. "On the Trail of the Woodsman in Minnesota," *Minnesota History*, vol. 13, no. 4, Dec., 1932.

Lee, Franklyn Warner. "The Hinckley Holocaust," *Midland Monthly*, vol. 2, no. 4, Oct., 1894.

Luthin, Reinhard H. *The Real Abraham Lincoln*. Englewood Cliffs, N.J.: Prentice-Hall, 1960.

Martin, Albro. *James J. Hill and the Opening of the Northwest*, New York: Oxford University Press, 1976.

Merling, Bert. *Sixtieth Anniversary Program: The Great Hinckley Fire, An Historical Pageant Drama Memorial*. Hinckley, Minn., 1954.

Minnesota Legislative Manual 1975-1976. Joan Anderson Growe, comp. St. Paul: State of Minnesota.

Mitchell, J. A. *Forest Fires in Minnesota*, State of Minnesota, Forest Service and U.S. Department of Agriculture, Forest Service, 1927.

Moody, John. *Railroad Builders*. New Haven: Yale University Press, 1919.

Orcutt, Wright T. "The Minnesota Lumberjacks," *Minnesota History*, vol. 6, no. 1, March, 1925.

Peckham, John M. *Fighting Fire with Fire*, Newfoundland, N.J.: Walter R. Haessner, 1972.

Pine County Historical Society. *Historic Sites of Pine County, Minnesota*, Askov, Minn., 1956.

Pine County Historical Society. *One Hundred Years in Pine County*, Askov, Minn., 1949.

Pitman, Benn, comp. *The Assassination of President Lincoln and the Trial of the Conspirators*. New York: Funk and Wagnalls, 1954.

Plummer, Fred G. *Forest Fires: Their Causes, Extent and Effects*, Bulletin 117. U.S. Department of Agriculture, Forest Service, 1912.

Poor, Henry V. *Manual of Railroads of the United States*, Annuals, vols. 26-28, New York: H.V. and H.W. Poor, 1893, 1894, 1895.

Prosser, Richard S. *Rails to the North Star*. Minneapolis: Dillon Press, 1966.

Rector, William Gerald. *Log Transportation in the Lake States Lumber Industry, 1840-1918*, Glendale, Calif.: Arthur H. Clark, 1953.

Report of the Minnesota State Commission for the Relief of Fire Sufferers, to the Governor, St. Paul, 1895.

Roscoe, Theodore. *The Web of Conspiracy*, Englewood Cliffs, N.J.: Prentice-Hall, 1959.

St. Paul and Duluth Railroad Company. *Annual Report for 1894, Fiscal Year Ending June 30*, vol. 171.

Singley, Grover. *Tracing Minnesota's Old Government Roads*, St. Paul: Minnesota Historical Society, 1974.

Sixtieth Anniversary of the Great Hinckley Fire, September 1, 1894, Hinckley, Minn., 1954.

Stover, John F. *The Life and Decline of the American Railroad*, New York: Oxford University Press, 1970.

Upham, Warren. *Minnesota Geographic Names*, St. Paul: Minnesota Historical Society, 1969.

Weichmann, Louis J. *A True History of the Assassination of Abraham Lincoln and of the Conspiracy of 1865,* New York: Alfred A. Knopf, 1975.

Wilkinson, William. *Memorials of the Minnesota Forest Fires,* Minneapolis: Norman E. Wilkinson, 1895.

Winser, Henry Jacob. *The Official Northern Pacific Railroad Guide for the Use of Tourists and Travelers Over the Lines of the Northern Pacific Railroad, Its Branches and Allied Lines,* St. Paul: W. C. Ripley, 1891.

UNPUBLISHED SOURCES

Allbert, Mrs. V. P. *Kansas State Historical Society Reference Report,* Nov. 19, 1976, Topeka, Kansas.

Crosby, Francis Marion. *Family papers, 1851-1953,* vol. 13, 1883-1907 (scrapbook), Minnesota Historical Society, St. Paul.

Freeman, David Allen. Letter to brother, Oct. 8, 1894, Hinckley Fire Museum, Hinckley, Minn.

Governor's Files, Minnesota Commission for Relief of Sufferers, 1894-95, boxes 1, 2, 3, 4 and 7, Minnesota Historical Society, Archives and Manuscripts Division, St. Paul.

Great Northern Railway Company, Eastern Railway Company of Minnesota. Samuel Hill Subject Files, file 366, Minnesota Historical Society, Archives and Manuscripts Division, St. Paul.

Great Northern Railway Company, Eastern Railway Company of Minnesota. Samuel Hill Subject Files, files 94, 108-115, 148, Minnesota Historical Society, Archives and Manuscripts Division, St. Paul.

Great Northern Railway Company. President's Subject Files, file 2679, Minnesota Historical Society, Archives and Manuscripts Division, St. Paul.

Haney, Frank. Two reports, one dated and signed Aug. 18, 1954, the other undated and unsigned. Hinckley Fire Museum, Hinckley, Minn.

Hinckley Monument Committee Minutes, Apr. 8, 1899, — Jan. 23, 1901, Hinckley Fire Museum, Hinckley, Minn.

Kuehnast, Earl L. *Preliminary Study — The Relationship of Major Fall Forest Fires to Previous July-August Precipitation,* Department of Natural Resources, Sept. 17, 1976.

Nelson, Irene Patrick. Letter to Mrs. Newman, Feb. 14, 1966. Hinckley Fire Museum, Hinckley, Minn.

Saunders, Mary S. Proal. *Reminiscences,* 1938 (?), 1962, Minnesota Historical Society, St. Paul.

Stanchfield, Mrs. Lydia Clark. Personal account of the Hinckley Fire, Hinckley Fire Museum, Hinckley, Minn.

Work Projects Administration Writers' Project Annals of Minnesota, box 223 (Pine County), Minnesota Historical Society, Archives and Manuscripts Division, St. Paul.

INTERVIEWS

Gummerson, Joe. Fire Management Specialist, Department of Natural Resources, Centennial Office Building, St. Paul, Minn., Oct. 28, 1976.

Kofoed, Mary Anderson. Fire survivor, Hinckley, Minn., Aug. 14, 1974, and Oct. 8, 1976.

Kuehnast, Earl. State Climatologist, Crops Research Building, U. of Minn., St. Paul, Minn., Oct. 15, 1976.

Patrick, Frank. Fire survivor, Hinckley, Minn., Oct. 8, 1976.

Sando, Rodney. College of Forestry, U. of Minn., St. Paul, Minn., Oct. 15, 1976.

Stephan, Angus. Son of Dr. E. L. Stephan, Hinckley, Minn., Oct. 9, 1976.

Pictures

SOURCES OF PICTURES AND MAPS

All places are in Minnesota
unless otherwise indicated.

A

Aitkin County, 4
Alcona County, Mich., 19
Alstrom, Mr., alderman (St. Cloud), 140
American Forestry Assoc., 215
American Railway Union, 16
Anderson, Charles (Brook Park), 87
Anderson, Rev. Emil (Sandstone), 38, 39
Anderson, Mabel (Hinckley), 197
Anderson, Mary. See Kofoed, Mary
    Anderson
Anderson, Mr. and Mrs. Nels & family
    (Hinckley), 197-200
Anderson, S. W. (Hinckley), 143
Anderson, Gov. Wendell R., 197
Andrews, C. C., state fire warden, 215,
    216, 217
Armstrong, Mr., police dept. (Duluth),
    64, 106, 203
Arnold Granite Co. (St. Cloud), 207
Ash, George E., surveyor general, 88
Ashland, Wis., 19
Askov. See Partridge.
Askov School, Denmark, 222
Atkins, Mr., auditor (St. Cloud), 140

B

Badoura State Forest, 218
Badoura Tree Nursery, 219
Bailey, William T., search party, 42, 88-9
Baker, Massey, baggageman, 46
Banning State Park, 221
Barnum, 90, 138, 164
Barnum, Dr. E. E. (Pine City), 57, 65,
    67, 68, 100
Barnum, Kate (Pine City), 100
Barry, Edward, engineer, 30, 32, 41, 44,
    45, 47, 48-51, 178, 179, 180-1, 208
Barry township, 181
Bartlett family (Hinckley), 94
Bates, M. W. (Duluth), 103
Baudette Fire of 1910, 159, 217

Beach, O. L., brakeman, 46, 49, 50, 178
Becker, George, politician, 14
Bell, R. M., depot superintendent
    (Duluth), 64
Bemidji, 136
Beroun, 160, 163
Best, Christian (Hinckley), 84, 93, 126, 131
Best, George (Hinckley), 85, 93
Best, Mr. & Mrs. John & family
    (Hinckley), 84
Best, John Jr. (Hinckley), 84, 92, 125, 130
Best, William, engineer, 11, 30, 32, 33,
    36, 41, 46, 47, 48-51, 63, 178-9
Bicentennial Commission, 212
Big Mary (Hinckley), 204
Bilado family (Sandstone), 39, 88, 104
Bixby, Tams (St. Paul), 114
Blair, John, porter, 52, 53, 55, 171,
    174-5, 176
Bly, Nellie, reporter (New York), 4, 57,
    139
Booth, John Wilkes, Lincoln's assassin,
    165, 167, 168
Boston Corbett. See Corbett, Thomas P.
Boyington, Mr. & Mrs. Dana (Partridge),
    41
Boyle, Edward (Mission Creek), 24
Braden, Major, 104
Brainerd, 164
Bramen, Jay (Brook Park), 87
Brewer, Nicholas R., artist, 92, 93
Brook Park, 58, 72-5, 140, 160; Baty &
    Seymour Mill, 20; burial, 86-7; fire,
    20-3, 42, 61; history, 221; monument,
    211, 214; rebuilding, 123, 154; relief,
    120, 132; rescue, 72, 182
Brown, E. L., transportation director,
    135
Brown, Olive, telegraph operator (Rush
    City), 68, 69, 71
Brown's Hill, 66
Bruckart, D. W., mayor (St. Cloud), 70,
    72
Buchanan County, 223
Buckley, John, conductor, 57, 65, 66, 67,
    68

246